CHRISTIANS IN THE MARKETPLACE SERIES
Biblical Principles and Economics: The Foundations

Richard C. Chewning, Ph.D., Series Editor

NAVPRESS Ⓝ®
A MINISTRY OF THE NAVIGATORS
P.O. BOX 6000, COLORADO SPRINGS, COLORADO 80934

The Navigators is an international Christian organization. Jesus Christ gave His followers the Great Commission to go and make disciples (Matthew 28:19). The aim of The Navigators is to help fulfill that commission by multiplying laborers for Christ in every nation.

NavPress is the publishing ministry of The Navigators. NavPress publications are tools to help Christians grow. Although publications alone cannot make disciples or change lives, they can help believers learn biblical discipleship, and apply what they learn to their lives and ministries.

Scripture quotations in this publication are from several translations: the *Holy Bible: New International Version* (NIV), copyright © 1973, 1978, 1984, International Bible Society, used by permission of Zondervan Bible Publishers; the *New American Standard Bible* (NASB), © The Lockman Foundation, 1960, 1962, 1963, 1968, 1971, 1972, 1973, 1975, 1977; and the *Revised Standard Version Bible* (RSV), copyright 1946, 1952, 1971, by the Division of Christian Education of the National Council of the Churches of Christ in the U.S.A., used by permission, all rights reserved.

The individual authors of this book have used the following translations: Chewning-NASB; Grudem-RSV (unless otherwise noted); Pierard-NIV; Jones-NIV; Brown-NASB; Mouw-RSV; Beisner-NIV; Moore-NASB; McKinney-NIV; Longenecker-NIV; Land-RSV.

Printed in the United States of America

CONTENTS

SERIES EDITOR

Dr. Richard C. Chewning is the Chavanne Professor of Christian Ethics in Business at the Hankamer School of Business of Baylor University in Waco, Texas. He received baccalaureate, Master's, and Ph.D. degrees, all in business, from Virginia Polytechnic Institute, the University of Virginia, and the University of Washington, respectively. He began formal academic training in business ethics and corporate social responsibility as a doctoral student and pursued postdoctoral study in comparative ethics at St. Mary's College, the seminary arm of the University of St. Andrews in Scotland.

Dr. Chewning began teaching at the University of Richmond in 1958 where he taught finance, served for some years as a department chairman, and also as an academic dean. In 1979 he was invited by the business faculty to develop and teach courses in the field of business ethics. He moved to Baylor University in 1985. He has published over forty-five essays and articles integrating Scripture with business and economics, and he has authored and coauthored books in the field of ethics and business from a biblical perspective, including *Business Ethics in a Changing Culture* and *Business Through the Eyes of Faith*.

For years Dr. Chewning has been a consultant to government bodies, trade associations, and corporations in matters of both finance and ethics, while maintaining a busy schedule of public lectures and seminar participation. He is the series editor of the CHRISTIANS IN THE MARKETPLACE books. Volume 1 is *Biblical Principles & Business*.

PREFACE

Does the Bible favor the establishment of a specific type of economic system? How does the biblical revelation of God's nature and man's nature relate to the complex economies in our modern society? What principles of Scripture should bear on our choice of an economic structure?

These questions will be thoroughly addressed in this book. Every effort will be made to avoid the pitfalls of bringing a specific economic system to the fore in order to "baptize" it with selected biblical passages. Scripture should reform our view of economics—we are not to rely on our marketplace experiences to tell us which scriptural passages should be used to justify our worldly wisdom.

We do start with an important presupposition, however, that nonChristians tend to reject: Man's nature is fallen. Because we all have sin natures, we contaminate and pervert any and every system of economics we could ever create. Our fallen nature gives rise to the consequences of human alienation, selfishness, greed, ignorance, and spiritual blindness, thus preventing all systems from operating in a perfectly just and righteous manner. Our task is therefore to ask, *Which economic system is in closest harmony with God's biblical aims and sets free the positive and constructive aspects of our human nature, while constraining the negative and harmful tendencies of our fallen nature?*

Humanly constructed "systems" are merely forms and channels that provide parameters within which we exercise our wills. Scripture does provide some structural guides but does not address, as such, particular economic systems. But it has a great deal to say about the attitudes and desires that drive our volitional decisions that are manifested in our behavior

7

in the business of economic world

and are operative in all structures. Any humanly devised economic system that fails to take into account the realities and consequences of our human nature can only frustrate and undermine God's best intentions for us, as the Pharisees and lawyers did in rejecting God's purposes for them in the days of Christ (see Luke 7:30).

Biblical Principles and Business: The Foundations, the first book in this CHRISTIANS IN THE MARKETPLACE Series, dealt with biblical principles that serve as the foundations for a Christian view of business. Specifically, it discussed the development of a Christian world view and then examined in depth six pairs of biblically related truths that often seem to be in tension with one another. Keeping these tensions in balance and harmony (or disharmony) profoundly shapes our attitude toward business and our behavior in the marketplace.

That first book candidly addressed (1) the tension many Christians feel between the biblical precepts that urge them to implement God's will in every walk of life, including the marketplace, thereby bringing every aspect of society under the standards of Scripture, *and* their obligation to carry out the Great Commission; (2) the relationship between the Old and New Covenants (Testaments) and the question of the superiority of one over the other as a guide for marketplace conduct; (3) the tension created by acknowledging the existence of biblical absolutes on the one hand while being confronted with the necessity of making moral judgments on the other hand, as a vast variety of ever-changing situations are encountered on the job; (4) the decisions that must be made about whether Christians should make their ethical appeals to nonChristians in the marketplace on the basis of natural law or scriptural law; (5) the implications of holding a particular eschatological view of the "end times" and its impact on our marketplace behavior; and (6) a preliminary excursion into the question: Are there biblical directives for the distribution of wealth?

It is this last subject, the distribution of wealth, that we will address head-on and in great depth in this book. We will not do this from an economics perspective, however, but from the perspective of those biblical principles that throw light on the basic and often hidden assumptions underlying all economic systems.

This book follows the same organizational format as the first one. The series editor opens with a chapter discussing the relationship between the nature of man and the development of an appropriate economic system. This is followed by six pairs of chapters (chapters 2-13), with each pair addressing the biblical evidence that rests on both sides of a single foundational economic issue. In this volume we once again experience the tensions that arise when biblical truths are placed on us by God as a part of His sovereign design to keep us balanced and on a straight course, serving His good intentions for us, both to His glory and to our ultimate joy.

The pairs of chapters will examine (1) the relationship between and compatibility (or incompatibility) of economic systems with biblical revelation; (2) some market theories of economic value that reflect classical utility theory and some modern theories of subjective value in the light of God's assignment of values; (3) the scriptural case for private and public property and how these interrelate with considerations of personal liberty and human equality; (4) human incentives operating in the marketplace that are compatible and incompatible with biblical norms; (5) the question, "When does Scripture assign the problems associated with poverty to the attention and care of the private sector and when are they assigned to the public sector?" (The poor exist in all economic systems.); and (6) the biblical ethic of love and the problems Christians face when they carry this ethic into a highly competitive marketplace.

The editor will then conclude with an integrating chapter outlining the aspects of an economic system that must be present and those that must be avoided if the system is to be viewed as compatible with God's revealed will.

Richard C. Chewning
Chavanne Professor of Christian
Ethics in Business
Hankamer School of Business
Baylor University
Waco, Texas

CHAPTER 1

HUMAN NATURE AND ECONOMIC EXCHANGE

Richard C. Chewning

The nature of God and the nature of man—we need to have a grasp of these two areas of knowledge if we truly want to establish and maintain an economic system that reflects God's will. People may have good intentions, but if they lack sufficient knowledge of God's nature and man's nature, their good intentions alone cannot create an economic structure where they can live and work together as God intended. Likewise, people's mere observation of the natural order cannot lead them to form an appropriate economic structure apart from (1) God's constraining and directing work of common grace in their lives, (2) an understanding of God's and man's true nature, or (3) their having inherited a sound economic system from previous generations. Those who do not truly know God lack the definitive standards, obedient will, and wisdom necessary for the development of an economic system compatible with God's revealed truths.

Although this is not the place to develop a treatise on the attributes of God and their normative importance to our economic business decision-making process, a few comments are in order. God's foremost declaration about Himself in Scripture is that He is holy. It is His only attribute that is emphasized so emphatically as to be repeated in the form of a trilogy, "holy, holy, holy" (see Isa. 6:3; Rev. 4:8). Frequently, His very name is called holy (see Ps. 99:3; Isa. 57:15), and even the place where He resides is sometimes called a holy habitation (see Deut. 26:15; Ps. 20:6). If there was but one thing God wanted to disclose about Himself, there is every reason to believe it would be that He is holy.

The root meaning of *holiness* is embodied in the idea of moral purity and perfection. It is the defining and controlling state of the very essence of God.

It is His central and permeating attribute. God is separated from anything impure. There is no mixture, for example, of pure and impure thoughts in God, as there is in our minds. God is even incapable of having an impure thought or of being tempted (see James 1:13). We, on the other hand, continually find it necessary to bring "every thought captive to the obedience of Christ" (2 Cor. 10:5). We are not pure.

Knowing that God is holy in His very essence is not just a theological nicety, though. Perceiving the true wonder of holiness, not merely being able to define it, will motivate us to implore Christ to reveal Himself to us even more fully through Scripture, for to see and truly know Him through the eyes of a heart of faith is the condition necessary to become like Him (see Eph. 1:18-19; 1 John 3:2). When we obey Christ and earnestly seek to know Him more fully, He has promised to disclose Himself to us (see John 14:21) through opening our minds so we can understand the Scriptures that reveal Him (see Luke 24:45).

If God's holiness is foremost in His self-definition, His *righteousness* is the next most important attribute and is the description of His behavior. His character is holy, and all His acts are righteous. Righteousness carries with it the concept of being straight; it promotes the true well-being of others; and it seeks peace and harmony among those who live together in a community. God's righteous behavior is the normative standard for our conduct.

CREATED IN THE IMAGE OF GOD

If God is by nature holy and righteous, what is the nature of man? At precisely this point Christians and secular humanists, who on a de facto basis put mankind at the center of reality, part company. Beliefs about the human *potential* are not where the critical and operationally important differences between Christians and secularists lie, however. Our true differences arise from our perceptions, beliefs, and assumptions about (1) the current state of our nature, (2) what has given rise to our immediate state of nature, and (3) the things necessary for us to reach our potential nature. The gulf separating Christians and others on these three critical issues is very wide.

One of the best known and most frequently quoted Christian beliefs about humans is that we are created in God's image. This is not surprising, for it is one of the first things God told us about ourselves (see Gen. 1:26-27; 5:1; 9:6). It is equally true, however, that when most Christians are asked, "What does it mean to be created in the image of God?" few can give a definitive explanation. This is a shame. When we do not know what it means, we will lack part of God's encouragement to look forward to and seek His renovating help so we can grow toward our full potential.

When God created our first parents, they bore His image perfectly. Since God is spirit, and not flesh and bones (see John 4:24), how does Scripture explain what it really means to bear His image? In the Old Testament there are no precise expositions, but in the New Testament the Apostle Paul tells us what lies at the heart of the meaning of our being made in God's image. In Colossians we read,

> Do not lie to one another, since you laid aside the old self with its evil practices, and have put on the new self who is being renewed [lit., renovated] to a *true knowledge* according to the image of the One who created him. (Col. 3:9-10, emphasis added)

And in Ephesians we read,

> Lay aside the old self, which is being corrupted in accordance with the lusts of deceit, and that you be renewed [lit., renovated] in the spirit of your mind, and put on the new self, which in the likeness of God has been created in *righteousness* and *holiness* of the truth. (Eph. 4:22-24, emphasis added)

These two passages present the three building blocks necessary to understanding what is involved in being the image bearers of God. The first one is that we have the capacity to have a *true knowledge* of God. No other earthly thing or creature, besides mankind, can truly know God and fellowship with Him. Since the fall of our first parents, however, this knowledge has not been obtainable by human effort or study but is a gift and special work of God in the lives of His children (see Eph. 1:15-19).

Because God is the standard by which all human character and behavior are to be evaluated, and He is the renovator of His children, it follows that as we truly grow to know Him we will partake of His nature (see Eph. 4:13; 2 Pet. 1:4; 1 John 3:2) and thereby grow in *righteousness* and *holiness* (the second and third building blocks). In essence, we were created with the capacity to truly know God; through knowing Him and His will, we can know and do what is righteous; and in living righteously, we will be separated from evil and be holy. We can truly know God, act righteously, and be holy. This statement describes our *potential,* but not our daily experience or practice.

The Colossians and Ephesians passages quoted above make it abundantly clear that people need to be renewed or renovated in their very nature before their true potential can become a reality. When our first parents fell, our image was deformed and became distorted so that God was not clearly reflected in the character and behavior of His image bearers. But the potential for people to truly know God and be righteous and holy was not lost. The Holy Spirit has the power to renovate, and God's children are empowered at the time of their regeneration to cooperate in the restoration following their new birth.

THE CONSEQUENCES OF ERRONEOUS PERCEPTIONS

Misperceptions about God's nature and man's nature give rise to many debilitating consequences that adversely affect mankind's efforts to establish and maintain sound economic, political, and social structures. Scripture tells us that people who do not know God are sons of Belial, which in the Hebrew means they are "without profit" or are incapable of doing what is truly right (see 1 Sam. 2:12).

When people, for example, suppress the truth of God that is evident within them (see Rom. 1:18-23) and create a "god" of their own liking, they will devise structures, procedures, policies, and laws that will ultimately work at cross-purposes with God's created order and purposes. To illustrate, if a person has chosen to believe that God is impersonal in character and has left His creatures without clear moral guidelines, but with the burden of discovering what is right and wrong by trial and error, that person is left to his or her own desires, experiences, and logic for moral direction. Ultimately, people's desires will govern their will, and when their will is not enlightened by the truths of Christ, they will take actions that oppose God.

People who do not love God do not perceive themselves as fallen and disobedient, for they are busy obeying their own wills and justifying their own actions. They do not think of themselves as having a sin nature that leads them to frequently do what they really know is wrong even before they do it; they justify their intentions and actions with self-serving rationalizations that allow them to do what they want. Because they choose to argue that "questionable" behavior flows from an evolved or natural nature, not a nature that has fallen from a state of moral perfection, their antidotes for dealing with the sin nature of humans are either inappropriate or inadequate.

Western culture is now abandoning many of the Christian presuppositions that governed our economic, political, and social institutions for many years. For example, the idea that people are morally accountable for their personal behavior has been greatly weakened by the self-excusing notion that our *nature* is fundamentally determined by the experiences we have as children in the home, neighborhood, or society in general. Blame shifting and denials of personal responsibility are seen when criminals blame the environment or their parents for their acts, when "no-fault insurance" and "no-fault divorce" are sponsored by many states, and when the majority of people believe that morals are simply a matter of personal opinion and not subject to a verifiable standard.

The belief in an objective standard of moral truth that is anchored in the validating acts of God in the midst of human history, and sealed in the people of God by the work of the Holy Spirit, is really passé today. Christians must reject the erroneous perception that moral truth is only a personal and ever-changing truth. God is unchanging and His revealed truths are unchanging, and these truths must govern our thinking about economic, political, and social structures and the conduct they nurture.

HUMAN NATURE: THE POSITIVE SIDE

Even though we are born with a sin nature (see Ps. 51:5), we still bear the image of God and are truly remarkable creatures with astounding abilities and potentials that are to be protected, encouraged, and developed. King David, under the inspiration of the Spirit, asked and stated,

> What is man, that Thou dost take thought of him?
> And the son of man, that Thou dost care for him?
> Yet Thou hast made him a little lower than God [Hebrew *Elohim*],
> And dost crown him with glory and majesty!
> Thou dost make him to rule over the works of Thy hands;
> Thou hast put all things under his feet. (Ps. 8:4-6)

When looking down on the evil intentions and work of the people at Babel, God noted, "Now nothing which they purpose to do will be impossible for them" (Gen. 11:6). We are wonderfully made as God Himself has said (see Gen. 1:31).

When we carry out God's will in our dominion role as we explore and rule in the universe (discovering its wonders, creating new forms, shapes, and substances from the basic materials) and tame it as we subcreate and *distribute* its benefits according to God's standards, God is glorified and we are fulfilled. Part of our reason for being created was to engage in these activities. We have a God-ordained obligation to seek the best way possible to rule the dominion He has given us, and the economic systems we establish are a significant part of our response to that aspect of God's assignment. We must determine the most efficient, just, and righteous means of producing, distributing, and caring for both the people and the things God has given us to serve and rule.

Any economic system inhibiting in a biblically unauthorized manner the creative purposes of God is in a state of rebellion against Him. God's children, therefore, must advance an economic system that will enable individuals to develop their God-given capacities. To inhibit this process is to injure our neighbors. To encourage and support it is to love our neighbors.

HUMAN NATURE: THE NEGATIVE SIDE

The foregoing discussion addresses only one-half of the reality regarding human nature, however, and that is its positive, noncontroversial side, which nonChristians also enjoy and applaud. But there is a negative, very seamy side of our fallen nature that must be confronted.

Before Cain killed his brother Abel, the Lord had a conversation with Cain about his sin nature. God told him, "Sin is crouching at the door [of your heart]; and its desire is for you, but you must master it" (Gen. 4:7). God was telling Cain he must exercise self-control to contend with his sin nature or else it would rule him. Every Christian understands this struggle. Before Christ was restored to the throne of our hearts, our self-will and ungodly desires ruled us. Then with Christ's help we entered into a lifelong inner combat (see Rom. 6:12-14; 7:15-25). Daily we fight evil from within, even as we grow in self-control, a fruit of the Spirit (see Gal. 5:23).

Adam and Eve did not have any such struggle before their fall. They were *innocent* and without any knowledge of good and evil (see Gen. 2:17; 3:2-7). In a pure state of innocence there could be no perverted (evil) intentions behind their actions. They could not be self-willed in the sense of being stubborn or rebellious. They could not experience greed or lust, attitudes emanating from self-centeredness and selfishness.

The Fall changed all this. Pure innocence, in the broader moral sense, was abolished. Now people are born with an innate moral ability to discern fairness and righteousness, especially as they impinge on them. We begin life with self-awareness and a self-oriented interest in ourselves. Undoubtedly, our social environment has some influence on how we choose to socialize and express our thoughts, desires, and feelings, but we are not environmentally determined and unresponsible creatures. Some people grow up expressing their will in socially acceptable ways as they try to get what they want, and others act in very unpleasant and destructive ways in an effort to gain what they want. The basic nature of both, however, is the same, even though their behavior is quite different.

For the purposes of this discourse, we need to be aware that people are (1) inherently self-willed and not inherently motivated to seek God's will; (2) inherently oriented toward personal well-being and not the interests of others (see Phil. 2:19-21); (3) motivated by values and desires that are filtered through a self-serving personal orientation, not filled with holy and righteous intentions and motives; (4) easily tempted to do what in philosophy is called "choose the lesser good," or do what is called "sin" in theology; and (5) prone to put their temporal well-being and its accompanying psychological pleasures ahead of setting their "mind on the things above . . . compassion, kindness, humility, gentleness and patience" (Col. 3:2, 12).

No matter how civilized the human race may be as a result of God's common grace, the fallen nature of man is manifested in the pervasive self-oriented intentions and motives of the human heart. Opportunities will present themselves frequently for individuals to reveal these intentions through self-serving and unrighteous behavior. This means that an economic system must do two things to reflect God's will. It must support and encourage the fullest possible opportunities for human development and maturity while it simultaneously establishes limits and controls to appropriately handle the negative realities of man's fallen nature.

ROBINSON CRUSOE ECONOMICS

We will now change our focus and examine a few basic economic realities that are compatible with biblical truths dealing with marketplace behavior, discernible by observations, but not explicitly revealed in the Scriptures. Many principles of economics are components of the natural order that mankind was to discover and work with while subduing the earth. They are not components of special revelation.

Robinson Crusoe, the hero of Daniel Defoe's novel of 1719, was shipwrecked on an island, where he was alone for a long time before his companion Friday appeared on the scene. Our interest is not in the story per se but in the economic reality one would face if alone in the world.

Undoubtedly, an observer could learn many economic realities from watching the survival efforts of a Robinson Crusoe, but we are going to consider briefly only two major ones. First, Robinson Crusoe found himself in a world full of *potential* but with little that would allow him to exist above a bare subsistence without a great deal of creative thinking and personal effort. This economic reality was established at the time of the Fall.

The economic consequences of the Fall are seen in these elements: (1) the land was cursed and would no longer cooperate with man, but would resist him instead; (2) human sweat and laborious effort would now be required to convert the earth's potential into rewarding benefits; and (3) God removed our first parents from their lush surroundings where they had been originally placed (an act of love to keep them from eating of the tree of life and living eternally in a state of sin) and put them in an environment of scarcity where they would have to strive to survive (see Gen. 3). The Fall thus had enormous economic implications and radically altered mankind's economic reality. Most of the economic activity in the world today reflects mankind's efforts to either overcome or deny the moral and economic consequences of the Fall.

We know from God's righteous treatment of Adam that the isolated person has no right, awarded by God by pronouncement or granted through the created order, to be cared for apart from individual efforts being applied to the natural *opportunities* for material sustenance and advancement. This point is critical to grasp and believe. God is the gracious provider of seemingly unlimited opportunities for the material well-being of His image bearers, but the adult individual has no principium or inherent right to be cared for by others. Any economic system that is to reflect God's will must support and cooperate with this principle of personal responsibility by providing and encouraging economic opportunities for everyone who is capable of working.

The second and final point to be drawn from this one-person-survival illustration is that there can be no material advancement without one (or more) of three conditions being met. If you were an isolated individual and were, by God's providence, located where there was adequate opportunity to not only subsist but also advance your standard of living, you would have to engage in one or more of the following to enhance your natural well-being: (1) increase your productivity by either working longer and harder or developing tools of technology to increase the rewards of your labor; (2) save from what you produce today and forgo (sacrifice) the immediate gratification of some immediate wants in order to enhance your opportunities for a higher standard of living in the future or to enable you to "rest" in the future; and/or (3) take time to plan creative and innovative ways to accomplish steps one and/or two.

Putting it simply, we must work hard and be smart while making sacrifices if we are to survive and have a better physical tomorrow. These are so basic and true that they can be called economic laws that govern our physical reality.

ECONOMICS IN A COMMUNITY

Few people in the modern world live in isolation as a Robinson Crusoe, and few of us, if we stop and think about it, would want to be challenged by such a lifestyle. We live as members of an interdependent community that is both blessed with the positive aspects of human accomplishment and adversely affected by the negative aspects of our human nature. We do not live in a utopia and will not before Christ's second coming because of our inherent fallen nature.

Many people are industrious, but some are lazy. Most people are healthy, but ever-increasing numbers of individuals are debilitated by choices that have enslaved them to alcohol, drugs, or other habits impairing them physically or mentally. Some people resist temptations to express their self-will negatively in the marketplace, but others take what they consider in the moment to be safe opportunities to "fudge" on the system. There are many expressions of our human differences, yet we all share a similar nature.

People also differ widely in their views about economics and the appropriateness and inappropriateness of certain aspects of the various economic systems. One person looks over his neighbor's fence, sees a new hot tub in the backyard, and concludes he has a *right* to one, also. Do any of us have a right to a specific or relative level of economic well-being, minimal or otherwise, or are we without any economic rights beyond the *right to an opportunity to work*? Work was mandated by God before and after the Fall, and any economic system that creates artificial barriers to work is resisting God's expressed will.

Economic complexities are great and many. Our intention here is to establish just a few basic economic principles that apply in a community setting, so that as we begin reading the following chapters we will have some theologically and empirically sound economic building blocks.

First, we will look at the popular concept of an existent, fixed "economic pie" because our presuppositions about this will govern what we believe is a just way to divide the available scarce resources. Many people are convinced that the economic pie (total available wealth) is fixed, so that when one person gets a share of the pie, the amount available for others is reduced. Or put more crudely, the first party's benefit is at the expense of the second party.

This concept of a fixed economic pie is a false perception of economic reality. It would be better to think in terms of a natural economic "reservoir" whose very volume of resources has not yet been determined but whose basic capacity is inexhaustible if properly managed. We have no idea of the limits of our available resources for several reasons: (1) many resources replenish themselves; (2) many resources are reusable; (3) many resources are substitutable; and (4) the human ability to adapt, restructure, and discover new resources and possibilities for the adaptation of known resources remains very much open-ended.

The point is simple but vital: There is no fixed economic pie. There is no inherent reason to believe that what one person gets for his or her labor is necessarily at the expense of what someone else might receive. One person's gain is not another's loss. The economic reservoir is fluid, and the benefits derived from it largely depend on mankind's rule and dominion skills, not the basic supply of raw resources. The resource base is large enough, diverse enough, and dispersed widely enough to offer untold opportunities for everyone's economic well-being.

This basic economic reality regarding the vast availability of nonhuman material resources and the latent opportunities associated with its correct management means that the "fingers" of any economic problem point directly at mankind and not the natural environment. This is the central reason that the economic, political, and social structures should adhere to God's standards, for deviating from them can bring only harmful consequences on everyone.

The greatest wasted resource on the face of the earth, and its existence represents a true moral tragedy, is the underdeveloped and underutilized human potential that remains locked up and enslaved to mankind's fallen nature. Human apathy, poor motivation, willful ignorance, and the failure to act on what we know is right are far more devastating to the human condition than earthquakes, famines, and hurricanes. Wasted opportunities and wasted talent maintain and nurture a host of debilitating personal economic problems. Make no mistake about it, economic systems either foster the continuation of such debilitating conditions or support the processes that encourage solutions to these harmful circumstances.

WHAT LIES AHEAD?

The closing two paragraphs of the Preface outlined the specific pairs of tensions, both economic and theological in character, that will be addressed in this book as we work to shed light on the basic question: What must an economic system contain and encourage on the one hand and limit and control on the other hand to reflect God's will?

Christians do not agree on an answer to this question. Why not? Do they disagree because of differences in biblical interpretation or degrees of theological ignorance? Do they disagree because they lack an understanding of economics? Do Christians fail to integrate Scripture with economics? Do the variations merely reflect the emphases on worthy but competing economic goals so that economic means and ends are simply balanced differently? Christians differ for all these reasons and for many others.

A few things need to be kept in mind, though, as we move into the chapters ahead so they can be used as touchstones of thought as we interact with the ideas the scholars offer. They include the following:

1. God's character and behavior are the definitive standards to be used in examining and evaluating all human conduct;
2. Humans are fallen in nature, having both positive and negative realities associated with that condition, and this fact instructs us regarding the need for both freeing and controlling characteristics in an economic system if it is to be compatible with biblical truth;
3. The Fall itself produced profound economic consequences in that the land was cursed, work was made hard, and scarcity replaced readily available abundance;
4. Economic progress depends on savings being accumulated for future use through the forgoing of immediate gratifications;
5. One person's economic gain does not inherently result in another person's economic loss—economics is a mutually beneficial process when justly carried out;
6. There is no fixed economic pie to be distributed but a flexible reservoir of economic resources and opportunities;
7. The greatest economic problems we face are directly related to our human character and conduct and are not related to inanimate resources and conditions.

Finally, Christians must be realists and not generators of utopian hopes that can have no basis in reality in a fallen world. No economic system can rid the human experience of sin and its consequences. No economic system can, therefore, ever abolish poverty (see Matt. 26:11). No economic system will ever eliminate all economic injustices for the simple reason that fallen people will pervert any system. Where mankind is, sin will be present and have its effects.

Basically, wherever we find an "economic baby" (system), we will find plenty of "dirty bathwater" (economic injustices). Our task as Christians is to identify and change the dirty water in an effort to keep the chosen system as clean as possible and to avoid throwing out the economic baby in the process. Christians must learn to distinguish between systems and people. We can change systems but cannot, at our insistence, change people. Systems channel, free up, and constrain human behavior, and we are to determine which system does the best job of accomplishing these functions in a biblically compatible manner.

CAN AN ECONOMIC SYSTEM BE COMPATIBLE WITH SCRIPTURE?

Christians have expended great energy in recent years either attacking or defending specific economic systems or major elements of them. Capitalism has been vigorously defended and also questioned; Christian socialism has been championed and scoffed at; a mixed economy (capitalism/egalitarianism) has been both ridiculed and supported wherever it has existed; and various types of reform have been recommended by "liberation" theologians who have usually been less explicit about delineating the economic system they would like to see put in place after the poor have been liberated than they have been about criticizing the existing system. It seems that more effort has been spent on justifying and attacking existing economic systems than in examining the Scriptures to discern the principles they contain, for without embodying these principles no system of economics can be consonant with the Word of God.

Scripture, to be sure, is not an economics textbook and has no role in trying to unravel most of the technical material that occupies the time and energy of professional economists as they seek to understand the array of natural-law phenomena associated with both macro and micro spheres of technical economics. Scripture, however, does need to be the controlling source of our ideas about the moral nature and content of mankind's intentions, motives, and conduct in the economic arena. Scripture alone contains the standards and has the authority to define what is just and righteous in the economic, political, and social relationships within the human family.

There are four other sound reasons, though, why Christians should earnestly study Scripture to discern God's will as it relates to economic endeavors.

First, we are to be instructed and reformed by Scripture; we are not to let our experiences in the world determine how we interpret the Bible. Biblical truths should govern our thinking, even when they contradict something we are accustomed to and have come to like.

Second, by beginning with Scripture and using its principles to examine our economic systems, we are likely to develop a fuller and more accurate understanding of God's thinking on the subject. To illustrate, if I bring only my worldly economic observations to Scripture for validation or correction, I will have no way of knowing if these constitute the limit of what I should be concerned about or if there are other areas of my thinking that need correcting. Our personal experiences and interests are too limiting and, therefore, unreliable indicators of God's total interests.

Third, we can grow in our understanding of biblical principles by observing both the context and the frequency of a particular type of economic consideration. We can gain insight into the intent, spirit, and weight of God's Word as we see His thoughts expressed in various situations with different frequencies. For example, we are reminded that God is righteous or we are called to do justice (righteousness) over four hundred times in Scripture, and many of these are expressed in the context of the marketplace (see Mic. 2:1-2; 6:6-8). This frequency adds weight to its significance and establishes it as a principle reinforcing the particular standard. All Scripture is important, but some things in it are of greater importance than others (see Matt. 23:23).

Finally, Scripture lets us see how God deals with perverted human attitudes and conduct in the context of historic social, economic, and political settings. The emphasis is on human attitudes and actions, not economic structures and institutions per se. Structures and institutions are brought into existence to support and serve people, not to enslave or have people serve them. It is amazingly easy to slip into a pattern of treating people as a means of accomplishing nonpersonal ends when this simple truth is ignored.

Economic systems are structured means of helping us achieve the ends of (1) glorifying God by carrying out His expressed will in all that we do; (2) assisting all people in developing their full potential as it relates to subduing and ruling the earth; (3) fostering economic justice for both the individual and the community; and (4) taking care of the physical needs of everyone. But the Fall has introduced sin in its many forms, and people's enormous capabilities are expressed through impure motives and faulty conduct. Our most fundamental perceptions of God and man ultimately shape our views of economic structures, so we must first know what God thinks about economic justice and then learn how to effectively carry His moral precepts into the marketplace. If we fail to do this, our impact on society will steadily decline, for the world has little or no interest in the first two points made at the start of this paragraph. As a result, we possess inaccurate standards for accomplishing the third point, which in turn causes a breakdown in effectively accomplishing the fourth one.

In this part of the book we are going to address and answer the question: Are there biblical standards by which specific economic systems and ideologies can be evaluated and judged? The answer, as we shall see, is yes. However, several biblical principles need to be present if an economic system is to be considered compatible with God's intentions. We will then look at some "live" economic systems and note some gaps between the standards of Scripture and the observed realities in the world. This in turn raises the question: Are these gaps between the biblical norms and observed realities the result of human sin, or are they caused by structural problems in the economic systems?

To help us sort through these issues, Dr. Wayne A. Grudem identifies and discusses the biblical principles that have to be present in an economic system if it is to be considered compatible with Scripture, and Dr. Richard V. Pierard points out some deficiencies and problems related to the actual seeking of economic justice within the framework of contemporary economic systems. (The question of whether these deficiencies are related to our sin nature or to structural shortcomings in our economic systems will be handled in later sections.)

All twelve scholars participating in the four-day colloquium where these chapters were freely discussed (debated) acknowledged that no economic system could create or sustain true biblical justice for an indefinite period of time because of the pervasive nature of sin. They did not, however, always agree on what problems were structurally caused and which troubles were primarily related to our fallen nature. Making this determination is critical to this entire study, though, and readers should keep this question in mind throughout the book.

Dr. Grudem's chapter should delight anyone in search of biblical principles that must be reflected in the operation of any economic system that is to be considered consonant with God's Word. He sets a number of such principles before us with beautiful organization and great clarity. He does not offer, though, an exhaustive survey of the biblical principles that have application to the field of economics. For example, all the great biblical doctrines associated with systematic theology and the message of salvation also have important implications (direct and indirect) for economics, and these are not explored. However, he explains and outlines many biblical truths dealing with the economic responsibilities of both the individual and the community.

CHAPTER 2

HOW AN ECONOMIC SYSTEM CAN BE COMPATIBLE WITH SCRIPTURE

Wayne A. Grudem

Wayne A. Grudem is Associate Professor of Biblical and Systematic Theology at Trinity Evangelical Divinity School in Deerfield, Illinois. He majored in Economics and received a B.A. degree from Harvard University, and a Master of Divinity from Westminster Theological Seminary in Philadelphia. His Ph.D. was awarded by the University of Cambridge where he concentrated his efforts on the study of the New Testament. He is the author of 1 Peter *in the Tyndale New Testament Commentary series and* The Gift of Prophecy in the New Testament and Today. *He is also the author of numerous articles. Wayne currently serves as the Secretary-Treasurer of the Institute for Advanced Christian Studies, and he is an ordained Baptist minister.*

INTRODUCTORY ISSUES AND QUESTIONS

We may assume that all human societies in this age will contain at least some nonChristians. We may also assume that all societies for which a consideration of biblical propositions and economics is relevant will contain at least some Christians. The Christians, in general, will know and be responsive to the special revelation from God that is found in the Bible. But nonChristians, in general, will not know or be responsive to this special revelation. They will instead have access to the general revelation from God that comes to all persons through human reason, conscience, and observation of the created world. In connection with such general revelation, the concept of natural law is often mentioned. For purposes of this paper, the term *natural law* will be used to refer to those moral principles that can be deduced from general revelation (that is, moral principles that can be known

27

apart from the written words of Scripture).

The recognition that there are both Christians and nonChristians in human societies will affect our analysis of economic systems. It will be appropriate to consider the influence of those systems on the economic behavior of Christians, who attempt to follow the teachings of Scripture, and of nonChristians, who respond in various degrees to natural law. Economic systems that tend to promote greater conformity to scriptural principles by Christians *and* greater conformity to natural law by nonChristians may be judged to be preferable to those that hinder such conformity.

But which of the moral principles of Scripture can be known through natural law? Paul apparently thinks that God's moral standards, in general, are accessible to unbelievers. After listing over twenty specific sins, he says, "Though they know God's decree that those who do such things deserve to die, they not only do them but approve those who practice them" (Rom. 1:32). The implication is that when unbelievers act contrary to God's standards, they have an awareness of offending God and being liable to punishment, even though they have not read the specific commands of Scripture. Then in the next chapter, in talking about Gentiles who do not have access to the written law of God, he says that they "do by nature what the law requires," and in doing this, "they show that what the law requires is written on their hearts, while their conscience also bears witness and their conflicting thoughts accuse or perhaps excuse them" (Rom. 2:14-15).

It seems appropriate to conclude that in the witness of conscience, and in the ability to reason and observe the natural world, people generally have access to the moral standards of God, which He expects them to live up to. In fact, the judgments of God that fell on people at the Flood or in Sodom and Gomorrah or in other situations indicate that God holds all people responsible for and accountable to those moral standards.

Of course, in the Old Testament some laws are specifically directed to the community of Israel, a special group among all the people of the world. And in the New Testament specific directions are given for people within the Church, a special group among all the people of the earth. So, for example, commands to preach the gospel, to baptize, and to participate in the Lord's Supper are rightly understood as applying not to all people but to those within the Christian community, showing them how to behave in that community.

But apart from such commands directed to specific communities of people, we may expect that the commands of Scripture regarding human activity generally, and economic activity in particular, are commands that reflect the moral will of God, which He expects all people to obey, and which

He has implanted in the conscience of mankind generally. Therefore, we may expect that the content of the moral commands of Scripture is the same as the content of natural law, rightly understood. If we want to understand more precisely what moral standards can and should be discovered by nonChristians through natural law, we may gain such a precise definition from a study of moral commands of Scripture applying to all people generally.

The distinction we have made between what may be expected of Christians and what may be expected of nonChristians becomes significant when we realize that the full biblical teaching on economic behavior is never limited to a perspective that is exclusively "earthly" or focused on this present world. Rather, biblical teachings related to economics always include *attitudes* of mind and *motivations* that have a "heavenly" or "spiritual" perspective and consciously take into account the individual's relationship with God.

For example, it is not enough to "work heartily." Paul says Christians are to "work heartily, as serving the Lord and not men" (Col. 3:23) and to do their jobs "knowing that whatever good any one does, he will receive the same again from the Lord, whether he is a slave or free" (Eph. 6:8). Similarly, it is not enough to work merely for rewards that will be given in this life, because the Christian is to do some things that have reward not in this life but in the life to come: "When you give a feast, invite the poor, the maimed, the lame, the blind. . . . You will be repaid at the resurrection of the just" (Luke 14:13-14). It is not enough simply to use the resources of the earth; we must use them with thanksgiving to God (see 1 Tim. 4:4). And it is not enough just to give to the needs of others, for such giving should rightly be motivated by a trust in God to supply our needs (see Phil. 4:18-19) and by an attitude of mind that sees such giving as a spiritual sacrifice "pleasing to God" (Heb. 13:16). Moreover, although material productivity is good because it is implicit in the mandate to subdue the earth (see Gen. 1:28), the parable of the rich fool reminds us that it is not an end in itself—it is the "fool" who "lays up treasure for himself, and is not rich toward God" (Luke 12:21). Therefore, those who are "rich in this world" are not to "set their hopes on uncertain riches but on God who richly furnishes us with everything to enjoy" (1 Tim. 6:17).

The point of mentioning these examples is that Scripture seems to view *no* economic activity from an exclusively "earthly" perspective. All economic activities—working, saving, spending, giving—are to be done while mindful of God and conscious of "spiritual" or "heavenly" rewards and punishments to be received sometimes in this life and sometimes in the life to come.

But can we encourage or expect nonChristians to follow this full-orbed biblical teaching? In many cases that would be inappropriate. To encourage an unbeliever to give to the poor in order to have treasure in Heaven, or to trust God for a future heavenly reward for faithful performance at a daily job, would be to encourage salvation by works rather than by trust in Christ. Such encouragement would wrongly suggest that the nonChristian can confidently expect a heavenly reward apart from Christ.

But then what *can* we say? Is it appropriate to give nonChristians *any* encouragement to live in conformity with moral standards revealed in Scripture? And is it appropriate for us to advocate economic systems that tend to promote conformity to the moral standards of God (whether revealed in Scripture or through natural law)?

Yes, I believe it is appropriate, so long as the encouragement does not imply that such moral actions will merit heavenly reward from God apart from salvation in Jesus Christ. Certainly it is better that people tell the truth rather than lie, that they remain faithful in marriage rather than commit adultery, that they protect human life rather than murder, that they are honest in business rather than dishonest. Even in the realm of attitudes, it is better that people offer thanks rather than grumble, that they be generous rather than selfish, that they enjoy rather than resent their work, and so forth. Therefore, it seems right for us to pray for, encourage, and work for laws, policies, and patterns of conduct among earthly societies that conform more rather than less to the moral standards of Scripture.

In fact, both Old and New Testament examples warn us that an immoral society is more displeasing to God than a largely moral society, and that a society given to immorality is in imminent danger of God's judgment (note Sodom and Gomorrah, Babylon, Assyria, Tyre and Sidon and, in the New Testament, 1 Pet. 1:17 [present judgment implied by present tense verb for "judges" in context of living this present life in the fear of God], and Rom. 1:18-32). In the words of the *Westminster Confession of Faith,*

> Works done by unregenerate men, although for the matter of them they may be things which God commands, and of good use both to themselves and others; yet . . . cannot please God, or make a man meet to receive grace from God. And yet their neglect of them is more sinful, and displeasing unto God. (18.7 or 16.7)

What should be our goal, then, in discussing biblical principles and economic systems? In the light of the considerations mentioned above, it seems that our goal as Christians should be to seek economic systems that

(1) best enable Christians to fulfill the whole range of biblical economic teachings, and (2) best enable nonChristians to conform to those moral demands of God that can be known through general revelation.

In the following discussion, the distinction between economic standards for Christians (which can be known through Scripture) and those applicable to all people (which can be known through Scripture *or* through general revelation) will inform our analysis. In discussing each aspect of economic activity, we shall ask (1) what the whole range of biblical teaching would require for those who have access to it and seek to follow it. After that, we can distinguish (2) what aspects of that teaching may be expected from a mixed society composed in large part of nonChristians. Then we can consider (3) what type of economic system would be most conducive to the fulfillment of those standards by Christians and by nonChristians.

BIBLICAL PRINCIPLES AND THEIR IMPLICATIONS FOR SPECIFIC ECONOMIC SYSTEMS

Three fundamental questions must be decided by every economic system:[1]
1. What goods and services should be produced?
2. How should they be produced?
3. For whom should they be produced?

1. What goods and services should be produced?
Principle 1: People should produce goods and services for the benefit and enjoyment of mankind. Why did God fill the earth with material abundance? Why did He make it fertile, creating it with thousands of different plants and animals good for food? Why did He fill it with color, with precious metals and gems, with raw materials that could be made into an infinite variety of consumer goods? None of this was really necessary if God had intended us merely to survive.

The biblical answer is that God gave us an abundant earth for our enjoyment. He is the God "who richly furnishes us with everything to enjoy" (1 Tim. 6:17). He created human beings to "subdue" the earth and "have dominion over the fish of the sea and over the birds of the air and over every living thing that moves upon the earth" (Gen. 1:28). The word translated "subdue" (Hebrew *kābash*) means to overcome or to force into subjection or service. This word and its related verb forms are used of forcing people into subjection (see 2 Chron. 28:10; Neh. 5:5; Jer. 34:11, 16), of defeating enemies in battle (see Num. 32:22, 29; Josh. 11:8; cf. 2 Sam. 8:11; 1 Chron. 22:18). The idea of forcefully overcoming someone or something in order to obtain service or benefits for oneself is almost always present when the word is used.

The phrase "have dominion over" (Hebrew *rādāh*) is almost always used of kings or government rulers who have others subject to them and who serve them (see Lev. 26:17; Num. 24:19; 1 Kings 4:24; Ps. 72:8; Isa. 14:6).

So God's purpose for human beings in relationship to the natural world is to develop its resources and make them useful for our benefit and enjoyment. In fact, "everything created by God is good, and nothing is to be rejected if it is received with thanksgiving" (1 Tim. 4:4; note also Gen. 1:31; Deut. 16:11, 14-15; 28:47-48; Neh. 9:25; Eccles. 5:19; 6:2; Isa. 30:29; Jer. 2:7; Acts 2:46).

NonChristians, as well as Christians, may know something of this purpose of God, for Paul and Barnabas told the Gentile unbelievers at Lystra that God "did not leave himself without witness" in previous generations, "for he did good and gave you from heaven rains and fruitful seasons, satisfying your hearts with food and gladness" (Acts 14:17). The abundance of the earth and its productivity, and the resulting gladness that comes to people's hearts, are a "witness" God has given and continues to give to all people.

We can conclude that productivity, even of material goods from the earth, is one legitimate criterion for evaluating economic systems. Better systems will be more productive and more efficient in enabling greater enjoyment of the abundance and variety of the earth's resources. Because of this, empirical studies showing that free market economies are in general more productive than planned (socialist or Communist) economies might be appropriately used to argue that at least at this specific point free market systems are more consonant with biblical economic principles.

Principle 2: People should produce goods and services for morally right purposes. Although God wants us to use the earth's resources for our enjoyment, He surely does not want people to use them in sinful ways. Examples of morally wrong goods and services that might be produced in an economy would be pornography, drugs, radar detectors (whose only purpose is to enable people to break the law), and prostitution.

Since unbelievers are also subject to the moral laws of God, it is right to expect that they would use the earth's resources for morally right purposes as well. This implies that desirable economic systems will not have *absolutely* free markets, but will have some governmental laws and policies forbidding or discouraging and penalizing immoral goods and services; they will not be entirely *laissez faire* systems. Scripture endorses such governmental restraints on wrongdoing when it says that governmental authorities are sent "to punish those who do wrong and to praise those who do right" (1 Pet. 2:14), and that they should be "not a terror to good conduct, but to bad" (Rom. 13:3). Such a principle would give legitimacy to government prohibition of such goods and services, and also to government laws forbidding such things as stealing, fraud, breach of contract, false advertising, and so on.

Principle 3: Some public goods and services should be produced through government taxation. To carry out their function of restraining and punishing wrongdoing, governments should be able to tax to support themselves, and thereby to maintain military forces (for defense) and police forces (for internal restraint of evil). Therefore, Scripture says, "You also pay taxes, for the authorities are ministers of God, attending to this very thing" (Rom. 13:6). It may also be argued that the orderly functioning of society is furthered by the provision of certain "public goods" (such as roads), which must be provided through government taxation.

Principle 4: Christians should produce goods and services for spiritual purposes. In addition to the material production mentioned above, Scripture encourages Christians to devote time and money to things such as evangelism and missions, the building of churches, the provision of Bible teaching and counseling (both personally and through Christian books and journals), and corporate times of worship and prayer. These things are economic activities in that they require an investment of time or money, or both—and the time and money might otherwise be given to production of material goods or more secular kinds of human services.

Moreover, if such spiritual goods and services are to be produced in a way consistent with scriptural teaching, the necessary time and resources must be given voluntarily by individuals: "Each one must do as he has made up his mind, not reluctantly or under compulsion, for God loves a cheerful giver" (2 Cor. 9:7).

Of course, the production of such spiritual goods and services is only required of and appropriate to persons in the Christian community; therefore it should not be encouraged or expected from unbelievers generally.

Because Scripture requires such spiritual goods and services, the implication is that those economies are more desirable in which individuals have the freedom to choose—if they wish—to give as much of their time and effort as they want for the purpose of producing such goods and services. But this suggests that economic systems (such as communism) emphasizing only the production of visible or earthly goods and services and compelling every citizen to contribute significantly toward those goals are less desirable. Moreover, the necessity of voluntary giving may be used as another argument showing one more specific advantage of a free market economy in which such purposes are fulfilled, not through compulsory financing by government taxation, but through voluntary giving by individuals.

In the context of Paul's encouragement that people should give "not reluctantly or under compulsion, for God loves a cheerful giver" (2 Cor. 9:7), the specific kind of contribution in view is *material* help for poor Christians in Jerusalem. This passage might be used to indicate that giving by Christians to meet the needs of the poor is better accomplished through the voluntary contributions of individuals rather than through compulsory taxation by government. Additional help to the poor through governmental programs would not be prohibited. But voluntary personal giving to the poor is categorically affirmed in Scripture; governmental giving does not receive such support.

Principle 5: Individual morality is necessary for the production of goods and services that are truly good. A final qualification must be made regarding the production of goods and services. In a free market economy, the decisions about what quantities of each good and service are produced, and what kinds of goods and services, are made by the economy's response to the aggregate of individual consumer demands (expressed through high or low prices that consumers are willing to pay for these commodities). The total output of goods and services in a society is really the sum of decisions of individuals within that society concerning what they wish to demand and pay for. Decisions will be morally good or bad depending on the judgments and the morality of the individuals within that society. Therefore, an economy needs not only government prohibition of immoral goods and services, but also sound moral character in its citizens so that producers are ultimately rewarded for producing true goods and services, not what Warren Brookes calls "bads and ripoffs."[2] (Modern advertising is not morally neutral, for it has considerable power to inform people as well as to alter their wants in directions that may be judged, according to biblical standards, to be morally desirable or undesirable.)

2. How should goods and services be produced? This section examines biblical teachings concerning the means by which resources are produced. In what proportions are land, capital, and labor allocated to produce the goods and services desired?

Principle 6: Resources should be neither wasted nor hoarded, but used efficiently. The Bible views the whole earth as ultimately belonging to God. It is His possession, and He places human beings on it only as His stewards to care for it. Paul asks the Corinthians, "What have you that you did not receive? If then you received it, why do you boast as if it were not a gift?"

(1 Cor. 4:7). No possession, property, strength, or ability is ours in an absolute sense. Whatever we have is given to us by God in trust, and we are to use it as faithful stewards.

This theme is familiar in the Old Testament, beginning with the affirmation that God created the heavens and the earth (see Gen. 1:1), and made man and put him on earth to rule over it as God's representative (see Gen. 1:26-30; 2:15-17). So David reminds us, "The earth is the LORD's and the fulness thereof, the world and those who dwell therein" (Ps. 24:1). And God tells His people, "Every beast of the forest is mine, the cattle on a thousand hills . . . all that moves in the field is mine . . . the world and all that is in it is mine" (Ps. 50:10-12). Similarly, the book of Haggai records, "The silver is mine and the gold is mine, says the LORD of hosts" (2:8). That was why the people of Israel could not object to God's laws for the restoration of land to its original owner in the Year of Jubilee: "The land shall not be sold in perpetuity, *for the land is mine*" (Lev. 25:23, emphasis added).

The idea of faithful stewardship always includes accountability for the management and use of the things the master has entrusted to the steward. In Luke 19:11-27 (the parable of the pounds, with each servant receiving one) and in Matthew 25:14-30 (the parable of the talents, with servants receiving varying amounts), the master returns and requires an accounting from the stewards. Whether we understand these "talents" or "pounds" to be spiritual gifts, areas of responsibility, opportunities for service, or material possessions (it is probably best to understand that Jesus had all these things in mind—anything He has entrusted to us), the principle of accountability is made clear. And in both cases faithful stewardship is seen to include attempting to increase or improve those resources as we are able. (Compare the teaching in Prov. 27:23-27 concerning the necessity of knowing well "the condition of your flocks.") Therefore, while God wants us to use our resources or give them to others to use, He condemns letting them lie idle (note the "worthless" and "slothful" servant who hid the talent in the ground in Matt. 25:24-30; cf. Luke 19:20-27).

Wasting resources is forbidden in passages that condemn gluttony (see Deut. 21:20; Prov. 23:20-21; 28:7; Titus 1:12), and an actual example of wastefulness is evident in the sin of the prodigal son who *"squandered* his property in loose living" (Luke 15:13, emphasis added). Jesus refused to waste the bountiful excess of His miraculous creation of loaves and fish, telling His disciples, "Gather up the fragments left over, that nothing may be lost" (John 6:12; cf. Prov. 21:20 [NASB]; 25:16; Luke 16:10-13).

On the other hand, we are not to hoard our resources, either. Hoarding means keeping things that we have no reasonable expectation of using and not letting those things be used by others. The rich fool said, "I will pull down my barns, and build larger ones; and there I will store all my grain and my goods" (Luke 12:18). God's perspective on this hoarding activity is clear in the contrast described in Proverbs 11:26: "The people curse him who holds back grain, but a blessing is on the head of him who sells it" (see also Eccles. 5:13-17; James 5:2-3). Eventually, hoarded goods will rot or become moth-eaten anyway (see Matt. 6:19-21; Luke 12:15), and then it will be evident that those who hoarded have been poor stewards of what was entrusted to them.

Yet one qualification is important here: Reasonable saving for the future is not hoarding but is part of good stewardship. People have a responsibility to support themselves and their families (see 1 Thess. 4:11-12; 1 Tim. 5:8), and they should make provision for a day when they cannot work due to age or illness (see James 4:13-17; cf. Gen. 41:25-57; Prov. 6:6-11; 15:6; 27:23-27; Luke 19:23). Our lives will likely follow the path that we observe in the great majority of people as they grow older, and we, too, will reach a time when we will be unable to support ourselves.

Therefore, putting nothing aside for unforeseen future needs is equivalent to demanding that God perform a miracle to meet our needs; it is like casting ourselves down from the Temple instead of using the stairs; it is to force a test on the Lord our God (see Matt. 4:7, NASB).

Similar to reasonable saving for future personal needs is the business activity of temporary storage of goods (for example, frozen vegetables) for later release to the market when these goods are more scarce. This procedure benefits the economy by making goods available through both high and low production seasons. It is not hoarding because the business has a reasonable expectation of using the goods later. (Note Joseph's wise grain storage in Gen. 41:46-57.)

NonChristians should be urged to use resources wisely, neither to waste them nor to hoard them. They may or may not see themselves as accountable to God for their stewardship in some sense, but most will agree that efficient or effective use of resources is a wise course for human action. It is appropriate for those who understand the biblical teaching about stewardship and God's ownership of the earth to encourage such wisdom. This consideration of efficient use of resources can become the basis of an argument to show that the allocation of labor and capital resulting from the pricing system in a free market economy is much more efficient than that seen in a centrally planned economy where resources are allocated by government decision (as in communism or more extreme socialism). This claim to higher efficiency can no doubt be documented through detailed economic analysis or can be empirically verified by any tourist who notices the amazing contrast in the availability of goods in geographically contiguous and culturally similar regions such as East and West Berlin, Hong Kong or Taiwan and the People's Republic of China, Helsinki and Lenigrad, North and South Korea, and so on. The necessity for efficient use of resources also provides an argument for a system of private ownership that gives more reward for such performance.

But it must also be noted that personal economic freedom allows freedom for individual immorality in economic choices. Irresponsible stewardship may lead to much wasting of resources by individuals, and personal greed may lead to much hoarding of goods. Private ownership and free markets alone do not guarantee biblically approved behavior apart from a base of personal morality in the society.

Principle 7: The earth has abundant resources that may be used for productive purposes. The Bible never hints at any limits to the earth's resources. Speaking of God's activity to "earth's farthest bounds," David says, "Thou visitest the earth and waterest it, thou greatly enrichest it; . . . Thou crownest the year with thy bounty; . . . The pastures of the wilderness drip, . . . the meadows clothe themselves with flocks, the valleys deck themselves with grain" (Ps. 65:9-13). When God brings future blessing on the earth, He promises that "the wilderness and the dry land shall be glad, the desert shall rejoice and blossom; like the crocus it shall blossom abundantly" (Isa. 35:1-2). Amos also foretells amazing productivity for *this earth* in a future time of blessing when "the plowman shall overtake the reaper and the treader of grapes him who sows the seed; the mountains shall drip sweet wine, and all the hills shall flow with it" (Amos 9:13).

Although the earth requires work, sometimes hard and difficult work, to extract its abundant resources and make them useful for man (note the curse of the Fall in Gen. 3:17-19), the abundance is there to be enjoyed—provided that we will work to develop it and provided that God allows His "favor" to be upon us and establish "the work of our hands" (Ps. 90:17).

We find in the Bible no suggestions of any limits to the abundant resources that God is able to provide from the earth for His people and for others if they will only seek His blessing on them. Rather, it describes great abundance that will be available to people whenever they are faithful to God (cf. Ps. 72:3; Isa. 30:23; 32:15-16; 51:3; 60:17-18). All these blessings are promised as things that would come forth from the earth, which God's people knew. God would bless and cause to bring forth abundantly *their* wilderness and *their* desert and *their* waste places.

But how would this happen? Whether this productivity would come through providential intervention, for example, by God's sending rain to desert areas to make them productive, or whether it would come through God's fulfilling His promise "to bless all the work of your hands" (Deut. 28:12; cf. 14:29)—so that through technological development and hard work people would be able to discover and use the resources God had hidden in the earth—Scripture does not always specify. It would seem that both kinds of blessing are contemplated in these promises (see Jer. 31:12-14; Ezek. 34:14, 26, 29; 36:29-30; Joel 2:24, 26; Zech. 1:17).

Moreover, several passages portray continual productivity of the earth. Amos pictures not only a "reaper," but also a "plowman"; not only a "treader of grapes," but also one who "sows the seed" (Amos 9:13). In such times of blessing there is no more famine or hunger (see Ezek. 34:29; 36:30).

This biblical teaching about the earth's abundance leads to the conclusion that its resources are potentially capable of providing abundant prosperity and doing so in a way in which they would not be exhausted or destroyed for future generations. There is a suggestion of the earth's ability to produce great wealth and still be continually renewed and replenished. "Subduing the earth" need not be carried on in destructive ways or in ways that fail to consider the needs of future generations.

But are these statements about the earth's abundant resources contradicted by factual data such as that found in the *Global 2000 Report to the President,* which appeared in 1980, or its precursor, *The Limits to Growth: A Report for the Club of Rome's Project on the Predicament of Mankind* (1972)?[3] Space does not permit detailed discussion here, but technically trained specialists in various areas of resource availability and use have severely criticized the *Global 2000* report for its dire predictions of resource shortages and overcrowding of the earth. Probably the best collection of such criticism is *The Resourceful Earth: A Response to Global 2000.* The book summarizes its five hundred pages of analysis by twenty-four world experts as follows: "We are confident that the nature of the physical world permits continued improvement in humankind's economic lot in the long run indefinitely."[4]

Of course, these considerations are not unique to Christians. Since evaluation of the resources of the earth is possible through empirical observation, it is appropriate that unbelievers would come to a similar conclusion. Indeed, none of the authors contributing to *The Resourceful Earth* indicate any religious commitment.

The issue of the abundance of the earth's resources is important for decisions about economic systems because our convictions about the relative scarcity or abundance of resources directly affect how much government regulation we advocate for the allocation of those resources. Government rationing of resources in wartime is a significant example. If essential resources really are in short supply, there comes a point where government allocation of a fair share to everyone must supplant allocation determined by the pricing system of a free market.

Moreover, Christians who advocate a simple lifestyle today often appeal to an assumption that the world's food, energy, and other supplies are running low. Therefore, they say, we should not take more than our fair share because when we use some of the scarce resources, we automatically deprive others of their use.[5]

But if there actually are *abundant* resources in the earth, resources we have not yet fully developed, we can be encouraged that it is possible to increase the amount we give to the needs of others *and* the amount we can thankfully use as a gift from God for our own enjoyment. When resources are abundant, large use of resources by one person or country does not deprive other persons or countries of their use of resources as well.

Related to this consideration is the reminder that God has given the earth to human beings so that we may develop and use its resources for our benefit. It is not an "untouchable earth,"[6] as some extreme environmentalists seem to believe; it is a "subduable" and "usable" and "renewable" earth.

These conclusions seem appropriate: A system that rewards increasing development and use of the world's resources is preferable to one that does not; and governments should be very hesitant to adopt national or international rationing of resources, since economic inefficiencies inevitably result and since such rationing is usually not necessary—genuine shortages will usually be averted by market forces encouraging the use of substitute goods and rewarding further technological development.

Principle 8: There should be some government restrictions on the use of resources. Although I have argued that the allocation of goods resulting from a free market economy leads to more efficient use of resources, such support of the free market is not absolute in Scripture. In fact, there are reminders that some restrictions should be placed on the economic activities of a free market. I list four such restrictions here.

(1) There must be some means of averting monopolistic control of land, capital, or labor since that would result in inefficiencies due to artificial shortages, artificially high prices, and the misallocation of the resource. So Isaiah says, "Woe to those who join house to house, who add field to field, until there is no more room" (Isa. 5:8). Probably some degree of monopolistic power is implied in the activity condemned in Proverbs 11:26: "The people curse him who holds back grain, but a blessing is on the head of him who sells it." The statement that such things are evil does not by itself

indicate that government must restrain the evil, but if governments are generally given to "punish those who do wrong" (1 Pet. 2:14), imposing a restraint would seem an appropriate governmental task.

Similarly, many Old Testament passages condemn or prohibit the oppression of the poor by the rich, which primarily involves taking advantage of persons in a weaker position. As Proverbs 22:22 states, "Do not rob the poor, because he is poor, or crush the afflicted at the gate; for the LORD will plead their cause and despoil of life those who despoil them" (cf. Exod. 23:6; Ps. 10:2, 9; Prov. 14:31; Amos 2:6; 8:6). And God commands government officials, "Give justice to the weak and the fatherless; maintain the right of the afflicted and the destitute. Rescue the weak and the needy; deliver them from the hand of the wicked" (Ps. 82:3-4). This obligation on government to defend those who have less power from those who have more and will abuse it would seem sufficient justification for saying that government restrictions preventing monopolistic control of resources or labor are appropriate.

(2) Another kind of government regulation would prohibit and punish stealing (note Exod. 20:15, "You shall not steal"). But a more subtle kind of stealing is also wrong, namely, dishonesty in dealing with others: "A false balance is an abomination to the LORD, but a just weight is his delight" (Prov. 11:1; 16:11). God specifically commanded the people of Israel, "You shall do no wrong in judgment, in measures of length or weight or quantity. You shall have just balances, just weights, a just ephah, and a just hin; I am the LORD your God, who brought you out of the land of Egypt" (Lev. 19:35-36; cf. Deut. 25:13-16; Prov. 20:10, 23; Amos 8:5).

Obtaining income through dishonesty or deceit is wrong and ought to be prohibited: "The getting of treasures by a lying tongue is a fleeting vapor and a snare of death" (Prov. 21:6; cf. 20:17). This kind of behavior is forbidden by the commandment, "You shall not bear false witness against your neighbor" (Exod. 20:16).

(3) Moreover, some government policies should protect the earth's resources for future generations. The command, "You shall love your neighbor as yourself" (Matt. 19:19), and the admonition, "Whatever you wish that men would do to you, do so to them" (Matt. 7:12), combine to indicate that we should consider the needs of others, including the needs of future generations as well as our own. Therefore, some measures must be taken to assure that we do not deplete resources needed for future generations. Although the earth's resources are abundant, careless and wasteful use can result in eroded farm land, dry wells and streams, poisoned lakes, stripped forest lands, and unbreathable air. It takes some government control

to prevent what is sometimes called the "tragedy of the commons"—where property shared by everyone is essentially no one's property, and it can be misused and depleted. Government restrictions on such depletion of resources would therefore seem appropriate.

(4) Finally, concern for the prevention of evil and the general protection of the safety of workers would allow for some governmental health and safety standards, restrictions on pollution, and so forth.

Principle 9: All use of resources should be accompanied by trust in God and thankfulness to Him. Both Old and New Testaments remind us that we depend on God for provisions to sustain and enrich our lives. We are taught to pray, "Give us this day our daily bread" (Matt. 6:11), and we are to remember the Lord our God, who gives us "power to get wealth" (Deut. 8:18). People are to depend on the Lord to grant success to the work of their hands (see Ps. 90:17; cf. Deut. 14:29; 28:12; Ps. 18:34; 75:7; 127:1).

Should unbelievers be expected to trust God to give success to their work and to give thanks to God? Paul tells us that unbelievers are morally culpable in part because "although they knew God they did not honor him as God or give thanks to him" (Rom. 1:21). So even unbelievers seem to be obliged to have a heart attitude of thanksgiving toward God and perhaps a general sense of creaturely dependence on Him as well.

Does this principle have any implications for economic systems? Though I realize not all Christians will agree, I think it might be argued that an economic system allowing or even encouraging people to take time from work (that is, to take one day in seven from work) to show dependence on God and to give thanks to Him—and, for believers, to worship Him—would be appropriate. The question of whether the observance of a day of rest each week is a moral command for all people or a specific command for God's people, and whether it is a specific command for God's people in the Old Covenant or one to be observed by Christians in the New Covenant as well, is a hotly disputed theological question, and I do not propose to resolve it here. (But I might add that living in England during the political dispute in which the evangelical community combined with the trade unions to defeat Margaret Thatcher's proposed liberalization of Sunday trading laws in 1986 has caused me to reconsider my previous acquiescence to widespread Sunday retail trading patterns in the United States.)

A related subject is that of womb-to-tomb governmental systems of complete economic support. Although Christians may also differ in their evaluations here, we might well ask if the actual result, and perhaps even part of the intended purpose of such systems, is to undercut dependence on God.

Finally, if indeed it is true that God "gives you power to get wealth"

(Deut. 8:18), and if this is a general truth applicable to all people, we might ask whether increasing immorality on the part of a society will lead to the withdrawal of God's hand of blessing and, conversely, whether national revival may be accompanied by God's allowing increased technological breakthroughs and higher productivity for the economy generally. At the very least, such a pattern might be argued from the natural consequences of moral and immoral behavior; honesty and hard work lead to higher economic output in the natural course of events, according to the way God has planned the world to function. But perhaps this consideration may be expanded to include expectations about God's special providential intervention to reward or punish as well. In either case, Michael Novak is right to note that "a free society . . . must insist upon a core of common and indispensable morality."[7] Such morality cannot be imposed by government legislation, but government can make policies and laws that are more or less conducive to moral conduct.

Does this mean that government should support religion generally, since religion provides the basis for morality in society? Although I certainly would not endorse the idea of any "state church"—adherence to any religious view is ultimately a matter of voluntary choice—nonetheless, it seems that some governmental support of religions generally, and perhaps specific religions fairly and proportionately, is good for a society. That affirmation encourages the "core of common and indispensable morality" without which a society cannot endure. Therefore, one might argue, it is appropriate for governments to provide such things as tax-exempt status for churches, chaplains in the military and the Congress, certain tax benefits related to clergy housing allowances, and even the inscription of a religious motto on a nation's currency. Promoting the same ends without risking at all the establishment of a state church would be the advocacy of basic morality (honesty, sobriety, sexual abstinence outside marriage, the dignity of work, respect for authority, respect for the family, etc.) by governments and government-sponsored schools.

3. For whom should goods and services be produced? This final area of inquiry asks how the use of labor, land, and capital should be rewarded. Once the society produces goods and services (section 1) and produces them by certain means (section 2), then to whom are these goods and services given? This section examines appropriate wages and rent, interest and profits. It also discusses the issue of appropriate distribution of income within a society.

Principle 10: Private ownership of property should be encouraged and protected. In the commands "You shall not steal" (Exod. 20:15) and "You shall not covet" (Exod. 20:17), God endorses the idea of private property. (In fact, in the distribution of sections of the Promised Land to the tribes of Israel [see Josh. 13–21], and in the subsequent allocation to families, as well as in the requirement to return each family's land at the Year of Jubilee [see Lev. 25:8-55], God Himself allocated private property to people and guaranteed that families would retain some private property.) What is my neighbor's is his own. It belongs not to society generally but to him, and I am neither to take it nor desire to do so.

The desire to own and thus to control property is sometimes criticized as mere selfishness, and therefore thought to be sinful. In this way people often allege that capitalism depends on human sinfulness to make it work.

Yet God Himself "owns" and "controls" property—"The earth is the LORD's and the fulness thereof" (Ps. 24:1)—so the ownership of property (or the desire to own property) cannot be something that is wrong in itself. Even in a sinless world it seems that Adam and Eve would have had some God-given desire to exercise control over property if they were to have desires consonant with God's command to "subdue" the earth and to "have dominion" over it (Gen. 1:28). Such a desire to own or control property is appropriately thought of as one aspect of our creation in the image of God, for in exercising good stewardship over property we reflect something of God's sovereignty, power, wisdom, and blessedness.

As with all God-given desires, the desire to control property can be (and often is) distorted to sinful ends. Scripture recognizes this tendency and warns, "You shall not covet" (Exod. 20:17) and "You shall not steal" (Exod. 20:15). But the desire for property should not be perceived as wrong in itself, and wise self-interest (that does not seek one's own benefit by harming others) should not be indiscriminately lumped together with wrongful selfishness (that seeks one's own good by harming others). Even in a sinless world we might imagine a productive atmosphere of friendly competition whereby each person seeks to excel at, and be rewarded for, individual activity.

Therefore, capitalism should not be thought to depend on human sinfulness. It can turn both wrongful selfishness and rightful self-interest (including the desire for property) to productive ends, but that fact should be seen as a benefit, not a reason for criticism.

And endorsement of the appropriateness of private property may also be expected by unbelievers generally.

This principle has significant implications for economic systems because it stands in contrast to the Communist doctrine that private property is evil in itself.[8] Scripture views private property as something good (though certainly subject to misuse through sin). Abolishing private property does not improve man; it makes him unproductive and reduces both the freedom God intended for him and his God-ordained ability to enjoy with thanksgiving the rewards of his work.

Principle 11: It is not wrong to earn profits by employing other people or by renting one's land. In direct opposition to Communist teaching that it is wrong for the "bourgeois" owners of factories or lands to make profits from the labor of the workers they employ (the "proletariat"), or from rent on land, Scripture says that Christians who work as servants or slaves should work "as servants of Christ, doing the will of God from the heart" (Eph. 6:6). Paul reminds them, "Whatever your task, work heartily, as serving the Lord and not men, knowing that from the Lord you will receive the inheritance as your reward; you are serving the Lord Christ" (Col. 3:23-24).

In fact, "those who have believing masters . . . must serve all the better since those who benefit by their service are believers and beloved" (1 Tim. 6:2), a command apparently indicating that Paul thought it right for believing masters to profit from the labor of their servants, and for servants to work so that their masters might profit. When we couple these statements with the directives concerning servants and masters in the Bible (see Eph. 6:5-9; Col. 3:22–4:1; 1 Tim. 6:1-2; 1 Pet. 2:18-20; and several of Jesus' teachings), there is no suggestion that employing others, paying them, and profiting from their work are wrong. Fraudulently withholding wages when they are due is wrong (see James 5:4), but paying wages and gaining benefit from labor are not wrong in themselves. Masters are never told to "gain no benefit" from the work of individuals who labor for them (an idea that would lead people never to hire anyone, for no personal benefit could come from it); rather, they are to treat their servants "justly and fairly" (Col. 4:1).

The Old Testament provides directions concerning the rental or lease of land until the Year of Jubilee: "If the years are many you shall increase the price, and if the years are few you shall diminish the price, for it is the number of the crops that he is selling to you" (Lev. 25:16). Yet, "the land shall not be sold in perpetuity, for the land is mine," God tells His people (Lev. 25:23). At least in this specific context, the rental or lease of land for a certain number of years is endorsed, and it would therefore seem impossible to say that private rental of productive land is in itself evil.

Principle 12: There should be greater reward for more work and for higher quality work. The statement that "the laborer deserves his wages" (Luke 10:7; 1 Tim. 5:18) endorses the payment of wages for work rendered. Appropriate reward for work is implied also in the fact that "the plowman should plow in hope and the thresher thresh in hope of a share in the crop" (1 Cor. 9:10; Paul applies this statement beyond the realm of agriculture to the appropriateness of getting paid for preaching the gospel and teaching God's Word, and this application broadens it to include specific kinds of economic activity). Paul asserts, "It is the hardworking farmer who ought to have the first share of the crops" (2 Tim. 2:6). And the parables of the talents and the pounds (Matt. 25:14-30 and Luke 19:11-27) support the idea that more work or more productive work receives greater reward.

The wisdom literature in the Old Testament affirms this idea as well: "He who tills his land will have plenty of bread, but he who follows worthless pursuits will have plenty of poverty" (Prov. 28:19), and "Lazy hands make a man poor, but diligent hands bring wealth" (Prov. 10:4, NIV; cf. 6:10-11; 15:19; 18:9; 19:15; 20:4; 21:5, 25; 22:29; 31:27). The theme in both Old and New Testaments is clear: laziness or slackness in work ordinarily diminishes one's reward, while diligence and industry are given greater reward.

In spite of the foregoing discussion, should there be an equality of rewards or possessions in a just society? The New Testament frequently teaches that there will be degrees of reward in Heaven and that we should work for a large heavenly reward (see 1 Cor. 3:14-15; 2 Cor. 5:10; see also Matt. 6:20; 19:21; Luke 6:22-23; 12:18-21, 33, 42-48; 1 Cor. 3:8; 13:3; 15:19, 29-32, 58; Gal. 6:9-10; Eph. 6:7-8; Col. 3:23-24; 1 Tim. 6:18-19; Heb. 10:34-35; 11:10, 14-16, 26, 35; 1 Pet. 1:4; 2 John 8; Rev. 11:18; 22:12). If this is so, it is not wrong for there to be inequality of reward (and thereby inequality of responsibility or perhaps of "possessions" in some way in Heaven). Inequality of reward is not wrong in itself.

There were rich people in New Testament churches, and the apostles— unlike some simple lifestyle advocates of today—never rebuked them for being rich. Nor were they told to become poor. Paul writes to Timothy,

> As for the rich in this world, charge them not to be haughty, nor to set their hopes on uncertain riches but on God who richly furnishes us with everything to enjoy. They are to do good, to be rich in good deeds, liberal and generous, thus laying up for themselves a good foundation for the future, so that they may take hold of the life which is life indeed. (1 Tim. 6:17-19)

Such instructions would not have been given unless Paul assumed that these people would continue to be wealthy and would need directions about the proper use of wealth (cf. Phil. 4:12 with Matt. 27:57-60; Luke 23:50-53).

We should not strive for equality of possessions, either within the Church or in society generally. This principle needs to be said clearly today because some Christians say the Church should work toward equality of possessions and because the Marxist ideology that has subtly affected so much modern thought would say that inequality of possessions ("capital") is a great evil. In fact, inequality of possessions is necessary in a world where God makes us to be different individuals with different gifts and different responsibilities.

Moreover, inequality of possessions is necessary for an economy to function well. Without the ability to keep more reward for harder work, people generally will not work to their maximum ability. Thus, Communist economies become notoriously unproductive, and so do modern-day "feudal" societies in Latin America where all the land and all the profits are held by only a few families. Socialistic economies that impose extremely high taxes on the wealthy hurt themselves, also, for the most highly skilled business and professional people will not work as hard (why should they?) or else will move to a country—such as the United States—that will let them keep most of what they earn. (Of course, this does not contradict the fact that most people in every society are *also* motivated by other goals than financial reward for work. Yet monetary return is still a large factor, and usually the largest, in motivation for work.)

The Jubilee Year in the Old Testament should not be urged against inequality of possessions, for a reading of the text (see Lev. 25) attests that only the family farm and house returned to their owners every fifty years. There was no equalizing of cattle or sheep, jewelry or money, stored grain or tools, or houses within walled cities.

Nor should Acts 4:32-37, which states the early Christians "had everything in common," be used as a pattern for Christians today. It was the result of an extraordinary, voluntary outpouring of love through the power of the Holy Spirit, but the Epistles never command anything like this for the New Testament churches. Even the context shows it to be entirely voluntary (see Acts 5:4), and private ownership of houses was maintained (see Acts 5:42; 8:3; 12:12).

The biblical idea of justice should not become an argument for equality of possessions. The very common Hebrew words for "justice" and "righteousness" in the Old Testament (*mishpat, sedek,* and cognate terms) never take the specific sense of "bringing about equality of possessions in society." Rather, "righteousness" concerns obedience to God's laws generally, and "justice" can refer either to the decision of a judge (a "judgment") or to right and fair decisions and actions toward others in human conduct generally.

This last sense would include caring for the weak, defenseless, and needy (see Ps. 146:7; Isa. 1:17), but should not be limited to that (cf. Gen. 18:25; Prov. 21:15; Isa. 5:7; 61:8).

Some simple lifestyle advocates have argued that the Church should work toward equality of possessions because of the point made in 2 Corinthians 8:14: "As a matter of *equality* your abundance at the present time should supply their want, so that their abundance may supply your want, that there may be *equality*."[9] Yet the word twice translated "equality" (*isotes*) in this verse is probably better translated "fairness." It takes this same sense in its only other New Testament occurrence, Colossians 4:1: "Masters, grant to your slaves justice and *fairness* [*isotes*]"(emphasis added)—not here implying that all slaves would be paid exactly the same amount, but that they would be treated fairly. And in 2 Corinthians 8:14, certainly Paul was not asking that the wealthy Corinthians divide their possessions *equally* with the poor Jerusalem Christians.

Will only Christians recognize the fairness of inequal rewards? No. The idea of greater reward for more or better work is generally shared by unbelievers because of a God-given sense of justice or fairness.

These conclusions have specific implications for economic systems. If it is not wrong to profit from employing others, the Communist "labor theory of value" is not to be endorsed. Indeed, the owners of any enterprise also deserve to gain some return on their planning and investing, and economies ought to be structured to allow this to happen.

An economic system is preferable if differences in amount and quality of work result in different rewards, and therefore in differing amounts of possessions. Of course, since people have various levels of God-given ability, energy, and desire to work, there will inevitably be degrees of possessions in any society that allocates rewards in this way.

Moreover, if these rewards are to be genuine, people must have the ability to enjoy them. Such enjoyment of rewards is not wrong; it is right and good. Material rewards and the ability to enjoy them are necessary as incentives to work: "The plowman should plow in hope and the thresher thresh in hope of a share in the crop" (1 Cor. 9:10; cf. Prov. 16:26; 28:20).

Support for this principle of greater reward for greater amount and quality of work may be sought and even expected from Christians and nonChristians alike, since it results from a God-given sense of justice or fairness. The appropriateness of such a principle for society will also receive empirical confirmation from observing the actions of Communist societies when they wish to increase productivity. Such increases can be accomplished by allowing people to keep the rewards of their work, though such programs are generally not called "capitalism" but euphemistically (or perhaps accurately) referred to with some other term—such as "the responsibility system" in recent years in China. The new constitution of the People's Republic of China (adopted December 4, 1982) no longer endorses the traditional Communist maxim, "From each according to his ability, to each according to his need." Instead, it says, "From each according to his ability, to each according to his work" (article 6, paragraph 2).[10] Yet this principle seems to have in it the seeds of destruction of the Communist system, for if people are generally rewarded according to their *work*, those who work more or who work more productively will gain greater and greater possessions. If these possessions are to be enjoyed, there will be increasingly large amounts of private property held by individuals.

But the larger point is that differing rewards for work are appropriate in a society that conforms to scriptural teachings. And such a society will also result in increased productivity because of the greater incentive to work where there is greater reward.

Principle 13: Society should value productive work. Closely related to the previous principle is the fact that one moral component of a scripturally approved economic system would be a society that values and praises industry, diligence, and skill in productive work. God has made us so that there is fulfillment in industrious work, for work is a gift from God. Though there is now some pain with work due to sin and the Fall (see Gen. 3:17-19), work in itself remains a blessing; it is something good to be sought, not something evil to be avoided. God created us to work; He gave Adam work before there was any sin in the world (see Gen. 2:15).

A scripturally directed society would not be one that grumbles about every Monday morning and tries to avoid work whenever possible, living for the weekend or a vacation. It would be a society of cheerful laborers, thankful to God for each day of work He has given. It would be a society of *producers*, not just *consumers*. So the Preacher asserts, "My heart found pleasure in all my toil, and this was my reward for all my toil" (Eccles. 2:10), and "There is nothing better for a man than that he should eat and drink, and find enjoyment in his toil. This also, I saw, is from the hand of God" (Eccles. 2:24; cf. 3:13; 5:19-20).

Principle 14: Christians who are workers and owners of property should also seek heavenly rewards, not just earthly possessions. Christians in any economy must add a "spiritual perspective" to the principles above. Work is to be done as to the Lord (see Col. 3:23); therefore, the goal of all our work should be not accumulating great possessions but gaining God's approval. It is wrong to make the acquisition of a large personal fortune the goal of our work: "Do not toil to acquire wealth; be wise enough to desist" (Prov. 23:4). And Jesus knew that we cannot make personal wealth our goal and be faithful to God: "You cannot serve God and Money" (Matt. 6:24; cf. 1 Tim. 3:3, 8). In fact, "those who desire to be rich fall into temptation, into a snare, into many senseless and hurtful desires that plunge men into ruin and destruction" (1 Tim. 6:9). Instead of wealth, high status, influence, or fame, the desire that motivates Christians each day should be seeking God's blessing, "Well done, good and faithful servant" (Matt. 25:21).

But it does not seem appropriate to encourage unbelievers to seek heavenly reward for their work or even to foster the idea that they can gain God's approval on their work apart from forgiveness in Christ. They must not get the impression that persons can earn merit with God apart from Christ.

This principle nonetheless has implications for economic systems. A system in which workers are free to choose the kind of work they will do, including the freedom to choose work that will benefit the Church and bring much heavenly reward (for instance, missionary work), is a more desirable economic system. Again the indication is that a totally materialistic system where people are compelled by the government to work for the material productivity of society exclusively (as in many Communist states today) is less consistent with biblical standards.

Principle 15: There should be reward for those who cannot work but not for those who will not work. Certainly Scripture encourages the giving of material assistance to the poor. The apostles in Jerusalem encouraged Paul to "remember the poor" (Gal. 2:10), and he urges Christians to "do good to all men, and especially to those who are of the household of faith" (Gal. 6:10). He also makes the point that a converted thief should no longer steal, but should "labor, doing honest work with his hands, so that he may be able to give to those in need" (Eph. 4:28). The second half of Paul's third missionary journey (see Acts 19:21–21:16) was almost entirely occupied with the taking up of a collection for the poor Christians in Jerusalem (cf. Rom. 15:25-27; 2 Cor. 8:9).

However, persons who were *unwilling* to work were not legitimate recipients of free handouts: "For even when we were with you we gave you this command: If any one will not work, let him not eat" (2 Thess. 3:10). The reasonableness of this precept in the economic world is obvious: If those who are simply unwilling to work received material rewards anyway, fewer and fewer would work, and nonproductivity would be rewarded.

The wisdom of such procedures for aiding the poor is also apparent in the general ordering of the world and should be clear to nonChristians as well, apart from the special revelation of Scripture.

The suggestion is that a desirable economic system will make some provision for giving assistance to the poor, particularly to persons who cannot work to support themselves, and to their families. (Whether this aid should come through government activity or private contributions or both, and in what proportion, is the subject of chapters 10 and 11, and I will not attempt to treat it here.) In addition, a desirable economy will punish with negative consequences persons unwilling to work so that such behavior will actively be discouraged.

Principle 16: Individuals should give generously to the needs of others. Whatever we may say about the appropriateness of government aid to those in need, all will probably agree that the Bible strongly encourages individuals to give to the needs of others. The New Testament advocates that Christians should do good to all people: "As we have opportunity, let us do good to all men, and especially to those who are of the household of faith" (Gal. 6:10).

But the New Testament emphasizes giving generously to Christians in need: "If anyone has this world's goods and sees his brother in need, yet closes his heart against him, how does God's love abide in him?" (1 John 3:17). ("Brother" in the New Testament refers only to a believer or to an actual brother in one's immediate family. Note also Matt. 25:40; John 13:35; Rom. 15:26-27.)

Yet the parable of the good Samaritan (see Luke 10:25-37) reminds us that sometimes people with urgent needs come to our attention, and these people are the "neighbors" whom we are to love as ourselves. Paul says Christians should "help cases of urgent need" (Titus 3:14; cf. Eph. 4:28). And generous giving to the needs of others is motivated by trust in God who will Himself provide for our needs (see Matt. 6:19-20; Phil. 4:19; Heb. 13:5).

The general moral obligation to love one's neighbor extends certainly to unbelievers as well as to believers, and its endorsement by unbelievers is seen in all kinds of charitable and community activities carried on by unbelievers throughout our societies.

This principle implies that an economic system allowing people the opportunity to give generously of time or money or both is preferable to one prohibiting or restricting them in this area. Although God is certainly thankful for the sacrificial contributions of poor people in societies that will not permit any person to accumulate much wealth (such as most Communist societies), very little actual giving can be done by those who are kept by their governments at subsistence level, and very few needs can actually be met by such giving. Once again, an economic system that allows individuals to gain ownership of and therefore stewardship over large amounts of possessions and thereby enables them to give large amounts of both time and money to the needs of others would seem to be more closely aligned with biblical principles.

CONCLUSIONS

An economic system may be said to be more compatible with scriptural principles if it includes the following factors:

1. It provides more productivity than other systems. [Principle 1]

2. It allows individuals freedom to give time and effort to producing "invisible" or "spiritual" goods and services if they wish to do so. (It does not compel citizens to emphasize entirely the production of material goods.) [Principles 4 and 14]

3. It permits a wide range of choice in individual occupations (this is a broader application of point 2 above [Principle 4], but may also be derived from the desirability of a market system for efficient allocation of human resources [Principle 6] and from the need for freedom of vocational choice as an expression of full humanity created in God's image).

4. It has the most efficient use of resources for production (this suggests the allocation of goods through the pricing system of a free market economy as opposed to a planned economy). [Principle 6]

5. It promotes development of the earth's abundant resources for the benefit of human beings. [Principle 7]

6. Perhaps it is one that permits or encourages—or even requires— people to take time from work, perhaps one day in seven, in order to rest and show dependence on God. [Principle 9]

7. It makes provision for and protects private ownership of resources and gives greater reward for more efficient use of these resources. [Principle 10]

8. It is one in which those who own land may receive rent from the use of that land and those who employ others in enterprises that produce goods and services may gain profit from those enterprises. [Principle 11]

9. It is one in which more and better work receives greater reward, thereby resulting in inequality in possessions. It also allows for the ability to enjoy those possessions. [Principle 12]

10. It is one in which hard work and diligence in work are viewed as valuable by the society as a whole. [Principle 13]

11. It is one in which assistance is given to those unable to work, but in which unwillingness to work is punished with negative economic conse-

quences. [Principle 15]

12. It is one that allows individuals opportunity to give generously to the needs of others. [Principle 16]

13. It is one in which there is a common basis of indispensable morality reflected in the lives and convictions of the people. [Principles 5, 6, 9, and 14]

In addition, we have noted certain appropriate kinds of restrictions that a government may put on an economic system:

14. Government should prevent the production of immoral goods and services. [Principle 2]

15. Government should produce some public goods and services through taxation. [Principle 3]

16. Government usually should not adopt any rationing or government-directed distribution of resources. [Principle 7]

17. Government should prohibit monopolistic control of resources by any individuals or small groups of people. [Principle 8 (1)]

18. Government should prohibit stealing and the acquiring of possessions through fraud or deceit. [Principle 8 (2)]

19. Government should ensure that people do not deplete resources that need to be used by future generations. [Principle 8 (3)]

20. Government should impose some health and safety standards. [Principle 8 (4)]

21. Government should support and encourage a common basis of morality. [Principles 4, 5, 6, 9, 14, and 16]

In combination, these factors indicate that a free market economy with some government restriction in significant specified areas, coupled with a commitment to basic indispensable morality by the individuals in a society, may be said to be an economic system compatible with Scripture.

EDITOR'S REFLECTIONS

Several questions cry out at this juncture: (1) Is it fair to take biblical precepts given to a people living in an agrarian society that was theocratically governed and apply them as a normative standard to a people living in a pluralistic society that is technologically dominated and urban in character? (2) Is it fair to develop ethical standards for the marketplace from biblical information that served as contextual material in which much of Scripture's salvation theology was developed? (3) Has Dr. Grudem selected only those biblical passages that seem to pertain to our economic system, or has he really surveyed Scripture in identifying sixteen principles, fourteen of which apply to individuals in the marketplace and ten that speak to the community and those who govern (eight apply to both)? These questions need to be addressed before we proceed any further, for if the answer to the first two questions is no, the balance of our work is both dangerously misleading and heretical.

Many people choose to believe that the precepts given by God to His people when they lived in an agrarian and theocratically governed society cannot be transferred to another culture. This assertion, however, is built on false assumptions and is, therefore, false. It assumes moral truth either changes with time and circumstances or is so narrowly constructed that it has no general or broader application. God's standards do not change, for His nature and character do not change. Human nature is also the same from generation to generation and from culture to culture, and it does not change. Human circumstances change, but external circumstances do not determine the inherent essence of what is righteous and constructive for moral development. Particular circumstances call for the application of specific moral principles, but circumstances do not alter or define the content of the moral principles that need to be applied.

One underlying premise of this entire series of books is that it is possible to glean biblical principles from God's Word by observing how God's precepts were repeatedly applied and discussed during the centuries of unfolding revelation and that these biblical principles have application in every culture for all times. Certainly situations, environments, and circumstances change repeatedly and rapidly in the modern world, but these realities do not alter God's revealed principles. The concept of discerning and developing biblical principles was discussed in some depth in the second half of the opening chapter of *Biblical Principles & Business: The Foundations*, and may be reviewed there by readers who want to refresh their memory about this subject.

Our real task is to correctly discern the intent of God's Word and carefully construct the principles to be derived from it. The time, place, and circumstances under which the original revelation was given, however, do not restrict or negate its future use. God did not restrict His clear revelation for the use of a single generation, social condition, or nation. This view is supported by the fact that Scripture was given to God's people over a number of centuries and has maintained the same consistent moral principles throughout those times. God's truth is timeless as to its salvation message and its moral principles.

What about the second question I raised: Is it fair to develop ethical standards for the marketplace from biblical information that was not recorded for the explicit purpose of teaching economic truths? Or put more bluntly, should not the use of Scripture be restricted to its salvation message and things spiritual? This question reflects either a narrow perception of what is embodied in God's plan of salvation or a mental compartmentalization of the sacred from the secular where one spends his or her time picking out the "spiritual" content of Scripture and separating it from its recorded application. Either misunderstanding leads eventually to spiritual immaturity and a quasiwithdrawal from the world.

Salvation is a reality at a point in time as well as a process. We are being continuously sanctified and conformed to the image of Christ so that Christ's mind can be manifested through our conduct as we grow in Him (see 1 Cor. 2:16). Christ redeems us so that we can have eternal life, but we are to live for Him in the world, too. We are to be set apart (sanctified) from the intentions, methods, and sinful ways used in the world as we live and work for Christ in the world.

Scripture does not teach us to compartmentalize life into sacred and secular categories. In fact, God addresses us in the context of the world as we work, raise families, play, and so forth. God has not given us His truth in some philosophical format. He has spoken to us at the level of our everyday needs.

God does not want us to withdraw from the world. When we love the Lord Jesus Christ, we strive to live as He would have us live. We know His will both by learning the propositional truths of Scripture and by observing their application in Scripture so we can follow Him and know clearly how we should think and act in situations calling for the same principles. Others must see Christ in our integrity, acts of compassion, forgiving spirit, and other manifestations that reveal His transforming presence in our lives, or else our testimony will be perceived as lifeless words that speak of godliness but deny its reality and power (see 2 Tim. 3:5).

Salvation's doctrines are to be applied in the practical events of life. The Apostle Paul sets forth the great doctrines of God and man at the beginning of some of his letters (see Rom. 1–11; Eph. 1–3), and then he immediately illustrates how we are to live out these doctrines in the world (see Rom. 12–16; Eph. 4–6). Godly behavior is to be the natural outgrowth of believing the message of salvation. We can, therefore, conclude that much of Scripture was purposely given to us in the context of everyday life to explicitly instruct us about ways to act as followers of Christ in the economic, social, and political arenas.

Finally, we need to address the question: Has Dr. Grudem really surveyed Scripture to determine the principles that have economic implications for us, or has he merely brought our contemporary economic system before Scripture and addressed a narrow range of selected economic topics? He has uncovered and defined biblical principles that apply to economics, and he has represented Scripture's content in a balanced, evenhanded manner. Some people may object that his analysis seems too supportive of a free market system. But when the economic activities and structures of the ancient Israelites are compared with those of their neighbors (characterized by slavery and authoritarian rule) and when these historic economic activities are compared with contemporary economic systems, we soon realize that the Israelites actually worked and traded in a very free marketplace.

We do not want to leap ahead too far or too rapidly in our evaluation of contemporary economic systems, but a significant difference exists between the operation of a theocratic state and a humanly governed state with regard to the demands placed on the economic resources by God and the requirements likely to be placed on those same resources by human rulers (see 1 Sam. 8:1–22, esp. vv. 11–18). Our nation's founding fathers sought to establish a representative democracy, in part, because they realized this difference and sought a means to control the rule of men.

Dr. Grudem has also done a good job of presenting the tensions between "freedom" and "control" in Scripture. The principles he has enumerated address both individuals and government. While it is true that Scripture has much more to say about individuals and their personal accountability before God in matters affecting economics than about the responsibilities of the community, it is nevertheless true that those who rule or govern are also clearly addressed and in definitive language. For example, the prophets did not hesitate to speak to neighboring heathen nations about moral issues.

We are, however, a long way from being finished in our efforts to identify biblical principles applicable to business and economics. We will discover many other specific biblical principles as we zero in on topics that relate to business and public policy, such as: (1) God is no respecter of persons (many applications in management and marketing); (2) accountability must always accompany the granting of authority (universal application); (3) Christian leaders are ultimately servants; and a host of other easily definable principles.

Now let's turn to the work of Richard Pierard and look at some gaps between the standards of Scripture and the consequences of operating a particular economic system in a fallen world where God's biblical principles are not sought by the majority of people. Dr. Pierard supports the basic tenor, objectives, and accomplishments of a free market economy, but he has a very sensitive heart for people who remain out of the economic mainstream and thus do not derive as many of the benefits from the system as do others with greater opportunities and/or abilities. He is attuned to God's call that we are to be concerned for the widows, orphans, poor, and others who have real difficulties coping in a fallen and frequently uncaring world.

Solomon has told us, "The righteous is concerned for the rights of the poor, the wicked does not understand such concern" (Prov. 29:7). God desires that we speak up for the afflicted, needy, and oppressed (see Prov. 31:8-9; Jer. 5:28), which is precisely what Richard Pierard is doing. We will discuss in later sections if the problems he identifies emanate from our fallen nature or are associated with the economic structure. At this juncture our attention is being drawn to some serious economic problems in our society.

CHAPTER 3

NO ECONOMIC SYSTEM FLOWS DIRECTLY FROM SCRIPTURE

Richard V. Pierard

Richard V. Pierard is Professor of History at Indiana State University, where he has served since 1964. He received the B.A. and M.A. degrees from California State University in Los Angeles, and the Ph.D. in modern history from the University of Iowa. He has held visiting professorships at various colleges and theological seminaries and was a Fulbright Professor in 1984-85 at the University of Frankfurt in West Germany. He has authored or coauthored seven books, the most recent being Civil Religion and the Presidency *(Zondervan, 1988), and over twenty book chapters and fifty articles in scholarly and popular journals in such wide-ranging areas as evangelical Christianity, right-wing politics and religion in both America and Germany, European overseas expansion, and Christian missions. He is an active layperson in the American Baptist Churches, U.S.A.*

"**M**an is an economic animal" is a trite phrase that has been heard since time immemorial. Economics is indeed a central part of human life because it involves society's use of scarce resources for the production and distribution of goods and services. This includes food, water, clothing, and shelter, things that are necessary for human existence, the innumerable comforts and conveniences that lie beyond the basic need for survival, and less measurable matters like education, government, and national defense that make a society viable.

All societies have economic systems that focus on the production and distribution of these things, as most of what we need or want is not freely available in nature. The systems also deal with the allocation of resources since there is not enough to go around for everyone. Choices must be made as to how much of the goods will be produced, whose wants will be satisfied first, and how the limited amounts will be divided among the members of the society. Thus, economic decisions are at their root social ones. Ethical questions and value judgments infuse every element of the economic process, even though some economists like to see their discipline as "value-neutral" and concentrate solely on analysis, the generation of hypotheses that can be tested objectively, and the implementation of public policy on the basis of their findings.

Christians who regard the Bible as the standard by which all human actions may be measured must certainly reject the idea of economics as a value-neutral science. They will of necessity have to perceive all economic arrangements as tainted by the Fall and infused by sin and to acknowledge as well that every system is subject to human finitude. Therefore, Christians are compelled by the very logic of their faith to conclude that no specific economic system is in itself biblically consonant and that all of them in some way or another fall short of scriptural standards. This is the case regardless of the system—free market (*laissez faire*) capitalism, monopoly capitalism, centrally planned state socialism, communitarian, traditional agrarian, or a mixed economy.

Unfortunately, many evangelicals today, particularly in the United States, reject or at least sidestep this axiom. They are fully aware of the failings of socialism and related types of "command" economies and have expended enormous effort both to explicate the glories of free market captitalism and to expose the inadequacies of its rivals. Most North American evangelicals would agree with Jerry Falwell's oft-quoted comment:

> The free-enterprise system is clearly outlined in the Book of Proverbs in the Bible. Jesus Christ made it clear that the work ethic was a part of His plan for man. Ownership of property is biblical. Competition in business is biblical. Ambitious and successful business management is clearly outlined as a part of God's plan for His people.[1]

Few Christians in the United States take any of the various forms of socialism seriously, and most evangelicals would probably resonate with another Falwellian dictum: "Atheism and socialism—or liberalism, which tends in the same direction—are inseparable entities."[2] Should the Lynchburg televangelist seem a little too extreme, consider the remark by George Gilder, one of the spiritual fathers of Reaganomics, made of all places in *Christianity Today*, that a socialist society "is inherently hostile to Christianity and capitalism is simply the essential mode of human life that corresponds to religious truth."[3]

However, as John C. Cort demonstrates in his stimulating book *Christian Socialism*,[4] a small group of Roman Catholics and liberal Protestants in the United States have espoused various socialist doctrines from time to time during the twentieth century. Moreover, with the emergence of liberation theology in Latin America, serious questions are being raised about capitalism, even within evangelical circles. It is safe to say that most indigenous evangelical theologians and missiologists in Latin America today are sympathetic with the general line of liberationist thinking, even though they may not subscribe to its use of Marxist categories. Their socialist leanings are shared by many biblical and theological conservatives elsewhere in the Third World and in such places as South Africa. They wonder why their North American and European counterparts have ignored the failings of the Western capitalist order except to offer a few minor correctional criticisms that do not touch upon fundamental problems in the system itself.

The Bible provides rather clear guidelines as to how an economic system should function. Unfortunately, the systems in real life deviate widely from these principles, a situation we naturally should expect to see in a finite and fallen world. Christians who seek to function as salt and light in this world must recognize the vast differences between God's ideal and human reality, and rather than simply affirm the various economic orders under which they live, they should work to bring these closer in line to the divine standard. In the process, they will almost certainly have to make some adjustments in the economic philosophies they have picked up from their sociopolitical environments.

THE POSITION OF GOD

From a Christian standpoint, any critique of economic systems must begin with a consideration of the position of God. He created the world and declared it to be good. He has not abdicated His sovereignty even though sin entered the world and, as some have said, it is currently "under Enemy occupation." Through the so-called cultural mandate, we have been given the assignment of establishing "dominion" over the earth and assisting in preserving and upholding what He has created. Further, we look forward to that day when the Kingdom of God will be established in its fullness over all the earth, the creation will be restored from the effects of the Fall, and all people will participate in a truly just and righteous social and economic order.

God has given us the final word of authority in His written revelation, the Bible. The particular teachings and stories of the great acts of God recorded in Scripture *are* the Word of God, not something we must go behind to find the real revelation. It stands above all political and economic systems, which by their very nature are relative, imperfect, transitory, and subject to change. Because the Word of the Lord abides forever, Christians have the right and obligation to hold all systems accountable to its principles. The Bible is not a book of systematic ethics or theology; it is the divine Word addressed to many different situations and crises that the people of God experienced. No human editor prepared a final copy reconciling the differences and ambiguities. What we find here is not a set of normative injunctions constituting a "letter of the law" to be followed assiduously by the believing community, but principles that must be dug out and applied to our present situation.

The universe is held together by the bonds of law inherent in the divine character. The Scriptures affirm that a fundamental attribute of the Sovereign Creator is justice (e.g., Ps. 99:1-4; Jer. 9:24; 10:6-12). In fact, God's law and concern with justice are inseparable entities, and they go forth as a light to the peoples of the earth (see Isa. 51:4). The specific law code He gave to His people Israel reflects the divine character. It was paradigmatic in that it was a model for His covenant community to follow that would enable them to live in harmony and justice and it also provided a standard of justice by which the performance of other peoples could be measured.

Moreover, the Scriptures describe a God of history who works through our social existence, is concerned about our welfare to the point that He sent His Son to die for us, and reveals ways in which His creatures are to relate to one another. They show a God who cares for humanity in its particular material and social existence. Because human nature is essentially unchanging over space and time, the problems humankind faces are more or less the same in every culture. Conflicts over the exercise of power and the oppression of the weak by the strong are recurring human experiences, and the Bible speaks to these matters.

Scripture must, however, not be forced to answer questions brought to the text that are culturally foreign to it. The apologies locating capitalism or socialism in the Bible grievously err in this regard. As Stephen Mott ably points out, one cannot automatically extrapolate from the property arrangements of an agrarian and tribal culture the specifics that should be applied to a complex modern industrial economic arrangement:

> The choice is not bipolar between private and collectivistic property
> so that the existence of private property in the Bible can be equated
> with capitalism or the existence of tribal controls on property can be

equated with socialism. Rather there exists a broad spectrum with great variations in the form and degree of community control of property. The fact that the biblical property pattern is neither capitalistic or socialistic in itself is not a biblical argument against either.

But the biblical support for a modern economic arrangement must be much more complex and indirect. One must discover the values that are sought to be expressed in the economic, social and political systems in the Bible and in theological reflection upon the Bible and the subsequent history of the church and indicate the modern arrangements which would best implement those values. Such a case will require empirical and historical information far beyond that which can be furnished from the Bible.[5]

THE IMPORTANCE OF HUMAN BEINGS

Humankind is God's central concern, and any economic system that diminishes or downgrades human life and values falls short of the divine standard. Each man and woman is created in the image of God and is called to a personal relationship with Christ. Each person possesses absolute value in the eyes of God, which is a truth David expresses in this psalm:

When I consider your heavens,
    the work of your fingers,
the moon and the stars,
    which you have set in place,
what is man that you are mindful of him,
    the son of man that you care for him?
You made him a little lower than the heavenly beings
    and crowned him with glory and honor.

You made him ruler over the works of your hands;
    you put everything under his feet:
all flocks and herds,
    and the beasts of the field,
the birds of the air,
    and the fish of the sea,
    all that swim the paths of the seas.
O Lord, our Lord,
    how majestic is your name in all the earth! (Ps. 8:3-9)

Thus, in economic life, the individual is not to be regarded as an object whose value is determined by the play of market forces and who may be bought and sold or dispensed with at the whim or will of those possessing economic power. He or she is to be treated not as a thing but as a free and responsible agent.

However, as important as each individual is in God's sight, one finds the highest personal fulfillment in community, not in isolation. God's call to faith and conversion is personal, but His plan is for the reconciliation of all humankind and the restoration of the created order. Hence, rugged individualism is a cultural, not a biblical value. Social contract theory regards society as merely a voluntary association of persons, one in which the individual retains his rights and power to maximize benefits for himself, regardless of how things might affect others in the society.

The biblical emphasis is on covenant and community. In this framework, every person is called to be a coheir with Christ in the community of God's people. The essence of community is that all will work for the fulfillment of each person's basic needs. To be sure, even though nonChristians technically do not share in this community, Christians still must respect the dignity of every person and have a sense of solidarity with the whole human race because the Scriptures clearly affirm that Christ died for the redemption of all.

Nowhere is the linkage between the divine and the human aspects of God's program more evident than in the summary of the law: "Love the Lord your God with all your heart and with all your soul and with all your strength and with all your mind," and "Love your neighbor as yourself" (Luke 10:27; Lev. 19:18; see Deut. 6:5; Matt. 19:19; 22:37-40; Mark 12:29-31; Rom. 13:9; Gal. 5:14; James 2:8). The vertical and horizontal relationships encompassed here are represented as well in that greatest of all symbols of God's grace, the cross on which Jesus suffered and died in order to effect the reconciliation of man with man and with God.

The vision of a better existence that God ordained for His creatures was expressed frequently in the Old Testament and articulated by Jesus at the inauguration of His ministry when He called on His listeners to repent and believe in the gospel, for the time had come (or was fulfilled) and the Kingdom of Heaven was at hand (see Mark 1:15; Matt. 4:17). Jesus proclaimed a "mode of flourishing" that could be called *shalom*. Nicholas Wolterstorff explains that for *shalom* to be instituted, first humans had to be reconciled to God and delight in fellowship with Him. In addition must come reconciliation among human beings and between them and nature, and delight by humans in the good things of nature. The content of the Kingdom of Heaven that Jesus preached was encompassed in the Old Testament concept of *shalom*. Through Jesus Christ, God broke into the world with this vision, the Church continues the work Jesus began, and we await the coming of God's Kingdom in its fullness, which will bring to fruition our struggle to produce here and now the signs of that Kingdom.[6]

Thus, the good news of the gospel is that of reconciliation—God and humanity, men with men, and humankind and nature. The first is a spiritual action—we turn to God in faith and are transformed into His children—and the other two follow, albeit slowly, painfully, and imperfectly. The reason is the all-pervasive nature of sin, which continues to infect all human material relationships with its demonic and corrupting influence. Stephen Mott captures its essence:

> Sin is not the self-harmonizing enlightened and rational self-interest of capitalist and other liberal forms of thought. Nor are human beings controlled by the communal and creative drives assumed in traditional socialist thought. Sin is a power which destroys and which must be restrained. Such a view of sin is reflected in the power of exploitation in social relations.[7]

All efforts to build a better social order will fall short of the mark because of the depth and permanence of human sin. Elements of personal selfishness and group self-interest inexorably find their way into our thoughts and policies, no matter how dedicated and well-intentioned we may be in our effort to carry out God's redemptive work. Despite these very real limitations, still the best economic system from a biblical standpoint is one that endeavors to promote the objective of *shalom*—reconciliation among humans and between humankind and nature.

STEWARDSHIP

The third aspect of a Christian critique of economic systems concerns the stewardship of the earth's resources. "The earth is the LORD's, and everything in it [or, the fullness thereof, KJV]," so reads Psalm 24:1, while Psalm 50 adds that God owns "the cattle on a thousand hills" and "the world is mine, and all that is in it" (vv. 10, 12). Thus, there is no such thing as absolute ownership of property, regardless of the claims of autonomous man. The land and all that pertains to it belong to God, and we human beings are the stewards to whose care He has entrusted it. We are, as Walter L. Owensby so pithily comments, "the managers of everything and the owners of nothing."[8] Our job is to preserve and wisely utilize the resources of this earth for the benefit of all God's creatures, not manipulate them for personal wealth and advantage.

As good stewards of God's creation, we are responsible for preserving the integrity of nature. It is not a mere "thing" to be disposed of casually. The creation, too, suffers under the burden of corruption and awaits the day when it "will be liberated from its bondage to decay and brought into the glorious freedom of the children of God" (Rom. 8:20-21). We are obligated to preserve it from irreparable damage.

By far the most fundamental biblical illustration of the interrelationship between divine ownership of the earth, environmental protection, and proper stewardship is the Jubilee principle set forth in Leviticus 25. The underlying assumption (v. 23) is that the *land* is the Lord's and the people are temporary occupants or "tenants." The first part of the chapter indicates that the Israelites were required to let the land lay fallow every seventh year so that it might regain its fertility. Then, every fiftieth year the land would be rested and the ones who had been compelled by economic necessity to sell their land would regain this property. It was a way of institutionalizing the equality of the original land distribution and guaranteeing to each extended family the possession of a piece of productive property so that it could be self-sufficient. Thus, the interests of the larger community were given primacy over those of entrepreneurial individuals who through clever business practices or the misfortunes of others had been able to move ahead economically.

Whether or not the Jubilee idea ever was implemented once the Israelites settled down in Canaan, the principle expressed in it surely is at odds with the Western concept of private property, which includes the power to *dispose* of it freely. In modern thinking, land is essentially a commodity to be bought and sold, and little consideration is given to its use for the best interests of society. The community is denied any control over the land other than to see through zoning or other restrictive agreements that it is not utilized in ways that would cause the neighboring pieces of property to depreciate in value.

Christians should have serious reservations about any economic order that does not take seriously the necessity of protecting the physical environment. In this respect, virtually all modern-day systems are deficient. Such disasters as the Chernobyl nuclear power plant explosion and the virtual death of Lake Baikal in the Soviet Union or the use of highly polluting brown coal in East German industries reveal that socialist economies have no more and probably even less respect for the environment and resource conservation than capitalist ones do. The overgrazing of marginal semiarid lands in Africa and the widespread cutting of the Amazon rain forest in South America are other examples of poor stewardship that will certainly lead to ecological disasters in the near future if nothing is done about them.

Furthermore, we are expected to be *productive* and not simply *possessive* of God's gifts. James Skillen comments that God commissioned and enabled humankind to serve Him by investing His gifts and our energies in the ongoing development of creation. Each successive generation can work and build on the efforts of its predecessors to advance the creation. We are to use God-given resources and talents (see the parable of the talents, Matt. 25:14-30) "for productive, stewardly use in the service of others, not for excessive consumption or to encourage the vain search for earthly security and self-sufficiency."[9]

Every person's work is important, and the shutting out of some people from exercising their productive potentialities through poverty, ignorance, and involuntary unemployment is a transgression of God's plan for His created beings. Also, savings and accumulation of wealth should flow back into the productive process instead of being hoarded. The current practice of amassing great amounts of money in order to buy out companies and build ever greater concentrations of wealth and power violates the design of the Creator, which is productivity on behalf of humankind. Such poor stewardship of wealth is simply covetousness and is just as much a breaking of the divine commandments as murder or theft.

MATERIALISM

Scripture gives considerable attention to material possessions and the primacy of material over spiritual values. Jesus' anger as He drove the merchants and moneychangers from the Temple (see John 2:13-16) is perhaps the most compelling example. The Bible is replete with warnings about the dangers of riches, as the following selections illustrate:

Whoever loves money never has money enough;
    whoever loves wealth is never satisfied with his income.
This too is meaningless. (Eccles. 5:10)

The name of the LORD is a strong tower;
    the righteous run to it and are safe.
The wealth of the rich is their fortified city;
    they imagine it an unscalable wall. (Prov. 18:10-11)

The Pharisees, who loved money, heard all this and were sneering at Jesus. He said to them, "You are the ones who justify yourselves in the eyes of men, but God knows your hearts. What is highly valued among men is detestable in God's sight." (Luke 16:14-15)

To the angel of the church in Laodicea write: . . . I know your deeds, that you are neither cold nor hot. I wish you were either one or the other! So, because you are lukewarm—neither hot nor cold—I am about to spit you out of my mouth. You say, "I am rich; I have acquired wealth and do not need a thing." But you do not realize that you are wretched, pitiful, poor, blind and naked. I counsel you to buy from me gold refined in fire, so you can become rich; and white clothes to wear, so you can cover your shameful nakedness; and salve to put on your eyes, so you can see. (Rev. 3:14-18)

But godliness with contentment is great gain. For we brought nothing into the world, and we can take nothing out of it. But if we have food and clothing, we will be content with that. People who want to get rich fall into temptations and a trap and into many foolish and harmful desires that plunge men into ruin and destruction. For the love of money is a root of all kinds of evil. Some people, eager for money, have wandered from the faith and pierced themselves with many griefs. (1 Tim. 6:6-10)

The biblical admonitions about the seductive quality inherent in riches are most appropriate. From an individual standpoint, the possession of great wealth can deaden human sensitivity to God's call, and Jesus' point about the impossibility of being able to serve two masters, God and Mammon (Matt. 6:24), is well-taken. Those who have gained this largesse may come to feel that it is truly theirs and that they merited it because of some innate superiority. They can become intoxicated by wealth and be so self-satisfied, self-reliant, and proud that they fail to recognize the source of all good things, which is God, and that He may at any time require a final accounting from them. Jesus' parable about the rich fool who stored up his grain and goods for many years to come and then sat back to enjoy life poignantly illustrates this reality (Luke 12:16-21).

A hallmark of contemporary economic systems is the central role of materialism. Every system, from the hard-line Marxist-Leninist through the democratic socialist to free market capitalism, is shot through by materialism. John White aptly observes,

Communist materialism is doctrinaire and oppressive. Capitalist materialism is pragmatic and cancerous. Communist materialism claims that matter is all there is. Western materialism assumes that matter is all that *matters*. Many people who would never consider themselves to be materialists in the strict sense of the term, nevertheless live as though material things were of supreme importance.[10]

Regardless of what their defenders might say to the contrary, both capitalist and socialist systems fail to measure up to the biblical standard because of their materialistic underpinnings and emphases.

JUSTICE

The sharpest debate in the Christian criticism of economic systems centers on the issue of justice. God's demand for justice lies at the heart of biblical ethics, and all economic systems are particularly vulnerable at this point because few of them even come close to the divine standard of justice. Chapter 4 in Stephen C. Mott's *Biblical Ethics and Social Change* provides one of the most lucid expositions of the matter from an evangelical perspective.[11] Like most other writers on Christian ethics, Mott insists that the requirement for justice in societal matters is stated repeatedly in both Testaments, and he cites numerous passages to reinforce this generalization.

The defenders of *laissez faire* capitalism find this situation distressing, and often try to rebut those who explicate the justice theme by spiritualizing the relevant passages, placing them in a dispensational compartment that renders them inapplicable to today's problems, or labeling their use as "prooftexting." Of course, the conservative polemicists engage in all sorts of prooftexting. One can make a case for almost anything from the Bible.

The argument for justice proceeds from what was said earlier—it is a major attribute of God, and accordingly He expects it of His people. For example, Paul told the Corinthian church with respect to their collection for the poor brethren in Palestine:

> "God distributes, God gives to the poor. *God's justice* lasts forever." Now God who supplies seed to the sower and bread for food will also supply and multiply your seed and cause the harvest of *your justice* to increase. (2 Cor. 9:9-10)[12]

Paul's point was that the just God enables us to do justly. We are to structure our lives along the lines He laid out.

Moreover, divine justice is inseparable from divine love. Justice is not simply retributive (punishment for one's just desserts); it is also distributive (extension of the benefits of society to all, not just a favored few). In the Atonement, God's just demand of death for sin is satisfied by His love through the vicarious death of Christ, and God's righteousness overcomes His wrath, thereby making the benefits of Christ's death available to all.[13]

God's demand for justice is most forcefully made on behalf of those who are poor or otherwise socially weak. They are symbolized repeatedly throughout the Old Testament as the widow, the orphan (fatherless), and the resident alien (sojourner). Some examples are found in these passages:

> He upholds the cause of the oppressed
>> and gives food to the hungry.
>
> The LORD sets prisoners free, . . .
> the LORD lifts up those who are bowed down,
>> the LORD loves the righteous.
>
> The LORD watches over the alien
>> and sustains the fatherless and the widow,
>> but he frustrates the ways of the wicked. (Ps. 146:7-9)

> You hear, O LORD, the desire of the afflicted;
>> you encourage them, and you listen to their cry,
>
> defending the fatherless and the oppressed,
>> in order that man, who is of the earth, may terrify no more.
>>> (Ps. 10:17-18)

> For the LORD your God is God of gods and Lord of lords, the great God, mighty and awesome, who shows no partiality and accepts no bribes. He defends the cause of the fatherless and the widow, and loves the alien, giving him food and clothing. And you are to love those who are aliens, for you yourselves were aliens in Egypt. (Deut. 10:17-19)

> This is what the LORD Almighty says: "Administer true justice; show mercy and compassion to one another. Do not oppress the widow or the fatherless, the alien or the poor. In your hearts do not think evil of each other." (Zech. 7:9-10)

Many commentators feel that the biblical passages on justice manifest a distinct bias in favor of the poor and weak of the earth. Their evidence to support this view is truly impressive. Both the Israelites in the Old Testament and the Christian believers in the New Testament were directed to imitate God's preference for the poor and downtrodden.

The Exodus is the story of God's liberation of a poor and oppressed people. Then, the Israelites became wealthy oppressors, and after repeatedly issuing calls for repentance through the prophets, God finally destroyed their nation and sent the people into captivity. Through various prophets— Jeremiah, Isaiah, Ezekiel, Amos, Micah—God announced that destruction was imminent for wealthy individuals and nations that oppressed the poor.

Jesus declared that one aspect of His ministry was to preach the good news to the poor, proclaim release to the prisoners, heal the blind, and free the oppressed (see Luke 4:18-19; Isa. 61:1-2). Jesus Himself was poor and identified with the outcasts and lower elements in Jewish society (see Matt. 8:20; 11:2-6; 25:35-40; 2 Cor. 8:9). The disciples He chose were, with the exception of Matthew, from the lower classes. In the Magnificat, Mary proclaimed that God would exalt the poor and debase the rich; and her Son in the Sermon on the Mount pronounced a blessing on the poor and a curse on the rich (see Luke 1:46-53; 6:20-25). The Apostle James warned the rich that they would weep and howl because of their impending misery for having cheated their workers (see James 5:3-5).

Ronald J. Sider has reviewed this body of biblical data in his seminal work (for the evangelical community, that is), *Rich Christians in an Age of Hunger*. He concludes that God is impartial in His love for all human beings, but because of *our* unconcern for the poor and *our* preference for the prosperous, He exercises a special concern for the weak and disadvantaged. God longs for the salvation of the rich and desires fulfillment, joy, and happiness for all His creatures, but genuine biblical repentance and conversion require a turning away from all sin, including that of economic oppression. Salvation includes more than just spiritual renewal. For the rich, it involves liberation from injustice, and for the poor, the satisfaction of their basic physical needs.[14]

Space forbids an extended analysis of this complex topic, but its implications for our evaluation of economic systems are crucial. Contemporary systems come up short in this regard. For one thing, biblical faith demands that we form our society in such a fashion as to alleviate the inequalities that cause the suffering of the poor and weak. Acts of personal piety and charity that blunt the harsh impact of poverty are not enough. As Micah suggests, the Lord requires us "to act justly and to love mercy and to walk humbly with [our] God" (6:8). The numerous directives and provisions in Exodus, Leviticus, Numbers, and Deuteronomy aimed at helping the economically powerless and victims of injustice in Israel are indicative of God's larger design. Owensby wisely observes, "It is the responsibility of the covenant community to help shape a society where the weakest and most vulnerable will be defended and uplifted."[15]

The advocates of *laissez faire* capitalism tend to either ignore or at least explain away the many biblical injunctions about the poor.[16] On the other hand, Marxists disregard the Scriptures entirely and claim that they promote social justice from purely secular principles. Yet, when they achieve political power, they invariably erect political systems that perpetuate old injustices and create new ones. It seems to me that a mixed economy might do better in approximating the biblical vision, but the evidence as of now is inconclusive.

The problem is that few, if any, economic systems have come to terms with the question of concentrated power. In the political entities where socialist and command economies have been erected, there is an almost universal abuse of power. The record is clear in country after country that power has been used for purposes of personal aggrandizement and the persecution of dissenters and unpopular minorities. Since the incentives to increase output or otherwise engage in productive activities are few or not particularly meaningful, the state finds itself exercising ever more power over its citizens. It becomes a tyrannical force in its own right that equals or surpasses the tyranny of the market in a capitalist order.

At the same time, most of these systems, based as they are on an Enlightenment understanding of man, adopt a utopian view of the future and a belief in the possibilities of human improvement and perfectibility. Since this never takes into account the reality of sin and human finitude, the wielders of power in the economic order turn to compulsion to get people to do what they will not voluntarily do. In effect, the system ends up having to "force people to be free," to use the ominous phrase coined by Rousseau. Moreover, Communist countries are guilty of a new elitism whereby those who are part of the privileged class have access to luxury commodities in the "hard money" stores and enjoy benefits denied to most of the general populace, such as country cottages, quality schools and hospitals, automobiles, and travel abroad.

Abuses of power are rampant as well in the capitalist systems that are based on private property and market processes. Business interests provide the money to elect legislators who are amenable to their will. They possess the legal and public relations staffs to counter the efforts of consumer advocates who pressure them to be more socially responsible. They manipulate prices through making deals with one another and establishing formal or informal cartel arrangements. They force smaller concerns to go out of business or to conform to their wishes through the actual process or implied threat of takeovers. They close plants at will or move their operations to other parts of the country or abroad and thus throw thousands of hardworking, productive laborers out of their jobs.

People gain a sense of alienation and meaninglessness as they discover that their place in the economic process is dramatically affected by actions of individuals and groups far removed from their scope of influence or control. Persons who have seen their livelihood destroyed through no fault of their own are likely to wonder if there really is much difference between the systems after all.

A further problem is the tie between capitalism and social Darwinism, something that should disturb every sensitive Christian. In the late nineteenth century the laws of nature that had given us Adam Smith, *laissez faire,* and classical economics were linked with "the survival of the fittest" and "the bloody law of tooth and claw." It was held that individualism and selfishness could produce good results if the providential laws of the market were allowed free rein. Those who survived in the struggle for economic existence were deserving of their good fortune and were blessed of God. Millionaires were, as William Graham Sumner argued, nature's elect. They were "a product of natural selection, acting on the whole body of men to pick out those who can meet the requirement of certain work to be done."[17]

On the other hand, Herbert Spencer maintained that those who did not pass nature's test of survival died, "and it is best that they should die."[18] Sumner added that the misery of those who faltered in the competitive struggle was evidence of the wisdom and beneficence of nature:

> Many are frightened at liberty, especially under the form of competition. . . . They do not perceive that here "the strong" and "the weak" are terms which admit no definition unless they are made equivalent to the industrious and the idle, the frugal and the extravagant. They do not perceive, furthermore, that if we do not like the survival of the fittest, we have only one possible alternative, and that is survival of the unfittest. The former is the law of civilization; the latter is the law of anti-civilization.[19]

Another significant failing of free market capitalism is its neglect of the *social nature* of human beings in favor of self-interested individualism. J. Philip Wogaman notes that society is not just the sum of individual transactions among people who seek to gain things from one another: "Human life is shared life. It is a sharing of perceptions and values and language and purposes and identity. We are born and nurtured in a social environment or we do not survive." The philosophy of *laissez faire*, on the contrary, is a kind of principled selfishness wherein people are led to believe that social good is merely a byproduct of individual good and that it is a sufficient goal for each person to look out for himself or herself.[20] This hardly seems compatible with our faith in the Jesus whom Dietrich Bonhoeffer so aptly labeled the "man for others"[21] or the Lord God who said through His prophet Amos, "Let justice roll on like a river, righteousness like a never-failing stream" (5:24).

IDOLATRY

Finally, we must reject idolatry—regardless of what shape it may take. The commandment, "You shall have no other gods before me" (Exod. 20:3), is just as valid today as it ever has been. We as Christians make only one absolute commitment and that is to God as we know Him through Jesus Christ. Anything else is open to question, and our allegiance to other things is tentative and conditional. Any ideology, system, or nation that is elevated to the status of an absolute is an idol.

In countries where some form of Marxism-Leninism prevails, the ideology and economic system occupy an exalted place that approximates (if not actually is) idolatry. Unfortunately, many persons in the United States have, perhaps unwittingly, absorbed the idea that biblical faith and free market capitalism are inseparable realities and that the rejection or even the serious criticism of market economics is somehow an affront to God, country, and logic. However, God did not invent capitalism, socialism, feudalism, or any other economic ideology.

We must ask the hard question of every system: Is it producing the kind of results that work toward achieving the biblical vision of God's creation? If it is, we may support it. But if it is oppressing people or not meeting the needs of all, we must endeavor to modify or even abandon it in favor of something else. The problem is exacerbated, of course, when the system is one under which we live and that has treated us well. But we dare not give our unqualified allegiance to any economic system, regardless of whether it has brought us personal affluence or has received the blessing of fellow evangelicals.[22]

CONCLUSION

Although the Bible has much to say about economic matters, one really cannot extrapolate any modern economic system from its pages. It is wrongheaded to speak of either the capitalism or the socialism of the Bible. One may appropriate principles and values from the Scriptures to judge contemporary economic and political systems, but it must be understood that modern secular societies lack the faith and power to fulfill God's directives that are presupposed in the biblical materials. Still, we as Christians pledge our allegiance to a God who calls the entire world to repentance, and we may not surrender ourselves to any value system that does not stem from the Scriptures. Our efforts to apply biblical principles must necessarily be only partial and must be realistically conceived in light of the hindrances to their full implementation, but we surely must not abandon the vision of the Kingdom of God that guides us in all we do.

EDITOR'S PERSPECTIVE

The impact of Dr. Pierard's paper, the first one presented and debated at the Scholars' Colloquium in June 1988, was immediate and polarizing! The scholars appeared to be so committed to particular economic ideologies and perspectives on the causes and nature of certain negative economic conditions that their listening filters cast their interpretation of Dr. Pierard's paper into one of several categories—the paper had an anticapitalistic, socialistic slant; it presented a well-balanced position in harmony with a free market system of economics; or it was the position of a sensitive Christian observer looking for an economic system that will effectively address the needs of the disadvantaged (a man without an economic system).

Why would so much emotional electricity be generated by a paper examining the compatibility of certain economic realities with biblical norms? Because the very dignity and worth of human life are enhanced, repressed, encouraged, denied, perverted, or supported by the economic systems we form and foster; therefore, the type of system we support and defend is vital. Some of the scholars were deeply convinced of the fundamental rightness of a capitalistic free market system. Others focused on concerns for those who are missing or are denied positive economic opportunities in the existing system and who are consequentially disadvantaged. This group was willing to call before the bar of economic justice any socioeconomic system that appeared to either deny or overlook the needs of those at the bottom of the economic ladder. This early division, however, slowly evaporated, and a form of consensus emerged among the participants. They recognized that two specific but complex and interrelated matters needed to be thoroughly understood, balanced, and maintained when people talk about examining economic systems in the light of Scripture as economic justice is being sought.

First, we need to remember that economic systems incorporate both natural and human resources that must be combined in a dynamic and legitimized framework of ownership, production (to include services), and distribution of both output and profits. The variables in this process are enormous, and the decisions implemented in any single dimension will in all probability have both intended and unintended impacts in other areas. Little in economics can escape the need for some form of "input/output" analysis or "cost/benefit" analysis because there is almost always some form of waste, inefficiency, pollution, sacrifice, and ordering of priorities involved in every element of economic activity. Some economic "outputs" are extremely hard to value—safety and health, for example—and the selection of economic priorities is always fraught with value judgments that individuals differ over—"guns" or "butter," or the balance of pollution costs with the desire for reasonably priced goods.

Understanding these complexities is important for two reasons. There is "what exists," and there is "what ought to be." Economics, *like Scripture,* needs to start with "what exists" and move toward what is possible, but not seek some theoretical normative that is unobtainable because of mankind's fallen nature and finitude. For example, no economic system can eliminate greed, self-centeredness, or unethical behavior. The Christian life is one in which we are continuously growing to be like Christ, but we will not be perfected in this life before His second coming. Economic perfection is even less obtainable in a fallen world, for God is not working for economic perfection apart from His common grace. Those who would set up idealistic economic models should consider what can be hoped for in a fallen world before they seek to change an existing system. God meets us where we are and works with what is available. Economic ideologies should do the same thing.

We need to be wise as we try to understand and tamper with what causes both positive and negative economic consequences. For example, is a pocket of chronic unemployment in a particular city due to poor motivation of the people, inadequate education, patterns of discrimination, economic recession, inappropriate skills, the inability to recognize and respond to available opportunities, requirements for employment that are beyond their reach (experience or education), or a multitude of other causes or combination of causes? Until we can answer such a question, any attempted solution may well cause more long-term harm than it will do good.

We must also determine the individual's responsibilities in such adverse situations and the responsibilities of those who have the economic resources at their command (private ownership and/or public control) to alleviate the misery caused by unemployment. Which problems are interrelated with structural problems in the economic system? Could an alteration in the economic structure be helpful? What is the government's role in seeking solutions to such problems? The questions are many; the answers are not easy to discover.

The second matter the scholars agreed on concerns the need for genuine discernment when dealing with the tension between our personal responsibility for our choices and conduct, and our responsibility to help others help themselves when they seem unable to, for whatever reason. No knowledgeable Christian denies that Scripture heavily emphasizes the obligations and responsibilities we individually bear for our conduct and the fact that we will all give an accounting before God for our every thought, word, and act.

Very little Scripture is devoted to passages encouraging us to focus on ourselves and our rights, for God urges us to be other-centered. But neither does Scripture ignore that individuals do have rights. Paul claimed his rights as a Roman citizen when it was appropriate (see Acts 16:19-23, 37; 22:24-29; 25:11-12). Marriage partners have rights (see Exod. 21:10; 1 Cor. 7:3-5).

However, an enormous amount of Scripture discusses poor, needy, downtrodden, afflicted, and unjustly treated persons. As noted earlier, we are called on to care for their rights (see Prov. 29:7; 31:8-9; Jer. 5:28). The real need for discernment comes when we seek to help others help themselves. The implementation of any so-called solution to a problem of need that fosters a form of unbiblical dependency among people cannot do anything but enslave the recipient of such help to another person or group, which will ultimately prove to be unloving, even if well-intended. Scripture calls for people to care for themselves and for others to help them only when they cannot help themselves. Our challenge is to work to eliminate the barriers that create the "cannot help themselves" conditions, whatever they are.

Who is best qualified to help others help themselves? How are we to decide and assign legitimately recognized needs to those who can best bring about a solution? When should people's economic needs be temporarily or permanently assumed by other individuals, private groups, private agencies, churches, businesses, or arms of the local, state, or federal governments? These thorny questions were not resolved by the scholars (it was not their assigned task), and its discussion will have to wait until later.

THE RELATIONSHIP BETWEEN ECONOMIC VALUES AND THE BIBLE

The stage has now been set for us to go one step further in our search for a definitive answer to the question: What specific characteristics must an economic system contain and foster if it is to be considered compatible with God's revealed intentions? This question will be answered in this section, but our answer must be a carefully qualified one, for it deals with making choices, setting values, and providing freedom, and these must always be qualified if they are to be properly understood in the light of God's objectively revealed standards.

To illustrate, in regard to the freedom of choice that one should give a mature, God-fearing adult, the same normative principles that apply to the adult would not apply to the freedom of choice that one should give a two-year-old toddler. The adult and the toddler are not equally prepared to make choices. Or put another way, people need to be prepared over time to receive, inculcate, and then implement God's optimum intentions for them. For example, the Israelites were kept in the wilderness for forty years following their Exodus from Egypt to prepare the next generation to occupy the Promised Land. The first generation was not equipped to accomplish God's larger purposes, so He waited for and trained the ensuing generation (see Num. 14:22-31; Deut. 1:34-36; 1 Cor. 10:1-13; Heb. 3:7-11, 15-19). The same can be true for the establishment of an economic system. A nation of people may not be ready for God's best economic intentions. They may need to be brought along over a period of time to a new level of understanding so a new world view can be formed that will enable them to enjoy what can be properly entrusted only to mature believers.

Therefore, the conclusions of this section will be qualified in the sense that we will look at God's best intentions or at what would be normative for a mature, self-constrained body of people who earnestly desire economic justice and who are willing to accept the principles of righteousness as presented in Scripture. God's best cannot be given in a meaningful way to people who reject His precepts and exchange His truth for their own wisdom, catering to their fallen nature; eventually the very constraints that are so necessary for constructive choice, relevant valuing, and true freedom to exist will be undermined.

God has given us many biblical principles that have direct application in the economic arenas. Wayne Grudem introduced us to some of these in the previous section, but empirical reality also reveals that no matter how prosperous and widely dispersed the economic benefits may be in a given society, many problems must still be addressed regarding economic justice because the opportunity to make economic choices has been either interfered with or abdicated. Richard Pierard discussed a number of these problems. The problem we will now tackle, though, is one of establishing theologically and empirically that there is a normative system of economics, or at least some normative principles that must be embodied in an economic system before it can be considered compatible with God's revealed will.

The two chapters of this section offer significant insights, and the two distinct analyses bring different but interrelated truths to our attention. Chapter 4 deals with economics from a "positive" or descriptive and nonjudgmental perspective (until the end of the chapter). It reports on what is actually taking place in the decision-making processes in both free market and planned economies. It describes what is going on (positive economics) and reserves its judgment about what is good or bad about this (normative economics) until the end. Its author, Dr. Ronald H. Nash, presents the *logical necessity* for a system of economics that fosters a *maximum allowable degree of individual free choice* in all aspects of the market—production and distribution. Natural revelation, logic, and empirical evidence are the foundations of his work here; Dr. Nash makes no appeal to special revelation.

Dr. Nash is deeply concerned about whose choosing and valuing of goods and services will be decisive in the marketplace. Should a few people (bureaucrats) or the citizenry be the determiners of what is produced and distributed? He unequivocally believes the choices of the citizenry should prevail. Scripture supports this view; therefore, the concept of providing the maximum allowable freedom of choice in the marketplace deserves to be considered as a principle or standard that must be met if an economic system is to be classified as biblical in character. However, a proviso must be added that we can legitimately answer in the affirmative two additional questions: (1) Is Dr. Nash's normative model of "freedom of choice" in the marketplace absolutely compatible with Scripture? (2) Is the central assumption underlying his thesis valid—economic value is determined subjectively, not objectively? The "Editor's Reflections" immediately following chapter 4 will address these questions and also a significant limitation that must be placed in our final conclusion.

Dr. David C. Jones has written the concluding chapter of this section, and it provides a beautiful balance to Dr. Nash's work. Dr. Jones does not involve himself at all with the "positive" or merely descriptive dimensions of empirical marketplace observations but brings us, once again, face to face with the normative standards of Scripture for a look at God's special revelation and its application to everyday economics. The two chapters powerfully reinforce each other.

Ron Nash's discourse and line of reasoning are deliberate and intense. His precise logic takes the reader through several interrelated economic concepts that establish the groundwork for his analysis and forceful conclusion. Into this framework of logic, however, he injects a paramount assumption about the essence of the *value of things* (not people) that the reader must really come to grips with. If the reader accepts Nash's premise that the definitive value of material objects is determined subjectively, not objectively, his conclusion is really irrefutable. The implications of this chapter are far-reaching for all that follows, not only for this book, but for the entire series.

CHAPTER 4

THE SUBJECTIVE THEORY OF ECONOMIC VALUE

Ronald H. Nash

Ronald H. Nash (Ph.D., Syracuse University) is a Professor of Philosophy at Western Kentucky University. He is the author or editor of some twenty books, including Poverty and Wealth, Social Justice and the Christian Church, Liberation Theology, Process Theology, Faith and Reason, *and* Evangelicals in America. *Dr. Nash is also a popular public lecturer and has spoken at more than fifty colleges and universities in the U.S. and Great Britain. In addition, he serves as a member of Kentucky's Advisory Board to the U.S. Commission on Civil Rights.*

Simple observation of how human beings act in economic exchanges makes it clear that some things are thought to have more value than others. But what is it about one thing that makes it more valuable than another? Why do people want some goods and services more than others? Why are some things so valued that people are willing to make significant sacrifices to obtain them?

Many people, including numerous economists and philosophers, have mistakenly believed that economic value is objective, that is, is inherent in the thing itself. Such a view is, I contend, a snare and a delusion. Attempts to view economic value as somehow objective are at the root of many serious errors in the history of economic thought.[1]

It was not until the late nineteenth century that a few economists began to question the objective theory of economic value. These critics included the Austrian economists Carl Menger (1840–1921) and Eugene von Bohm-Bawerk (1851–1914). Following the lead of these men and others like Jevons and Walras, a growing number of economists argued that economic value is entirely subjective; it exists in the mind of the person who imputes value to the good or service. If something has economic value, it is because someone values it; it is because that good or service satisfies a human want. According to one writer, this new subjective approach to economic value

> represented a completely new, revolutionary approach to economics. For the first time, the *individual actor* himself became the unit with which economics was concerned. His actions, his responses to specific units of particular goods or services at certain places and times, were recognized as the key to explaining market phenomena. At every instance, an individual has in his mind a mental cutoff point, an invisible dividing line which separates the *units* of a good or service that he considers worth striving for from those that are not, and the units of a good or service that he wants to retain from those he is willing to relinquish. . . . Economics had been concerned previously only with *physical* goods and services and the means men used for the satisfaction of the various *material* wants. It had dealt with the relatively narrow fields of monetary transactions.[2]

However, the subjective revolution in economic theory changed all this. Once economists recognized the personal and subjective ground of economic value and the importance of thinking in terms of marginal utility,[3] "the science of economics was broadened to encompass all human (purposive/conscious) actions. It became a study of any and all the peaceful (nonviolent) means men use to attain any and all of their various ends."[4]

A simple example may make the plausibility of the subjective theory more obvious. Consider two diamonds of equal size and quality. Imagine that one is simply found in the ground by chance; no effort or danger was involved in its discovery. Suppose that the second diamond comes out of a diamond mine where an enormous investment has been made building and operating the mine. The men who work in such mines have a difficult and dangerous job. And so we have two diamonds; one cost little or nothing, but the second was produced at enormous cost. Imagine next that our two diamonds happen to be offered for sale at the same auction. The two diamonds might easily sell for similar prices. This shows that the value of the two diamonds bears no necessary connection to their respective "costs."

At this point, someone might raise an objection to the subjective theory of economic value. The example illustrates that value and cost are not necessarily related. But does it not also show that value still bears a relationship to the objective properties or characteristics of the thing? Our example stipulated that the two diamonds were similar in size and quality. Does it not follow that their similar "value" reflects the fact that their objective characteristics are so much alike?

It is true that the two diamonds had similar objective properties. It is also true (in our example) that they sold for prices reflecting a similar value. In this particular case, the closely related prices that indicate that two buyers placed much the same value on them might well have been a function of the objective characteristics of the diamonds. After all, if two things are practically the same, they can be substituted for each other. The hamburgers I can buy at the McDonald's on the north end of town are similar to those I can buy from the McDonald's at the south end of town. Because they are so much alike, most potential buyers will treat them as equal in value. But the economic value is not inherent in the hamburgers any more than it is in the diamonds. The value is imputed to the article by an individual valuer. Obviously, people take the objective characteristics of things into account when imputing such value.

One more thing needs to be said about our two diamonds. It would be a mistake to assume that just because two diamonds sell for the same price, they must therefore be equal in "objective value." What two buyers are willing to exchange for something reflects their separate personal valuation of that good. It is possible that two diamonds of different size and quality might also sell for the same price. Any number of personal, subjective considerations might lead two buyers to offer the same price for goods with different properties.

An important qualification needs to be made, however. When economists state that economic value is subjective, they do *not* restrict the subjective ground of economic value to personal tastes. In other words, the fact that Jones and Smith impute different value to the same good does not necessarily reflect just their differing tastes about that good. The value that people impute to things is also related to such factors as different knowledge, different interpretations of information, different expectations, and different quantities they already possess. It may also reflect varying degrees of alertness to new opportunities. Far more is involved in the subjective approach to economic value than personal taste. But it is clear that economic value is always imputed value.

People value things differently for a variety of reasons that include (1) different tastes; (2) different perceptions of available opportunities; (3) different interpretations of other people's actions; (4) different interpretations of current events; (5) different expectations about future events and people's future actions; and (6) different degrees of alertness to previously unrecognized opportunities.

An adequate analysis of economic value had to await the discovery that subjective utility plays an essential role in determining economic value. As long as economists and philosophers mistakenly believed that the value of any economic good lies in the thing itself, the search for the ground of economic value was bound to be frustrated.

A RELIGIOUSLY BASED OBJECTION TO THE THEORY

Many Christian and Jewish thinkers have expressed reservations about the subjective theory of economic value because of what they regard as its incompatibility with essential elements of their religious world view, namely, that God is the creator of all value, that value therefore has an objective ground, and that some values must be absolute and unchanging. Surely, such Christians and Jews argue, it is important to point out how some rankings of alternatives and how some economic choices are more compatible with Judeo-Christian values than others. Although these religious concerns are proper and understandable, none of them are really incompatible with the subjective theory of economic value. Even if we should discover that *some* values are subjective, it would not follow that this is the case with *all* values. Nor does the theory we're considering imply that every value-choice is as good as any other; nor is it incompatible with the belief that some economic choices are morally wrong.

Much of the confusion over this matter results from the ambiguity of some key words: *good, value,* and *desirable.* In economics, the word *good* refers to anything that people want or desire.[5] If a person prefers having more of something to having less, that thing for him is said to be a good. Some people fail to distinguish that some person indeed desires something from the quite different question of whether that thing is desirable, that is, whether it *should* be desired. When we say that X is desired, we report what is the case. When we say that X is desirable, we prescribe what ought to be the case. Statements about whether or not something is desirable are normative claims. When an economist says that something is a good (in this economic sense), all he means is that someone wants it, desires it, or values it. But saying that something is good in this way does not imply that it is the sort of thing the person ought to want.

The word *value* is ambiguous in a similar way. It may refer to (1) what people do in fact value or (2) what people ought to value. We all recognize that many people value things that they ought not to value, and that they often fail to value things they ought to value. We sometimes express the difference between these two senses of value by using the words *desired* and *desirable.* All that is required for something to be desired is for someone to desire it. But just because something is desired, it does not follow that it is *desirable,* that it ought to be desired. In positive economics, value reflects the extent to which something is desired; it does not mirror that thing's desirability. Economists have ways of measuring the degrees to which people desire things; obviously, this is something quite different from attempting to measure its desirability.

The word *desirable* can be used in two different senses. I have already stated that we sometimes use *desirable* to refer to what people ought to desire. In this sense, something is desirable if it is worth seeking, if it merits preference. But many people use *desirable* to describe anything that arouses desire. Because things like cocaine, heroin, and pornography have the power of arousing desire in some people, they are sometimes said to be desirable. I will avoid using *desirable* in this second sense. Whenever the word appears in my discussion, it is used in the sense of being worthy of desire.

No matter how desirable something may be—no matter how much people ought to desire it—the economic price of that thing will reflect how much some individual is willing to pay for one additional unit. The price of an economic good reflects the extent to which individuals desire it;[6] and this is something quite apart from the question of how desirable it is.

Economically literate Christians and Jews need to keep two things distinct. The first is the degree to which an individual may want X, a fact that reflects where X ranks in that individual's personal scale of values. The second is the need of individuals to alter the rankings in their personal scale of values to conform to what they *ought* to want. Christians, for example, are undoubtedly correct when they judge that the Bible obliges them to change the personal value scales of themselves and others to bring them more in line with the ultimate values associated with the Christian world view. But as important as this second task may be, it is an activity that falls under a different heading than positive economics. Economic exchanges in the real world will mirror only the actual subjective value that individuals have imputed to the good being exchanged. Any number of things, including religious conversion, may affect the way people rank things in their personal value scales. The occurrence of such changes in subjective value will have an obvious impact on the judgments people make about such things as marginal utility.

The theory of subjective economic value does not imply that all economic choices are equally good in a moral or religious sense. An acceptance of the theory does not commit anyone to believe that all values are subjective or relative. A Christian, Jew, or anyone else[7] is within his or her rights, in principle, to criticize particular economic choices. It seems clear, therefore, that any objection to the theory of subjective economic value on theological or moral grounds is mistaken. Positive economics does not presume to tell people that certain values ought to be ranked higher in their preference scales. That is more properly the task of the pastor, moralist, theologian, or spiritual counselor. Positive economics simply deals with how people actually make their choices with regard to the allocation of scarce resources.[8]

One other point should be noted. Even those individuals who may not yet see how a subjective analysis of economic value can be squared with their religious world view should welcome the way in which the theory has expanded the horizons of economics to include values other than *material* goods. Many people value such things as love, honor, friendship, virtue, and help for the less fortunate more than they value such material things as money, cars, clothes, and houses. Because such people rank things like love and honor so high in their personal value scale, their economic choices will reflect this ranking, and their conscious purposive actions can be explained by economists who hold to a subjective theory of economic value.

SOME THEORETICAL IMPLICATIONS

Opportunity cost—In every economic choice something is gained, but something else must be sacrificed. What economists call "opportunity cost" is the subjective value of the highest valued option or opportunity that someone forgoes to obtain some good. Most people think of the cost of some good or service solely in terms of the money they must surrender to acquire it. Such thinking confuses money price with cost. If I had not used scarce resources to acquire good A, I could have used them in many other ways. Suppose in this case, that of all the available options, one alternative (call it B) is my first preference to A. When I decide to acquire A, I forgo my opportunity to acquire B. My sacrifice of B, then, is the opportunity cost of my buying A. Since people's value scales differ, it follows that different people who acquire A will have varying opportunity costs. For one person, the opportunity cost of buying A might be a vacation in Monument Valley; for another person, it might be a large donation to starving children in Ethiopia. It is important, therefore, to recognize that the cost of anything involves more than money costs; it is actually the cost of forgone opportunities.

Imagine a person living on a limited but well-planned budget. Suppose further that this person is aware that his purchase of two movie tickets a week has the opportunity cost (to him) of a meal in a fine restaurant. If he buys the tickets, his opportunity cost is the forgone opportunity of eating in that restaurant. On the other hand, if he chooses to visit the restaurant, his opportunity cost is the two movie tickets. Of course, he might decide that he has other options. He might decide to buy just one movie ticket that week and dine instead at McDonald's. It is helpful to see the way in which the values of various economic goods are interrelated in the preference scales of particular people.

Because the opportunity cost of acquiring the same good will vary from person to person, it is impossible to predict for large numbers of people how much various individuals will be willing to sacrifice to secure some quantity of a good. This point helps explain the general uncertainty accompanying economic decisions. There is no way of predicting with certainty how many people will respond to a particular offer to sell a particular good or service at a particular price at a particular time. One can only wait and see.

The limits on economic knowledge—Because of the unavoidable subjective element in economic choices, human attempts to gain knowledge about future economic choices is severely limited. Economist Charles Baird introduces this point by writing,

> The subjectivist nature of economics refers to the fact that economics is about the formulation and consequences of the plans and actions of people as they attempt to do the best they can for themselves within a context of imperfect information and scarcity. The focus of attention is on the subjects, not the objects, of human action. Each individual's plans and actions are formulated on the basis of perceived costs and benefits. Both costs and benefits are subjective. That is, they both have whatever significance the individual's mind attaches to them. Neither costs nor benefits are objectively observable or measurable by third parties.[9]

We can never be sure of the economic value of things in the future. Natural catastrophes may make some resource more or less valuable. Human tastes, customs, and fashions may change. New highways may change traffic flows. Huge new shopping malls may lead people to develop new shopping habits. Inner cities may decay as people move to the suburbs. In all such changes, some people will win and others will lose. The scarcity of information means that economic decisions must always be made with some degree of uncertainty. No one, not even the largest and previously most successful businesses, can be completely sure what the future holds.

The problems resulting from limited human knowledge have been treated in the work of such economists as Ludwig von Mises, Friedrich Hayek, and most recently Israel Kirzner. These economists, one interpreter explains,

> work within a framework where the market is understood as a process of entrepreneurial adjustment to constant change and characterized by the piecemeal elimination of pervasive ignorance and error. Individual economic actors always operate under conditions of uncertainty, and in such an environment, error is the norm and the correction of error the raison d'être of markets. In this setting, there can be no question that subjective evaluations of cost bear little predictable relation to objectively measured outlays. Each person evaluates alternatives open to him within the context of uncertainty about the likelihood of expected outcomes, ignorance of the total realm of alternatives open to him and the possibilities of error in judgment about the value to him of the alternatives he does perceive. In such a world, it would seem to be purely happenstance if two separate individuals were to evaluate the same set of alternatives in the same ways. Thus the central problem of economic analysis in this context is to explain how millions of separate individuals with differing perceptions of reality and differing valuations and expectations about the future ever manage to achieve any kind of coordination of economic activity. With such an understanding of the purpose of economic theory, it is the very subjectivist ignorance, error and uncertainty confronting man that helps to explain the development and persistence of markets as corrective and coordinating institutions. That is, markets enable individuals to compare their subjective judgment with the evaluations of others in a continual process of giving and receiving information relevant to economic decision making.[10]

The ideas being presented here differ significantly from what has previously been regarded as the economic mainstream. Israel Kirzner contrasts the older economic orthodoxy with the recognition of "the open-endedness of knowledge as a source of economic understanding." He writes,

> To the standard mainstream view in economics, since about 1930, the view of the world has been one in which the future is essentially known, in which the participants in markets are in effect completely informed about the relative decisions made throughout the market by

fellow participants. This is a world of equilibrium, a world in balance, a world in which quantitative economic predictions are entirely feasible. Austrian economics has a quite different view of the world, and a quite different view of the way in which economic relations can be grasped.[11]

The views that Kirzner criticizes led many economists to believe that sufficient knowledge about the future was possible and that they could therefore predict successfully the future effects of governmental intervention on a nation's economy. Because of these economists' failure to take account of the impossibility of such knowledge, their effort to encourage governmental intervention in economic activities has had disastrous consequences. It explains the worldwide depression of the 1930s.[12] It also explains why socialism inevitably fails.[13]

A new understanding of cost—The subjective theory of economic value also provides a new understanding of cost. Many modern businessmen, along with some older economists, believe that the cost of some good is determined by the total outlay of money needed to produce it and make it available. According to the subjective analysis of economic value, this older view is clearly mistaken. The cost of production is determined by the subjective value of the goods that are produced. Economist James Buchanan comments,

> Simply considered, cost is the obstacle or barrier to choice, that which must be got over before choice is made. Cost is the underside of the coin, so to speak, cost is the displaced alternative, the rejected opportunity. Cost is that which the decision-maker sacrifices or gives up when he selects one alternative rather than another. Cost consists therefore of his own evaluation of the enjoyment or utility that he anticipates having to forgo as a result of choice itself.[14]

Buchanan then carries his analysis further by noting some implications of his emphasis on opportunity cost:

1. Cost must be borne exclusively by the person who makes decisions; it is not possible for this cost to be shifted to or imposed on others.
2. Cost is subjective; it exists only in the mind of the decision-maker or chooser.
3. Cost is based on anticipations; it is necessarily a forward-looking

or ex ante concept.

4. Cost can never be realized because of the fact that choice is made; the alternative which is rejected can never itself be enjoyed.

5. Cost cannot be measured by someone other than the chooser since there is no way that subjective mental experience can be directly observed.

6. Cost can be dated at the moment of final decision or choice.[15]

Buchanan is not claiming that cost exists only in the eye of the potential buyer. Prior to any voluntary economic exchange, both parties are constantly weighing cost *as they see it*. Suppose a businessman knows that he already has invested $25 in an article he wants to sell. Suppose further that the one prospective buyer he can find for that article is willing to pay only $20. In other words, the potential buyer's subjective valuation of the article weighed in terms of *his own* opportunity costs (his highest ranking alternative) results in $20 being the highest cost he is willing to incur; $20 is the magic line that separates his choosing or not choosing the article. The businessman realizes that if he doesn't exchange his commodity for the best possible deal, he will be even worse off than he is. For the businessman *at that moment of decision,* the "cost" that counts is the psychological obstacle or hurdle he must leap in reaching his decision about whether or not to accept $20 for the article. In this case, his alternative to accepting $20 is being stuck with an article he wants to sell. According to the subjective analysis, costs are forgone alternatives based on personal subjective appraisals of the value of those sacrificed options.

A new understanding of price—The most important way in which people can acquire objective knowledge about the subjective value that individuals place on various economic goods is to study changing prices. Prices are determined as prospective participants in economic exchanges buy or refuse to buy (or sell or refuse to sell) in response to their personal assessment of their opportunities. As countless individuals, each acting in line with their subjective value scales, exchange units of goods, services, and money, market prices evolve. One commentator remarks,

In time, out of the melee of bids and asks, "higgling and haggling," competition for all goods, services and/or money among countless persons, each offering something he or she has for something he or she prefers, money prices emerge. On a free market economy—when no person or group of persons uses force or threat of force to inter-

fere with the peaceful and moral acts of others—these money prices
tend to reflect the relative importance to people of specific units of
goods, services and/or money.[16]

The degree to which an individual wants some good or service will have
an obvious effect on the price he will pay to acquire it. The more he wants
something, the higher the price he will be willing to pay. Of course this price
will always reflect not just his eagerness to acquire that good, but also his
assessment of his situation and his other alternatives at that particular time.

SOME PRACTICAL IMPLICATIONS

Human economic behavior—Human wants are always greater than the
available resources to satisfy those wants. Economics studies the ways in
which people attempt to satisfy their wants with the resources at their
disposal. It is concerned with how people choose to bridge the gap between
what they have and what they want. Because our resources are never
sufficient to supply all our wants, we have to make choices about how to use
our resources to satisfy the wants that we judge to be most important. The
scarcity of economic goods means that people will always have to make
choices among several alternatives.

As human beings seek ways to get the most from their limited resources,
they are forced to rank their available alternatives. This ranking will reflect
the individual's personal order of values. Everyone has a scale of values by
which his needs, wants, and goals are ranked in order of the importance and
urgency the person attaches to them. However, this scale of values is not
always something of which the individual is conscious. But whether or not a
person happens to be aware of his scale of values, he will always aim at
whatever goal or end he regards as most urgent or important at the moment.
Even though we may be unaware of the process, we all engage in a constant
ranking of the relative value of things we want but do not possess and of
things we possess that we might be willing to trade for something else.

The internal scales by which people express their preferences and rank
their alternatives differ greatly. Since different people value some things
more highly than others, several things follow. For one thing, if person A
values X (some economic good) more highly than person B does, A will be
willing to sacrifice more to secure an additional unit of X. Moreover, since
person B values X less than A does, B may be willing to trade some quantity
of X to A in exchange for something else that B desires more.

Not only do different people's value scales differ, but the value scales of individual persons are constantly changing. As people's interests, wants, and information change, their preferences change. The things that a person puts forth the greatest effort to secure at any given moment are those that rank highest on his personal scale of preference; they will be the things that he values most highly at that time and in those circumstances.

Economic choices are geared toward maximizing benefits and minimizing costs. (It should be clear that the word *cost* has more in view than an outlay of money.) The more someone believes he is likely to benefit from an action, the more likely he is to act in that way. Greater benefits (utility) will make a choice more attractive; higher costs will make it less attractive and make it less likely that he will select the more costly option.

This analysis of economic choice entails neither materialism nor selfishness. It does not assume that human beings seek only their own welfare. But it is based on the observation that even when a person seeks the welfare of others, his choices reflect the fact that in those instances the well-being of others is the thing he most wants. To say that people choose in accordance with their highest ranked preference does not imply that they always rank money or selfish wants first. Economists Armen Alchian and William Allen elaborate on this topic:

> Economics does *not* assume that men are motivated solely, or even primarily by the desire to accumulate more wealth. Instead, economic theory assumes that man . . . desires more of many other things as well: prestige, power, friends, love, respect, self-expression, talent, liberty, knowledge, good looks, leisure. Day to day, economic theory is usually applied to the production, sale and consumption of goods with money expenditures via the market place. But economic theory does not ignore, let alone deny, that man is motivated by cultural and intellectual goods, and even by an interest in the welfare of other people.[17]

Alchian and Allen also explain that some people want more goods for the express purpose of being able to use those goods for the benefit of other people. They do not assume that such a person

> is oblivious to other people, that he is uncharitable or not solicitous of other people's welfare. Nor is he assumed to be concerned only with more wealth. If these assumptions had been made, the resultant theory would be immediately falsified by the fact that people do engage in charity, are solicitous of other people, do consider the

effects of their behavior on other people, and are interested in more than marketable wealth.[18]

Some people regard many things as more important than money. Some give a higher priority to serving others than serving themselves, and their economic choices will reflect these priorities.

People's economic behavior, then, simply reflects, first, their needs to make choices and, second, the relative value they place on their options. When it is impossible for someone to have both *A* and *B*, the choice that a person makes will reflect the relative value placed on *A* and *B*. People's actions, then, are a reflection of their value scales. Their choices are made to help them secure the alternatives that accord more closely with their values. If a Christian wants to change the economic choices of another person, he will first have to alter that person's scale of values.

Market exchanges—People exchange goods and services in a market precisely because they place different values on them. If everyone in a market regarded a particular good or service as having the same value, there would be little or no incentive for trade. Each person in a market has gone through the mental process of appraising goods and services in terms of his own preference scale. Each has set out to find someone who has something he wants more than the good or service he is willing to trade. As people weigh their options, they sometimes find that offers are unacceptable (for example, the cost is too high) and the exchange is not made. But when two parties reach that point where their subjective appraisals of what is best for them meet, an exchange takes place. What economists call the market is the framework within which countless individuals make choices in terms of those things they value most.

There are several ways in which voluntary exchange (as opposed to forced exchange) produces value. First of all, voluntary exchange produces value by moving some good or service from someone who values it less to someone who values it more. If you pay $5,000 for a used car, you and the person who receives your money demonstrate the differing values you place on the car and the money. The prior owner of the car values your money more than the car; you value the car more than the money or other things for which you could have traded the money. After the voluntary exchange, both of you are better off in the sense that you have exchanged something you value less for something you value more. It is a mistake to equate wealth with material things such as cars, houses, and lands. Things become wealth when they become the possession of someone who places a value on them.

Economic exchange also creates value because it enables people to specialize in ways that make the best use of their abilities and knowledge. Some people are better electricians than carpenters. It is to the mutual advantage of electricians and carpenters to specialize in what they do best and exchange their service for that of the other. Such specialization often works to the advantage of nations that can produce some things better than others.

Voluntary exchange also makes possible increases in the quantity and efficiency of production. If free exchange were not possible, individual persons or households would be forced to spend their time and effort producing all the things they might want. Under such conditions, production would obviously take place on a very small scale. But because free exchange encourages a division of labor so that each person can specialize in what he does best, production can occur on a much larger scale. Both labor and machines end up being used much more efficiently. The resulting increase in the kinds of goods and the quantity of those goods gives people a greater range of choices and thus enhances their freedom.

Entrepreneurial activity—Earlier in this chapter, it was noted that subjective economic value is not exclusively a function of personal taste. Another factor to be considered is knowledge—or more properly the lack of knowledge. Israel Kirzner discusses the element:

> The crucial element in market competition is the circumstance that knowledge is never concentrated in a single mind—always dispersed. We never know everything. None of us. No single mind can possibly know everything. No single mind can possibly grasp the entire economic problem that tends to be solved through spontaneous market processes.[19]

But as significant as human ignorance and the limitations of human knowledge are in understanding economic behavior, another related notion should be recognized. The acknowledgment of this feature is one of the most important contributions that members of the Austrian school of economics have made to economic theory. This second insight is, in Kirzner's words,

> an appreciation of the propensity within human action to discover what was hitherto unknown—what I like to call the *entrepreneurial* propensity in human action. It is this propensity that is responsible for entrepreneurial alertness for pure profit opportunities, for entrepreneurial discovery, for bursting asunder the limits of existing

knowledge. It is upon this alertness that we rely for the manner in which the market continually propels prices and decisions in the direction of greater mutual coordination. It is entrepreneurial alertness to existing errors that leads to their discovery and their eventual tendency to be corrected.[20]

An entrepreneur is someone who believes he sees an opportunity that others have not yet recognized.[21] The key to understanding competition is realizing that no one knows everything; different people have different information. The market process gathers and communicates information about the most important wants of buyers and sellers. As astute entrepreneurs pay attention to the information provided by changing market prices, they often perceive new opportunities. These new opportunities may take the form of new products or services that consumers want or of new ways of using scarce resources.

Stephen Littlechild expresses his regard for the Austrian school's emphasis on entrepreneurial activity:

Austrian economics takes as its starting point the behavior of people with incomplete knowledge, who have not only to "economize" in the situations in which they find themselves, but also to be on the alert for better opportunities "just around the corner." This alertness, missing from "mainstream" economics, is called entrepreneurship. It leads to the revision of plans and forms the basis of the competitive process, which in many ways epitomizes the Austrian approach. For [members of the Austrian school of economics], the *changes* over time in prices, production, plans, knowledge, and expectations are more important than prices and output at any one time. Similarly, from a "normative" point of view (of what policy should be), the adequacy of an economic system is judged not by the efficiency with which it allocates given resources at a point in time, but by the speed with which it discovers and responds to new opportunities over time.[22]

It goes without saying that entrepreneurial ability is hard to find. Not everyone has it; and even those who seem to have it in some areas lack it in others. But it is impossible to overestimate the worth of entrepreneurial activity. As entrepreneurs recognize hitherto unrecognized opportunities and assume risks in an effort to maximize their well-being by taking advantage of those opportunities, their actions result in distinct benefits to large numbers of people through the creation of new jobs along with the provision of new goods or services.

The superiority of capitalism over socialism—Everything stated above constitutes a powerful argument for the superiority of capitalism over socialism.[23] The miserable performance of socialist economies is no accident. There is a fundamental reason why socialist economies do not work: *They cannot work*. The argument supporting this contention was discovered in 1920 by the Austrian economist Ludwig von Mises.[24]

According to von Mises, socialism can never work because it is an economic system that makes economic calculation impossible. And because economic calculation is impossible, socialism turns out to be an economic system that makes rational economic activity impossible. As Giovanni Sartori observes, under socialism it is

> theoretically and practically impossible, for the collectivistic planner, to *calculate costs*. His costs and prices are, and can only be, "arbitrary." To be sure, arbitrary not in the sense that they are established at whim but in the sense that they are *baseless*: they cannot be derived from any economically significant base or baseline.[25]

A great advantage to a market system is the constant supply of information it provides by means of the price mechanism. That information is not available in a socialist system. Tom Bethell explains the socialist's problem this way:

> It is one thing for central planners to draw up a plan of production. It is quite another to carry it out. . . . How can you (the planner) know what should be produced, before you know what people want? And people cannot know what they want unless they first know the price of things. But prices themselves can only be established when people are permitted to own things and to exchange them among themselves. But people do not have these rights in centrally planned economies.[26]

Without free markets to set prices, socialists can never attune production to human wants. The impossibility of precise measures of cost accounting under socialism will result in economic disaster. Von Mises did not deny that rational action might still be possible under socialism with regard to small and insignificant matters. But under a system that ignores the factors of profit and loss, under a system that negates or destroys the essential informational function of markets, it would be impossible for production to be consciously economical. Rational economic production would be impossible. The problem of economic calculation under socialism grows increasingly more serious as national economies become more complex. Thomas Sowell has stated, "Where conditions are constantly changing in the economy, as in most modern industrial nations, the ability of a price system to make use of the scattered and imperfect knowledge that exists at any given time is one of [a market system's] primary advantages."[27] But this advantage is lost in socialist economies.

Socialism therefore presents us with the picture of a system of planning in which rational planning turns out to be impossible. Without free markets and the vital information supplied by markets, economic activity would become chaotic and result in drastic inefficiencies and distortions. The great paradox of socialism is that socialists need capitalism to survive. Unless socialists make allowance for some free markets that provide the pricing information that alone makes rational economic activity possible, or monitor the pricing information available from nations where free markets are allowed to function, socialist economies would have even more problems than those for which they are already notorious. In practice, socialism cannot dispense with market exchanges. Consequently, socialism is a gigantic fraud that attacks the market at the same time it is forced to utilize the market process.[28]

CONCLUSION

The theory discussed here is difficult for many people to understand because it requires them to alter radically old patterns of thinking. Unfortunately, some old patterns of economic thinking are responsible for a great deal of confusion and mischief in the contemporary world. The theory of subjective economic value, once accepted, opens new vistas to understanding economic behavior. As Christians attend to the theoretical and practical implications of the subjective theory, they will find that it provides them with fruitful new ways of understanding the economic behavior of the persons they deal with, both in their business activity and in their efforts to exercise a Christian influence on society.

EDITOR'S REFLECTIONS

How compatible with Scripture is Dr. Nash's strong conviction that freedom of choice in the marketplace is absolutely essential for an economic system to function effectively? Scripture does not directly address questions of this type, but an overwhelming body of biblical evidence indicating God's abiding interest in our having a true freedom to make choices clearly supports Ron Nash's contention that, as a normative goal, an economic system should provide as much freedom of choice in the marketplace as possible.

For example, if someone sat down to read the Bible from cover to cover in search of evidence to support the contention that human choice is a basic concern of God's, the reader could not get through the first three chapters of Genesis without noting that our first parents were given absolute free choice, even to the extent that its inappropriate use would ultimately require the humiliation, suffering, and death of God's own Son if mankind were to be saved from the consequence of our first parents' fateful choice that resulted in their and our fall. Giving freedom of choice to His image bearers was obviously extremely important to God, for He was willing to pay an infinite price for it to be an integral part of our nature. Choice and morality are inseparable; people have an innate moral nature; choice is an essential part of our humanity; people are dehumanized when choice is diminished.

Furthermore, throughout Scripture we see that living in bondage or under the control of kings or rulers was considered to be an inferior state of existence to that of living under God's rule. This fact does not weaken the truth, however, that God sovereignly establishes governments and those who rule (see Rom. 13:1-7; Titus 3:1; 1 Pet. 2:13-17) or that He expects us to honor and obey them. Governments exist because there is a need for public justice and righteousness in a fallen and self-centered world and God knows that those who reject Him need to live under some imposed constraints if the community is to function with some degree of order. But God's higher end is for us to be set free from our sin natures so we can enjoy the freedom of exercising moral choice in an environment of justice and righteousness. We can, therefore, conclude that God's perfect creative acts and special revelation reveal His earnest interest in our ability and opportunity to exercise true moral choices, and this truth reinforces Nash's observations about the marketplace.

The second question we need to address concerns the validity of Dr. Nash's central assumption that the economic value of things, *not* people, is inherently subjective, not objective, in character. The editor accepts Ron Nash's position, but with an important qualification. Nash would have to ultimately argue that it is the purchasers (not producers) making marginal purchases who can correctly be said to be completely subjective in their value determination. We must surely acknowledge that costs or the cost/ price relationships, which are to a large degree objective in character, deeply influence producers' willingness to create and make available goods and services. The availability and nonavailability of these goods and services in the market affect their products' relative position on the decision makers' subjective value scales because perceived scarcity and abundance have their psychological impacts. So it must be admitted that objective costs, which are the locked-in results of prior subjective choices on the part of producers, influence the availability and substitutability of goods, which in turn affects the final subjective priority rankings of goods by purchasers in the marketplace. But having made this qualification, the editor concludes that Nash's position is very sound. (The debate between objective and subjective values is much more complex than what has been presented here, but the burden of proof—logical and empirical—that economic values are objectively determined must rest on the objectivists to establish because all so-called objective values in the marketplace are nothing more than the summation of the calculated conclusions of prior subjective judgments, which can only be objective in the ex post facto sense.)

One additional caution is in order: We should not carry the concept of subjective economic value so far in our thinking as to make all other values associated with human endeavors a subset of economics so that some form of economic determinism is established. For example, when Dr. Nash acknowledges that other values like love, honor, friendship, and virtues have an impact on economic values, he is correct, but this does not mean that these nonmaterial values are subsets of economics so that they (honor and love, for example) are to be typically conceived of as having economic value. The concept of subjective economic value is helpful in highlighting the holistic and interdependent relationship between all components of life, but it should not become the controlling or dominant standard for evaluation.

The two questions we needed to answer before accepting Dr. Nash's conclusions have now been answered. It was noted earlier, though, that a limitation would need to be considered. Everyone in a particular economic system is not prepared to cope with the same levels of freedom and control. Dr. Nash's conclusion that it is normatively right for people to have genuine freedom of choice in the marketplace is correct in the ideal and normative sense, and this points us in the right direction; but left by itself in the normative mode, it ignores the need for possible public constraints in a fallen world where economic power can become concentrated and abused. (Dr. Nash does not ignore, in his larger world view, the necessity for appropriate government participation in world affairs, but this reality was not included in this chapter, for he was making a particular case for the fundamental necessity for freedom of choice in the marketplace.) It would be very wrong to assume that full market freedoms can be enjoyed in every society or that all markets are capable of enjoying the same level of freedom.

It is one thing to agree that it is a good long-term goal to seek expanded levels of freedom in the marketplace, but it is quite another thing to naively seek such an economic state through worldly philosophies or legislative action without regard for the fallen nature of man, which has such a profound impact on human behavior. Unless God's common grace is at work supporting a free economic structure, freedom will be abused and perverted, for freedom is, at its heart, a byproduct of spiritual vitality and common grace.

Freedom is a gift from Christ (see John 8:31-36; Rom. 8:2; 2 Cor. 3:17; Gal. 5:1, 13; James 2:12; 1 Pet. 2:16), and spiritual freedom from guilt, enslavement to the old nature, and unrighteousness is the true foundation of all relevant freedom. Freedom must be manifested in a large proportion of the population through God's special grace before God's common grace is likely to extend far enough to create the side effects where extensive freedom in the marketplace will be either long enjoyed or constructively used. The very implications of this are not pleasant to consider, for it means that Christians cannot simply work for more freedom in the marketplace without regard for the ability of their neighbors to use such freedoms righteously. Freedom should not be sought where it is likely to be abused. People need to be prepared for freedom. Societies do decay; therefore, simply calling for or working for more marketplace freedoms in the presence of that decay is not necessarily wise or godly.

Now it is time to consider the work of Dr. David C. Jones. His chapter is a marvelous balance to Dr. Nash's work. He brings us back again to Scripture and forcefully points out that God has prescribed certain standards for right conduct in the form of a duty-bound ethic and He has also given us a goal-oriented ethic that sets before us certain objectives, including at least four normative economic values to be fostered. They are (1) an appropriate temporal self-interest that does not exclude the best temporal interests of others; (2) the good of gainful employment; (3) the good of profits; and (4) the good of material wealth. We need to take Dr. Jones's insights to heart, for they point directly to the biblical standards supporting the appropriateness of an economic system promoting these qualities.

CHAPTER 5

ECONOMICS IN TELEOLOGICAL PERSPECTIVE

David C. Jones

David C. Jones is Professor of Systematic Theology and Ethics at Covenant Theological Seminary in St. Louis. He was appointed to the Covenant faculty in 1967 and served as Academic Dean from 1977 to 1988. He holds the Th.D. degree from Concordia Seminary in St. Louis. An ordained minister in the Presbyterian Church in America, he has served on various committees developing position papers on contemporary ethical issues, including chairing that church's committee on nuclear weapons.

INTRODUCTION

George Stigler, the Nobel class economist, begins his intriguing essay "The Economist as Preacher" by observing that "economists seldom address ethical questions as they impinge on economic theory or economic behavior. They (and I) find this subject complex and elusive in comparison with the relative precision and objectivity of economic analysis."[1]

This is entirely understandable; ethicists (at least I) also find the subject complex and elusive, the more so lacking a thorough background in objective economic analysis. But somebody has to do the preaching. As Stigler points out, "The ethical questions are inescapable; one must have goals in judging policies, and these goals will certainly have ethical content, however well concealed it may be."[2]

That being the case, I intend to take up the question of normative goals in economics, knowing that it casts me in the role of "the preacher as economist." That has a foolish ring to it, and a more suitably academic subtitle might be "Toward a Normative Economic Theory." But the former is more apt, and I am consoled by the thought at least of being in good company, if not apostolic succession, as a preaching fool.

THE STRUCTURE OF ETHICS

Human conduct is subject to a threefold evaluation from the moral point of view. First, is the goal that the agent seeks to realize good, worthy of human pursuit? Second, is the motive of the agent also good, so that the goal is sought because it is worthwhile? Third, is the means to the goal good, that is, does it conform to the standard of what is right?

The assumption underlying the third question is that neither a good end nor a good motive will justify a bad means. So important is this issue that ethics is sometimes conceived narrowly as dealing only with the standard of right and wrong. The result is a duty-governed (deontological) rather than a goal-oriented (teleological) ethic.[3] Because of the confusion of teleological ethics with consequentialism (that the rightness or wrongness of an action is determined solely by its consequences for good or evil), evangelical Christians tend to emphasize the absolute rules of moral obligation. This is laudable, but it is a mistake to think that a goal-oriented ethic necessarily excludes absolute principles of duty.[4] In the broader teleological framework of the biblical ethic, the moral rules provide guidance for the true fulfillment of human nature as the image of God.

The teleological tradition in Christian ethics may be traced from Augustine through Thomas Aquinas to the familiar opening questions of the *Westminster Shorter Catechism*:

What is the chief end of man?

Man's chief end is to glorify God, and to enjoy him forever.

What rule hath God given to direct us how we may glorify and enjoy him?

The Word of God, which is contained in the Scriptures of the Old and New Testaments, is the only rule to direct us how we may glorify and enjoy him.

The assumption of the catechism's first question is that there is some supreme purpose for human beings, some ultimate goal that fulfills human nature, some absolute value that is intrinsically worthwhile and totally satisfying. In the history of moral philosophy this is called the "highest good" (*summum bonum*).

By the time Augustine was converted to Christianity, the question of the highest good had been the subject of philosophical discussion for several hundred years. Aristotle, for example, taught that the highest human good was *eudaimonia* or "happiness" (fulfillment and satisfaction) through moral and intellectual excellence—plus a little bit of luck.[5] Luck was necessary because Aristotle could not guarantee that excellent activity by itself would produce happiness if too many creature comforts were lacking. Even philosophers require bed and board as minimum conditions of a happy life.

Augustine took for granted the quest for happiness as a human given. The philosophical problem was to know what to desire in order to be happy and how to obtain the object of that desire. His conclusion is summed up in the celebrated saying from the opening paragraph of the *Confessions*: "Thou hast made us for thyself and restless is our heart until it comes to rest in thee." In other words, God is our highest good. The desire for happiness, for human fulfillment and satisfaction, has been implanted by Him and is intended to lead ultimately to Him. As Augustine put it more fully in the *City of God*:

> God himself, who is the Author of virtue, shall there be its reward; for, as there is nothing greater or better, he has promised himself. What else was meant by his word through the prophet, "I will be your God, and ye shall be my people," than, I shall be their satisfaction, I shall be all that men honourably desire—life, and health, and nourishment, and plenty, and glory, and honour, and peace, and all good things? This, too, is the right interpretation of the saying of the apostle, "That God may be all in all." He shall be the end of our desires who shall be seen without end, loved without cloy, praised without weariness.[6]

Augustine thus agreed with the classical philosophers that all human action arises from the pursuit of happiness. But he denied that this quest can be satisfied in this life and by oneself alone.

What this has to do with economics I hope to be able to show in due course.

UTILITY: THE ECONOMIST'S HAPPINESS

"We believe that man is a utility-maximizing animal."[7] So runs the credo of economists, who use the term *utility* in a specialized sense for "the usefulness of a good or service, or the satisfaction it yields."[8] Actually, this definition contains an ambiguity (usefulness is objective; satisfaction is subjective), lending support to the conclusion that "after centuries of intellectual striving to arrive at a definition of utility, economists still have not completely settled on a meaning."[9] However, the subjective meaning is now regnant, and "utility-maximizing animal" is roughly equivalent to "wants-satisfying creature."

Economists speak in terms of utility largely for historical reasons. The term found its way into the discipline through the influence of Jeremy Bentham (1748–1832), who defined *utility* as "that property in any object, whereby it tends to produce benefit, advantage, pleasure, good, or happiness."[10] For Bentham, pleasure was the highest good; thus, the pursuit of happiness was equivalent to the pursuit of pleasure. This system, known as hedonism (from the Greek *hedone*, "pleasure") or more precisely as hedonistic utilitarianism, was a marked departure from traditional teleological ethics. As applied to society, nothing in the utilitarian theory prevented "the greatest happiness of the greatest number" from being sought at the expense of "liberty and justice for all." In the wrong hands, the goal of social welfare could be used as an excuse for overriding individual human rights and perpetrating all sorts of injustice. Historical examples are not hard to come by.

The use of the term *utility* in economic analysis does not necessarily imply a commitment to the theory of utilitarianism in philosophical ethics; the explanation for the continued use of the term lies elsewhere. One historian of the discipline observes, "The importance of the concept of utility for economic science stems from the desire to find the cause of economic value." Early on, economic theory supposed that human preferences might be measurable in "utils" of pleasure or satisfaction, but this idea had to be abandoned as the incommensurability of different values and the "interpersonal non-comparability of utility" were recognized.[11]

With the development of the subjective theory of economic value (see chapter 4) the concept of utility has been considerably broadened to become practically synonymous with "human well-being."[12] What economists call "maximizing utility," others call "the pursuit of happiness." Neither expression is particularly useful or felicitous; both seem to imply that the sense of satisfaction is the whole of human fulfillment, whereas in reality satisfaction depends on a broader realization of the purpose of human nature.

Adam Smith is renowned for his attention to the motive power of human self-interest. "The uniform, constant, and uninterrupted effort of every man to better his condition" is one of his better-known observations. Milton and Rose Friedman in their best seller, *Free to Choose,* interpret it as follows:

Smith, of course, meant by "condition" not merely material well-being, though certainly that was one component. He had a much broader concept in mind, one that included all of the values by which men judge their success—in particular the kind of social values that gave rise to the outpouring of philanthropic activities in the nineteenth century.[13]

Whether or not this represents Smith accurately (it looks revisionist on the surface), modern economic theory tends to interpret self-interest more broadly than is generally assumed to be the case. To cite the Friedmans again:

Narrow preoccupation with the economic market has led to a narrow interpretation of self-interest as myopic selfishness, as exclusive concern with immediate material rewards. Economics has been berated for allegedly drawing far-reaching conclusions from a wholly unrealistic "economic man" who is little more than a calculating machine, responding only to monetary stimuli. That is a great mistake. Self-interest is not myopic selfishness. It is whatever it is that interests the participants, whatever they value, whatever goals they pursue. The scientist seeking to advance the frontiers of his discipline, the missionary seeking to convert infidels to the true faith, the philanthropist seeking to bring comfort to the needy—all are pursuing their interests, as they see them, as they judge them by their own values.[14]

One of the correlatives of the subjective theory of economic value and its broader perspective on human self-interest is the tendency to view all human action as essentially economic in nature. According to von Mises,

The boundary that separates the economic from the noneconomic is not to be sought within the compass of rational action. Action takes place only where decisions are to be made, where the necessity exists of choosing between possible goals, because all goals either cannot be achieved at all or not at the same time.[15]

Economics is typically defined nowadays as "the study of allocation decisions about scarce resources." Resources are understood to include time and talent as well as material goods. Thus, all human actions may be regarded as economic inasmuch as they involve choices between competing values, not all of which can be realized. Although some businesses may operate on the assumption that the economic life may be reduced to "purchase cheap, sell dear," economists by and large are a long way from making monetary gain the sole rule of economic practice. This highlights the need to explore the ethical foundations of economics. Allocation decisions imply a goal: Is it good? Is the motive right? Are the means just? At this point economics and ethics coincide.

ECONOMICS AND CHRISTIAN ETHICS

As indicated in the previous section, given the broad conception of economics as allocation of scarce resources, the whole of human life may be viewed as economizing activity. Human beings are called to be stewards in this life, not only of material goods but also of spiritual opportunities— "redeeming the time" (Eph. 5:16; Col. 4:5, KJV). Thus, one could define *economics* as "a study of mankind in the ordinary business of life."[16]

Nevertheless, *economics* is ordinarily understood to refer to something more specific, namely, "the production, distribution, and consumption of wealth," *wealth* being "(1) everything having economic value measurable in price or (2) any useful material thing capable of being bought, sold, or stocked for future disposition."[17]

Even though it is impossible to cordon off a part of life as though choices in that area had nothing to do with anything else, for the purposes of this chapter I will follow the definition of Thomas Chalmers, the nineteenth-century Scottish Presbyterian clergyman and economist: "Political economy aims at the diffusion of sufficiency and comfort throughout the mass of the population, by a multiplication or enlargement of the outward means and materials of human enjoyment."[18] Chalmers did not believe this to be possible apart from the realization of other values, even going so far as to say that "for the economic well-being of a people, their moral and religious education is the first and greatest object of national policy."[19]

As we saw earlier, according to Christian ethics the final goal of human life transcends all created goods. Human nature finds its ultimate fulfillment in glorifying God and enjoying Him forever. God is the absolute value who alone is capable of satisfying every human desire. All created goods are finite and relative and are properly pursued only in relation to the Creator. Moses may be taken as an example of one who made a right choice on the basis of a true system of values:

> He chose to be mistreated along with the people of God rather than to enjoy the pleasures of sin for a short time. He regarded disgrace for

the sake of Christ as of greater value than the treasures of Egypt, because he was looking ahead to his reward. (Heb. 11:25-26)

This being the case, what does a Christian teleological ethic have to do with economics? Why should "the diffusion of sufficiency and comfort throughout the mass of the population" be one of its concerns?

The final end of glorifying and enjoying God is not to be taken only in an eschatological sense. Though *consummated* in the celestial city, God's purpose for humans begins to be fulfilled in this life. A comprehensive guiding principle of Christian activity is this: "So whether you eat or drink or whatever you do, do it all for the glory of God" (1 Cor. 10:31). God is glorified in the proper use of His created goods (see 1 Tim. 4:4-5), which He has richly provided for our enjoyment (see 1 Tim. 6:17). To receive God's gifts with gratitude is to glorify Him as the Giver; to enjoy His created goods is to experience something of His goodness as the Creator, a point emphasized by Paul and Barnabas in presenting the gospel at Lystra (see Acts 14:17).

Created goods are worthy of human pursuit. To think otherwise is to impugn the Creator who intends them as instrumental to human fulfillment and satisfaction. Of course, they are not to be valued absolutely; for Moses to have chosen pleasure rather than suffering under the circumstances would have been idolatry. Nevertheless, God is glorified and enjoyed through the right use of His creation.

Living the Christian life calls for a good deal of discernment in the absence of detailed legislation with respect to finite ends. The values are objective, but they are also relative to individuals in particular circumstances. Depending on the situation, someone might judge it better to attend a ball game than a missionary conference. Or to break an expensive vial of perfume to release its fragrance rather than sell it and give the proceeds to the poor. We have not been given a greater good calculator to tell us precisely what we should do in each situation. We must become wise by God's Word and Spirit, just as Paul prays for the Philippians: "That your love may abound more and more in knowledge and depth of insight, so that you may be able *to discern what is best* and may be pure and blameless until the day of Christ" (Phil. 1:9-10, emphasis added).

Scripture provides direction for all life's choices, but it cannot be made to yield specific instructions for all the various circumstances of life. However, it is not necessary to know *infallibly* that one course of action is *absolutely* better than any other. What is required is that we act to the best of our knowledge, based on an understanding of the general priorities of the Kingdom of God and in dependence on God in prayer.

NORMATIVE ECONOMIC VALUES

Granted that man's chief and highest end is to glorify God and to enjoy Him, are other subordinate ends normative in the economic sphere? I suggest the following goals are intrinsically worthy of human pursuit.

1. The good of temporal self-interest—The Eighth Commandment may be interpreted broadly as requiring "the lawful procuring and furthering the wealth and outward estate of ourselves and others" and forbidding "whatsoever doth or may unjustly hinder our own or our neighbor's wealth or outward estate."[20] This implies a high view of temporal self-interest, though certainly not to the exclusion of the temporal interests of others. Indeed, the proper emphasis of the commandment is to challenge us "to endeavour, by all just and lawful means, to procure, preserve, and further the wealth and outward estate of *others, as well as our own.*"[21] We are more biblical in our orientation when we put and keep others forward in our thinking.[22]

Still, a healthy and godly self-interest is encouraged in the Scriptures and even serves as a paradigm for conduct toward others. "Love your neighbor as yourself" presupposes an ethical stance involving self-regarding duties directed toward the fulfillment of one's nature and calling for the glory of God. The commandment is neither "Love your neighbor as [you now *sinfully* love] yourself," nor even "Love your neighbor as [you just *naturally* love] yourself," but "Love your neighbor as [you *rightfully* love] yourself," that is, as a person created in the image of God and responsible to Him.[23]

As already noted, the importance of self-interest in economics is usually traced to Adam Smith. John Kenneth Galbraith, for example, remarks, "Economic motivation for Smith centers on the role of self-interest. Its private and competitive pursuit is the source of the greatest public good." He continues,

> It was a huge step that Smith here took. The person concerned with self-enrichment had hitherto been an object of doubt, suspicion, and mistrust, feelings that went back through the Middle Ages to biblical times and the Holy Scripture itself. Now, because of his self-interest, he had become a public benefactor. A major rescue and transformation indeed![24]

At least two qualifications are necessary. First, not all "self-enrichment" is regarded with such negative feelings in the biblical and Christian tradition. The desire for "a competent portion of the good things of this life," so far from having to be suppressed, is actually encouraged to be expressed to God in prayer, coordinate with the desire "to enjoy his blessing with them."[25]

Second, Smith appears to have been made the "guru of self-interest" by overzealous followers who reduced economics to this one principle.[26] Whereas they argued that the individual pursuit of self-interest would of itself result in the greatest general welfare, Smith's view of prudence was considerably broader than the maximization of self-interest, and even so, not prudence, but the other virtues, "humanity, justice, generosity, and public spirit, are the qualities most useful to others."[27]

The pursuit of temporal self-interest is intrinsically worthwhile from a Christian point of view; it involves the practice of certain self-regarding duties, which are no less duties for being self-regarding, leading to fulfilled human lives as God intends. The principle is significant for economics, though it is not the sole economic principle. It calls for the exercise of individual responsibility; it calls also for the recognition of individual rights and the protection of individual liberties. As one appreciates the value of temporal self-interest and what is necessary to its fulfillment in the economic sphere, one is compelled on Christian principles to consider how the same might best be achieved for others. No one has ever proved that the simple and single-minded pursuit of self-interest will automatically achieve the same end for others, and there is good reason to suppose it will not.

2. The good of gainful employment—Labor has intrinsic value for human beings created in God's image and mandated to exercise dominion over the earth in His name. Work was designed originally to be fulfilling, which continues to be true even after the Fall. The overarching principle for work as well as worship is this: "Whatever you do, whether in word or deed, do it all in the name of the Lord Jesus, giving thanks to God the Father through him" (Col. 3:17).

In addition, numerous biblical texts emphasize the *instrumental* good of gainful employment:

Our people must learn to devote themselves to doing what is good, in order that they may provide for daily necessities and not live unproductive lives. (Titus 3:14)

If anyone does not provide for his relatives, and especially for his immediate family, he has denied the faith and is worse than an unbeliever. (1 Tim. 5:8)

He who has been stealing must steal no longer, but must work, doing something useful with his own hands, that he may have something to share with those in need. (Eph. 4:28)

If it is true, as Galbraith says, that the decisive problem of economics is not price determination or income distribution but "how the level of output and employment is determined,"[28] then given the intrinsic and instrumental value of work in the biblical ethic, the issue of unemployment, "demonstrably the prime social anxiety of our time,"[29] lays claim to special attention on the part of Christians working in the field of economics.[30] What is the most promising means to the fullest employment? The answer is likely to be coordinate with the subject of the next section.

3. The good of profitable business enterprise—As laborers are deserving of their wages (see 1 Tim. 5:18), so persons in business are deserving of their profit. This precept is largely taken for granted in the Scriptures, which assume the coordination of business or labor and its appropriate reward: "All hard work brings a profit, but mere talk leads only to poverty" (Prov. 14:23).

There is nothing wrong with the goal of profit as such from the biblical perspective. The problem with those who say, "Today or tomorrow we will go to this or that city, spend a year there, carry on business and make money" (James 4:13), is not their desire for profit, but their assumption that their life is in their hands rather than God's. They ought to say instead, "If it is the Lord's will, we will live and do this or that" (James 4:15).

There is no point in running an unprofitable business. Profit is the indicator of whether a business venture is a success or failure, whether or not it is self-sustaining. It is the *sine qua non* of a business enterprise, though not its entire *raison d'être*.[31] A business may have multiple reasons for its existence—to produce something worthwhile, to provide gainful employment, to serve a community or nation—but if it cannot turn a profit, it cannot stay in existence, and so cannot fulfill any of its other ends.

It is thus a mistake to pit profits against persons. Of course it is wrong to seek profits by unjust means, whether by fraud or by exploitation of workers. Nevertheless, assuming that the means are just, the goal of a profitable business enterprise is person-serving, fulfilling of human nature in many respects: the satisfaction of the entrepreneurial impulse by those who start the business, the realization of cooperative endeavor by those who participate in the business, and the meeting of the wants of those who sustain the business by purchasing the product.

4. The good of material wealth—The New Testament, while cautionary with respect to material wealth, is not condemnatory. As the converted thief is encouraged to work so as to be able to share with others, so the converted rich are similarly exhorted:

> But godliness with contentment is great gain. For we brought nothing into the world, and we can take nothing out of it. But if we have food and clothing, we will be content with that. People who want to get rich fall into temptation and a trap and into many foolish and harmful desires that plunge men into ruin and destruction. For the love of money is a root of all kinds of evil. Some people, eager for money, have wandered from the faith and pierced themselves with many griefs. (1 Tim. 6:6-10)

> Command those who are rich in this present world not to be arrogant nor to put their hope in wealth, which is so uncertain, but to put their hope in God, who richly provides us with everything for our enjoyment. Command them to do good, to be rich in good deeds, and to be generous and willing to share. In this way they will lay up treasure for themselves as a firm foundation for the coming age, so that they may take hold of the life that is truly life. (1 Tim. 6:17-19)

The Bible condemns not the production, but the idle accumulation of wealth, along with its bosom companions: nonpayment of wages, luxurious self-indulgence, and oppression (see James 5:1-6). The rich are condemned for their *unused* wealth, which through their selfishness has become rotten, moth-eaten, corroded. To think material wealth is an end in itself, to be accumulated to no further purpose than luxurious self-indulgence, is foolish (see Luke 12:16-21). The good of wealth lies in its use, beginning with just distribution to the workers and harvesters by whose labor it is produced, and beyond that to relieve the poor and oppressed.

For wealth to be distributed, it must first be produced. Chalmers's definition of the task of economics is remarkable for its coordination of ends and means: "Political economy aims at the diffusion of sufficiency and comfort throughout the mass of the population, by a multiplication or enlargement of the outward means and materials of human enjoyment."[32] The goal is the material well-being of the populace, which Chalmers recognized could be attained only through greater productivity.

Perhaps the goal comes not from economics as a discipline but from ethics. This is of little consequence so long as economists bend their efforts toward societal economic goals that conform to God's will for human beings living in community. These may be understood to include (1) adequate food, clothing, shelter, medical care for all; (2) employment as a means of providing for individuals and family units; and (3) an environment of clean air and water, with conservation of natural resources and aesthetics.

Economists have a crucial empirical role in determining which economic system has the brightest prospects of being productive and which economic policies offer the most hope for contributing to Chalmers's "diffusion of sufficiency and comfort throughout the mass of the population." Obviously, this task is not easy, especially since economics is rightly understood as "the science of tracing the effects of some proposed or existing policy not only on some *special* interest *in the short run,* but on the *general* interest *in the long run.*"[33] The long ranger writhes again! Nevertheless, empirical data by which economic systems may be compared are not lacking, and Peter Berger has assembled them in impressive array in *The Capitalist Revolution.*[34]

CONCLUSION

Temporal self-interest, gainful employment, profitable business, and material wealth do not constitute "the chief end of man." But it is not the case, as is frequently supposed, that they are unrelated to it. When rightly pursued in light of our final end, they are fulfilling of human nature created in the image of God, "who richly provides us with everything for our enjoyment" (1 Tim . 6:17).

The plural should not go unnoticed. As we are bidden in the Lord's Prayer to ask *our* heavenly Father for *our* daily bread, so the corporate dimensions of economic life may never be forgotten. Persons are fulfilled only in human communities, sharing in the stewardship of creation and in its bounty.

EDITOR'S PERSPECTIVE

The closing portion of David Jones's chapter places tensions between the individual's and the community's economic interest in a beautiful balance that we need to comprehend, appreciate, and pray that God will help create on both an individual and a community basis. The freedom every individual needs to pursue temporal self-interests, to be gainfully employed, to pursue economic profits, and to create and accumulate material wealth and a genuine interest in the general welfare of the community, cannot be realized apart from God's grace, however. The tensions between individual freedoms and community interests are a theme permeating Scripture. (Henry Krabbendam addressed it in the sixth chapter of the first book of this series.)

Ronald Nash's chapter, on the other hand, points to the kind of economic arrangement that must exist in the community if the particular normative features outlined by David Jones are to be given an environment in which to take shape. Citizens should have the chance to make choices regarding opportunities to own property, create goods and services, freely distribute the outputs, and share in the benefits and rewards of the economic processes in an equitable manner.

So what kind of economic system is inherently closer in its structure, opportunities, and goals to God's disclosed intentions for a just economic system? It is a system that provides as much freedom of choice to people as possible and simultaneously supplies the mechanisms of constraint that must operate in a fallen world so that the efforts of individuals are fairly rewarded and the needs of the larger community are met.

This is a biblically responsible answer but not an easy one to establish or maintain in a fallen world. Apart from a combination of God's special grace

113

and common grace, it cannot be created. One of the difficulties (there are many) involved in making the moral judgments necessary to have such an economic system can be illustrated by addressing this question: What is a just wage? This simple question is fraught with moral difficulties. We generally assume that the natural forces of a free market will produce a just wage. This assumption is not necessarily correct, however, for some so-called natural forces at work in the world reflect the negative consequences of our fallen nature.

The Israelites enjoyed a type of free market system when they were not in captivity or exile, and the prophet Malachi was moved by the Spirit of God to declare that God would draw near to them to judge those "who oppress the wage earner in his wages" (Mal. 3:5). When is a wage earner oppressed in his wages? When the wage earner's contribution to the welfare of the owner(s) is not fairly rewarded, the worker is being exploited and thus oppressed in his or her wages. This moral judgment is not universally rectified by the decisions made in a free and open market. Ignorance, unequal positions of economic power, immoral discrimination, misplaced cultural values, and other forces at work in the market often mirror both our fallen nature and our finitude that interfere with justice more often than many of us like to acknowledge.

We can conclude that Ron Nash has pointed us in a direction that is consonant with biblical truth—God desires His people to have as much free choice as prudently possible, and a free market offers the best opportunities for this to be accomplished. David Jones has clearly noted that God's normative standards encourage a good form of temporal self-interest, the good of gainful employment, the good of profit, and the good of material wealth, all of which are best sought in the context of a free market.

Christians must always keep their economic eyes looking in the direction of freedom, and they must be willing to pray and strive for its furtherance. But the balance between freedom and control that is needed for children, for mature Christians, and for a society made up of a pluralistic and diverse body of people with differing world views is not easy to determine. It is comforting to remember at this point that God is also absolutely sovereign, even in such matters, and that His ultimate will is being manifested in the economic realities we discern around us.

From the human perspective, though, determining legitimate property ownership is a fundamental issue to be faced and resolved in any economic system, and a major determinant of economic justice. How do we legitimize our claims on property, private and public? When the children of Israel were about to enter the Promised Land, they were reminded that the land they were about to inherit was God's and not theirs—they were to be stewards, not owners (see Lev. 25:23).

The distribution of wealth must rest on some system for determining how the basic undeveloped wealth will be divided up into divisible units so different groups and individuals can lay defensible claims to either their stewardship or their ownership. This is absolutely fundamental. The next section examines property ownership from a biblical perspective.

PROPERTY, WEALTH, AND ECONOMIC JUSTICE

Many issues related to economic justice are tied to concepts of property ownership, not the least of which are points in question like these: (1) How are we to establish the legitimacy of our claims on private and public property? (2) How are we to preserve, guard, control, manage, and dispose of property? (3) What are we to do with our individual and collective economic surpluses? The answers to these questions ultimately rest on our basic assumptions about life's obligations and rights regarding property. People fundamentally conceive of themselves either as *owners* or as *stewards* of property. Ownership carries with it the notion of property rights— particularly for those whose world view excludes God at its center—but stewardship clearly indicates that someone other than the steward has the right to determine what ought to be done with the property while the steward assumes the appropriate obligations and granted rights. God is not only the Creator; He is also the Owner who has revealed many of His intentions about our stewardship responsibilities. God has given us many freedoms with regard to our stewardship, but not without accountability. Stewards should, therefore, want to know the will of the Owner; self-proclaimed owners care little about the real Owner's desires.

Living in a fallen world, though, makes it absolutely necessary for us to establish a system whereby we can legitimize our claims on property. My memory is filled, for example, with incidents in my childhood where "finders keepers, losers weepers" was the standard set by my friends when they were staking a claim on something they had just found, but they were not interested in discovering who owned it. Others in history have experienced a life where everything they possessed was the property of a feudal lord, as

117

they were. Ideas about property can and do change over time when people ignore God's standards. In my lifetime there has been a radical shift in the use of the laws of eminent domain—the "right" of those who govern to take private property for public use. For example, in the past quarter century the land needed for highway construction and the development of urban renewal projects has often been secured through the use of the laws of eminent domain. Even when the original owners are paid a fair market price, as approved by the courts, this does not necessarily meet the requirements of God's justice (see 1 Kings 21:1-16).

Scripture abounds with passages about property and wealth. Dr. Harold O. J. Brown, the first author in this section, shares some insights into the difference between property (possessions) and wealth, and the world's frequently twisted ideas about them. Wealth and possessions are never condemned in Scripture or treated as if they are somehow inherently bad. We are warned about greed and idolatry, the love of things. When our personal identity becomes attached to our possessions and worldly achievements, or when we place our trust in our wealth, we are in danger of being self-deceived and of alienating ourselves from God, one another, and our true self.

Dr. Brown has a very scathing commentary on the unbiblical notion that private property should be abolished. Scripture clearly reveals that God wants individual stewards to have dominion over discretely defined pieces of property, and Joe Brown correctly observes that the abolition of private property can thwart the moral development of the individual, and thereby become dehumanizing. He concludes, therefore, that Christians should seek a just way to broaden the base of ownership when property is under the control of only a few people, but the solution to problems that may be associated with the concept of private property are not to be found in its abolition (see Isa. 5:8-10; Amos 5:11-12; Mic. 2:1-2).

Dr. Richard J. Mouw, the second author in this section, while being in virtual agreement with Dr. Brown and with Ronald Nash, goes even further in pointing out that a kind of family and community obligation is also associated with the concept of private property as enunciated in the Bible. The biblical tension of being individuals and simultaneously members of a community is not always easy to resolve, but Christians are to take both seriously.

Dr. Mouw asserts that those who govern society are to have a concern for people who are in economic distress and who have no family to speak up for them or to see that their rights are considered (see Ps. 72:1-4, 12-14). Individual citizens are not to leave these matters to those who govern though. To the contrary! Biblically, the king was to make certain that the needy were protected and helped when they were ignored or abused in the private sector. The Bible consistently calls the righteous to have a heart for the needy before the responsibility is assumed by the king (see Job 29:12-17; 31:16-22; Prov. 29:7; 31:8-9; Jer. 5:28; and many more). The king was considered unjust when he failed to ensure that the leaders under his authority aided the afflicted and needy in their midst. We will not develop this point any further here, however, because in Section E we ask and answer the questions: When does Scripture assign poverty problems to the private sector, and when are they assigned to the public sector?

Dr. Brown brings our thinking back to the broader biblical concept of property—which includes both wealth creating commercial assets as well as one's personal possessions, the latter usually not being conceived of in terms of their market value. Wealth is generally associated with commerce; personal property need not be thought of this way. He provides a good overview of the Bible's attitude toward property and wealth as well as its warnings to those who would identify with their wealth as a means of reinforcing their sense of personal importance and success. And finally, Dr. Brown opens up an understanding of the clear relationship that necessarily exists between property, freedom, and economic justice.

CHAPTER 6

PROPERTY AND JUSTICE

Harold O. J. Brown

Harold O. J. Brown occupies the Forman Chair of Ethics and Theology at Trinity Evangelical Divinity School in Deerfield, Illinois. He studied at Harvard College, Harvard Divinity School, the Universities of Marbur (Germany) and Vienna (Austria), and Harvard Graduate School of Arts and Sciences, from which he holds the Ph.D. in Reformation History. He holds ministerial standing in the National Association of Congregational Christian Churches and has served pastorates in Centerville and North Beverly, Massachusetts, as well as at Boston's Park Street Church and in Klosters, Switzerland.

Together with C. Everett Koop, M.D., Dr. Brown founded the Christian Action Council in 1975. The Council, of which he is still Chairman, is committed to creating a Christian witness in the forum of public law in life-related issues such as abortion, euthanasia, fetal research, genetic engineering, and others. He has written a number of books including Heresies: The Image of Christ in the Mirror of Heresy and Orthodoxy *and* Christianity and the Class Struggle. *He is a member of the Christianity Today Institute and a contributing editor to* Chronicles; *he has published extensively in secular and Christian magazines. He is also an Adjunct Professor of Theology and Human Rights in the Simon Greenleaf School of Law summer institute in Strasbourg, France.*

FORGOTTEN PRINCIPLES

North Americans and many Western Europeans are suffering increasingly from problems that we cannot solve because they result from factors that we cannot understand. Our ability to understand is limited by the fact that we have learned to disregard, deny, and forget things we once knew. Because we are still dimly conscious that we knew them once, and that we have chosen to leave them behind, it is difficult to turn to them once again when we really need them—which is the situation today. Among the things that we used to know well, things that made up the furniture of our moral habitat, we might name negative things such as violence and positive values such as virtue, fidelity, and property.

Prior to the student rebellions and antiwar demonstrations of the 1960s and early 1970s, there were concepts and values that seemed to have the permanence of fixed stars on the moral horizon. Peace, for example, meant the absence of war and violence. Since the end of World War II, the United States has engaged in two major wars, but they were never officially declared or officially acknowledged to be wars.

Domestic tranquility—one of the chief ends of government, according to the Preamble to the United States Constitution—used to mean the absence of violence, governmental or private. Today we define violence in terms not of the nature of the acts but of the quality of the perpetrator. For students to throw rocks at police, for terrorists from one of the many "liberation movements" to place bombs in public places, was, according to the older understanding, just plain violence, with no buts or maybes. Many who might otherwise have sympathized with the cause of the students or of the liberation movement objected to it when confronted with the violence.

How did the advocates of violent protest deal with this moral reaction, which questioned their legitimacy? Not by claiming that their violence was justified in terms that the older morality could have recognized, but by denying that their actions were violent, by changing the meaning of the term *violence* so that what their opponents regarded as peacekeeping became *institutional* or *structural violence* and their violent actions only *counter-violence* on the level of self-defense. We were urged to accept the thesis that the existence of outward tranquility and order does not necessarily mean absence of violence. The government and the institutions against which action was being taken might appear to be calm and tranquil, and thus innocent of violence; nevertheless, because they were perceived and defined as unjust, their very existence was said to constitute structural or institutional violence. In consequence, to strike out against them, however violently, was not to initiate violence—which would be wrong—but to respond to violence, which is all right. A familiar concept has become its opposite. It is just as George Orwell envisaged in *Nineteen Eighty-Four*, when "War Is Peace" was one of the three great maxims of the totalitarian state. The curious thing about the slogan was that it worked only one way; it permitted war to continue, but it made peace impossible.

Fidelity—faithfulness—is another concept that has virtually been changed into its opposite, whether we mean fidelity in marriage, in friendship, in employment, or in national allegiance. Marital faithfulness used to be a simple idea. It meant, in the words of the marriage service, "forsaking all others" to have sexual relations only with one's spouse. Today, some "theologians" argue that the act of "forsaking all others"—previous or potential lovers—constitutes infidelity, with the result that exclusive faithfulness vis-à-vis one's spouse really is a form of infidelity. If we operate with such a definition of terms, faithfulness becomes an impossible ideal and can be disregarded.[1]

Property is another concept we thought we understood—until recently. Although we are accustomed to distinguishing *private* from *government* or *public* property, the original and logical meaning of *property* is private property. The old understanding of property is that which really pertains to me, which is my own and which characterizes me—as opposed to my possessions, which I can give or sell to another so that they become as much his as they were mine before. For most, although not all, societies, property ownership is a natural right, and taking someone else's property constitutes robbery or theft and is a crime. It was, as the Germans say, *selbstverständlich*—self-understandable.

More recently, however, we are being told that the ownership of property by its very nature constitutes theft. Indeed, property *is* theft, and taking it from those who have it becomes a moral duty. In such a case, if force is used, we can assume that the force will be defined not as violence, but as the redressing of preexisting structural violence of property ownership.

FORGOTTEN ALLIANCES:
THRONE AND ALTAR, CHURCH AND COUNTINGHOUSE

In addition to several concepts that used to be taken for granted but now are being forgotten—to our loss—our moral habitat contained other furnishings such as traditional alliances. It is time to reexamine them because they may be doing more harm than good, costing more than they are worth. For example, it used to be natural to assume an alliance between the throne and the altar, between government and religion. Whether such an alliance was ever good or desirable is not the question; the fact is, it existed, and it molded civilizations and peoples. Many religions regularly support a political status quo, and Christianity has seldom been an exception. (When the Germans reformed their spelling in the nineteenth century and dropped the *h* from words with *th* in them, it was retained in the words *Thron* and *Theologie*. This gave rise to the joke that no one was allowed to take or subtract anything from either the Kaiser or the Deity.)

In Romans 13:1-7, Paul gives a massive declaration of support for the powers that be, which sound suspiciously like the status quo. Paul's endorsement of what was then a corrupt and vicious imperial system has led Christians to adopt a generally conservative attitude toward government, in most cases even if it is intolerant of Christianity. This alliance is carried over into American life, for although we no longer have a throne, we have a kind of mutual support agreement between Church and state. (This *modus vivendi* is under increasing pressure from militantly secularist groups and has suffered severe strains, but to some extent it still functions.)

Also, it has often seemed—at least to those of us in Europe and North America, in the so-called Christian West—as though there were an unspoken alliance between the Church and the countinghouse, between religion and business. In *Protestant Theology in the Nineteenth Century,* Karl Barth contends that during the Enlightenment Protestantism more or less enlisted in the service of the bourgeoisie and the bourgeois values that undergird capitalism.[2] Similar insights led Max Weber and R. H. Tawney to propose the theory that Protestantism is responsible for the rise of capitalism. As long as capitalism and the free market were favorably regarded by society, this identification redounded to the credit of Protestantism. Numerous theologians credited Protestantism with progress per se, in an era when it was taken for granted that progress is a good thing.

Today, capitalism and everything connected with it is widely considered an evil, even by those who could hardly survive, much less enjoy the affluence that is theirs, if it were not for capitalism and the bounty it produces. We all recognize that in the West generally the favored offspring of the upper and upper middle income groups become the intellectual adversaries of capitalism and the free market. They often gain fame and fortune as a result; they enjoy a kind of *succès de scandale* and get rich on the royalties and speakers' fees paid by those they want to expropriate. Particularly for the established and mainline churches associated with the World Council of Churches, but also for many evangelicals, especially in Protestant Europe, the immorality of capitalism and the free market is taken for granted, and the superior morality of any and every socialist system is assumed. For such people, the idea that Christianity has helped to create capitalism is perceived as a liability, even by those who would be very unhappy if they were deprived of the material abundance that capitalism brings them.

FAITH AND FORTUNE

What is the basic biblical attitude toward wealth? Do riches constitute an all but impassable barrier to entry into the Kingdom of God, as the needle's eye did for the richly laden camel? The Old Testament is generally more sympathetic than the New to the idea that wealth can or even should go along with faith and obedience. At least a few of its central figures were men of great wealth, such as Job and Solomon. The central figures of the New Testament, the Lord Jesus Himself and His disciples, were men of modest means. The Son of Man, we are told, had "no place to lay his head" (Luke 9:58, NIV). No less a saint than Francis of Assisi assumed that Jesus and His disciples lived in total poverty. Although this assumption is almost certainly wrong, it is evident that they were neither wealthy nor concerned with obtaining wealth.

Wealthy individuals were among their first followers, but surely the majority of early Christians were poor, and many were even slaves. Until the reign of Constantine the Great, the Church was subject to frequent persecution, and as an institution it could not accumulate real estate or other wealth. But as soon as Constantine established religious toleration, wealth came to many churches and to not a few clergy, and nothing prevented Christian laymen from getting rich. Even before Constantine, so many Christians in some communities were becoming worldly minded that a reaction set in, and thousands abandoned the "world" and its temptations for the austere life of desert hermits—the beginning of the monastic movement. On the whole, however, the Church was not opposed to wealth for itself or for others. Later generations, especially those inspired by Francis and the mendicant orders, saw in this a fatal compromise, but at first it did not appear so.

We should distinguish between the wealth of the Church and that of individuals, for even though subject to abuses, the wealth of the Church can be said to be in the service and for the honor of God rather than for the pleasure of individuals. Before Europe became Christian, individual Christians possessing wealth and power were rare. Costly gifts to convents and monasteries were considered to be given to God; this display provided worshipers with an intimation of the majesty and grandeur of God and of the glory of Heaven. Despite the abuses, the wealth that was accumulated in general belonged to the Church and not to individuals. Nevertheless, from Reformation days onward, the figure of the frugal, hardy Protestant minister living in a modest parsonage with a large family contrasted favorably with the stereotype of the worldly Catholic prelate feasting extravagantly if celibately in a baroque palace.

Today, with the rise of mass-media religion, we are confronted for the first time with religion, particularly with evangelical religion, used as a moneymaking venture on a large scale. We see televangelists attempting to outdo Renaissance popes in luxury (if not in taste) provided by tens of thousands of proverbial widow's mites. This flagrant abuse of spiritual influence provides critics of enthusiastic evangelical religion with additional reason to dismiss it as fraudulent. The fact that some Christians have justified what looks like religious exploitation in terms of a "gospel of wealth" or "prosperity theology" does not answer all our objections or relieve us of all suspicions.

Such criticism could not have been leveled, we know, at Francis of Assisi who claimed to be in love with "Lady Poverty." He imposed the most rigorous rules on his followers, who were not allowed to carry money on their persons; a friar found dead with two pence in his purse was to be disowned by the Franciscan order. The papacy, faced by a movement that cast it in a very bad light, explicitly condemned the assertion that Jesus and His disciples had owned no property but had lived in poverty, an assertion giving the impression that all ownership of property is sinful in itself and clearly indicting the Church and churchmen with their vast holdings. Although the Franciscan movement remained limited to a dedicated few, the idea that wealth is evil, and probably all those who are wealthy as well, has always been present in Christian spirituality.

WEALTH AND PROPERTY

The biblical critique of wealth and the suspicion of and hostility toward wealth evident in so many reforming movements throughout Church history are addressed to wealth, not to property. Wealth is a quantitative concept; property, a qualitative one. Wealth refers to the extent of one's possessions; property, to the quality of the act of possessing. Wealth creates or at least permits a high standard of living; property creates or at least permits a certain quality of life. Christian moralism, as we have noted, is critical of excessive wealth, but it actually *favors* property ownership, at least within certain limits. Socialism and communism, by contrast, seek to abolish property (private property), but often permit the accumulation of wealth. Strictly speaking, an individual may own much property but have little wealth; conversely, a wealthy man may own little or no property. By "property" we mean not only real estate, but everything that is so intimately one's own that one is unwilling to trade or sell it. In this sense, the furniture in a dealer's showroom is not his "property" as the family heirlooms in his house are, but is merely his "goods and possessions."

The Christian criticizes wealth because it threatens to turn a man's heart away from God and from his neighbor. Marxist criticism often sounds similar, but it has a different source. Marxism is really opposed to *property*, as it is to every artifact and institution that permits an individual to be himself, indeed, that permits the individual to exist as an individual and not as a cog in the state's economic machine. Marxism does not object to the accumulation of wealth and the privileges accompanying it, provided such wealth is derived from service to the state. The existence of a propertied class with "independent means" allows a measure of personal independence vis-à-vis the state. Of course it can be abused. Individuals can establish petty personal tyrannies, but even such abuses represent a check to the monolithic power of the state. The historical record, going back to Rome and beyond, shows clearly how tyrannical rulers, posing as protectors of the poor, regularly seek the support of the poor against the propertied classes, but actually they are more concerned with protecting their power against those who might otherwise have a measure of independence.

Because Christians must heed the biblical critique of wealth, they often develop an uneasy conscience with regard to property and thus unwittingly join hands with Marxists in tearing down an institution that is a vital protection for many things Christians consider valuable, chief among them freedom. Marxism, like other totalitarian systems, seeks to destroy property because property hinders the creation of one of the prerequisites of totalitarian control, the formation of what Hannah Arendt calls the "atomistic mass." In the atomistic mass, individuals are neither related to one another nor secured by property ownership; their only relationship is to the government, and their only hope is in the government. Individualism is not tolerated.

Property ownership, by contrast, is almost essential for individuality. Individuals can abuse property ownership and through poor stewardship make it seem as though property itself is a bad institution. Property in this respect is rather like but more important than money. Where money is used, it can be amassed and can be used to control and to exploit, but where money does not exist, the only alternative is a primitive barter economy or something resembling a prison or concentration camp, where everything is managed and no freedom exists. Unless the institution of private ownership exists and is utilized by many members of society, it is hard to prevent the population from degenerating into ciphers dependent entirely on the state.

Some commentators have wisely observed that the power to tax is the power to destroy. Property, in this sense of land and heirloom possessions that an individual will not alienate because they pertain too intimately to him, represents an obstacle to the total sovereignty of the state and hence a support for individual freedom. Even though property-less individuals in a property-owning society have less scope for their freedom than property owners, the very existence of property ownership gives them the potential to expand their scope in ways that would not be possible if the institution were not available.

Ancient slavery presents another parallel. A free man had the right to represent himself in court, to choose his employment, his place of work, and his citizenship, thus in a sense to dispose of or to administer his person as though he were private property. The fact that in such a society some do not have this right and are slaves does not alter the fact that unless the right to such private ownership of the self is recognized, everyone will be a slave and no one will be free. When this right of personal ownership of the self is limited by law, with the result that some are not free, the way to extend freedom lies in extending the right, not abolishing it. In a property-owning society, when the freedom of some is limited because they do not own property, the way to extend freedom lies in extending the ownership of private property.

In Europe the concentration of property ownership in the hands of a few has been seen as a limitation on the freedom of the many, and many societies attempted to remedy this by abolishing property or at least the ownership of the means of industrial and agricultural production. But it is increasingly being realized that the result of this action is the diminishing of freedom for everyone, not just for the previous owners. A better solution has been the attempt to *expand* private ownership, first of housing, but also of the means of production by broadening the base of ownership of production, that is, by widespread ownership of stock. Even when a small number of people own most of the share in industry, the fact that vast numbers of people own at least some shares dramatically increases freedom. This is not to say that one must possess wealth to be an individual (although it sometimes helps!), but to say that without property, without something that really belongs to a person and characterizes him, it is difficult to be more than a cipher or a cog.

The concept that wealth is evil per se and that those who possess it must be illegitimate is the spirit underlying the assertion of liberation theologians: God is on the side of the poor.[3] One gets the impression that Christians should favor the poor against the rich in justice and judgment, despite an explicit biblical warning against this (see Lev. 19:15). Scripture does show a certain bias in favor of the poor. For example, it is cognizant that the danger that the rich may use bribes to corrupt justice in favor of their causes is greater than the danger that an ideology will corrupt judges to favor the poor. However, neither being rich nor being poor is meritorious in God's sight; the Bible clearly indicates that both the rich and the poor need God's grace and forgiveness. God judges the wealthy not because of their wealth, but because of the way in which they acquire it and use or abuse it. But in like manner He does not favor the poor because they are poor. To say that God has compassion for them and summons Christians to act compassionately is not to say that God looks on poverty as a virtue. There are two errors, not one, to be avoided here.

In recent decades, we have seen a flourishing of the "gospel of wealth," the idea that God will reward with earthly prosperity those who serve Him. Some individuals have become wealthy by proclaiming this sort of "gospel"—among the foremost exponents of this view are some now fallen idols of televised religion. Their passing success does not prove that God's reward is this-worldly prosperity; it shows merely that people like to think that it is and are willing to pay to hear it.

On the whole, people are less willing to pay to hear the opposite. Harvey Cox's *Secular City*[4]—which does not say exactly that, but which claims that God works through Marxist ideologies as well as through capitalist technologies—became a best seller, but few of the proponents of the cause of liberation theology have become rich because of royalties earned by their repeated declarations that God is on the side of the poor.

Wealth is not to be seen as the badge of virtue or piety—often the wealthy "possess" neither—but it is also not to be contrasted with virtue as though it were its opposite or prevented it. God's people are not promised earthly abundance here and now as the reward of their faith, but neither are they called, as Francis of Assisi believed he was, to marry themselves to "Lady Poverty."

PROPERTY, FREEDOM, AND ECONOMIC JUSTICE

The Bible does not contain a blueprint for an economic system, but it does proclaim fundamental principles that an economic structure must embody to be just. These principles do not produce or require capitalism—particularly not our modern form of computerized international capitalistic finance—but they provide for property and for profit and presuppose the right to engage in industry and trade. Biblical principles, expressed in the language and concepts of an early Near Eastern economic and social order, indeed appear naive in the modern world. But naivete can mean charming and effective simplicity as well as unrealistic innocency. Old Testament economic concepts translate amazingly well into the language and situations of our day, and these concepts are far more compatible with the institutions of personal ownership of property and with the free market than with those of state ownership, state socialism, and the controlled or directed economy.

That Scripture encourages people to think in terms of private ownership and a free market, even if in a naive sort of way, is no doubt one reason why socialist governments wage constant war on biblical religion. The tyrannical totalitarians of the Communist world often attempt to root out biblical religion by force, but even the *new totalitarians* of socialist Sweden (the term is Roland Huntford's)[5] seek to starve and stifle it. Biblical religion does not explicitly prescribe private property nor explicitly ban socialism, but the statists rightly sense that its world view is not very compatible with their program.

AN IMPORTANT DISTINCTION

Public discourse—not the least, public discourse on economic matters—is frequently dominated by catchwords and slogans that people mistakenly think they understand when they actually do not. The concept of private property is one example. To many people, it suggests what we have already mentioned, an absolute right to use, abuse, or dispose of that which one has as one sees fit. If that were what private property means, we would have to say that it is not biblical. But that is not what it means, and the restrictions on the abuse of private property lie not in the abolition of the institution of property, but in the elevation of the duty of responsible stewardship.

In the very beginning, God granted our first parents "dominion" over the unspoiled earth, which meant stewardship and accountability: the right to use, not to abuse; to develop, not to exploit and exhaust (see Gen. 1:26-31; cf. Gen. 2:15).

The Christian discussion of rights in the West is polluted, so to speak, by the atmospheric fallout of revolution, particularly of the French Revolution, not the American one. For the French, with their Declaration of the Rights of Man, rights are an absolute principle, given in the nature of man as understood by the rationalistic humanism of the Enlightenment. Unfortunately, there is nothing compelling about the Enlightenment understanding of the essential nature of man; thus, there is nothing to enforce the concept of human rights derived from it.

The Scripture, by contrast, does not know the concept of rights at all, at least not in a primary sense. For Scripture, man is not and cannot be *ton panton metron*, "the measure of all things," in the expression of Protagoras.

Man really does not know what and who he is apart from the biblical revelation that places him *coram Deo* (before God). Man is defined in terms of his responsibilities vis-à-vis God, before whom he cannot speak of any intrinsic rights of his own. However, this does not leave him without standing and without rights. God in His covenant love gives us reliable promises, and through His covenant He prescribes our duties toward one another in such a way that rights will effectively derive from them. In what is probably an unconscious imitation, the United States Bill of Rights—the first ten amendments to the Constitution—does not express rights positively and abstractly, saying, for example, "The people have the right to keep and bear arms." Rather it says, "The right of the people to keep and bear arms shall not be infringed" (by government; I should note that I choose the Second Amendment not to endorse any particular understanding of the right to keep and bear arms—its terse and economical formulation simply makes it easy to make my point).

Fundamental to our concerns here is the Eighth Commandment (by Jewish and Reformed count; Seventh by Roman Catholic and Lutheran numeration): "Thou shalt not steal." The Bible nowhere says that "each person," "each man," or "every head of household" has the right to own private property; it says only that no one may take another's property or goods from him. Thus, the right is not constituted absolutely or abstractly, but derivatively. This is an important theoretical and a practically relevant distinction. As a matter of legal and social practicality, it is easier to prevent others from infringing one's rights than it is to confer the full enjoyment of those rights as such.

An illustration is given by testimony before the Subcommittee on Constitutional Amendments of the House Judiciary Committee, which I witnessed in the spring of 1975. Harriet Pilpel, an attorney and activist for the American Civil Liberties Union, and an ardent advocate of abortion on demand, denied—quite correctly—that the Constitution contains a right to life (for the unborn or for anyone else). Arguing against all versions of a right to life amendment, she contended that placing such an amendment in the Constitution would then require the government to provide food, housing, health care, and all other such necessities and enhancements of life necessary or desirable for living. I believe that recognition of a human right by government does not require the government to provide all the necessary means to exercise that right. Even the Declaration of Independence, which mentions rights more directly than the Constitution, speaks of the right to life and to liberty, but not to "happiness"—only to "the pursuit of happiness."

If one followed Harriet Pilpel's argument to its logical conclusion, for the government to write a right to life amendment into the Constitution would obligate it to abolish death, something that exceeds the competence of even the most ardent advocates of federal power. But it would be proper and possible for the government to deny to citizens the right to take innocent lives where the not-yet-born are concerned—as it already does, although not with 100 percent effectiveness, on behalf of born children and adults. It would be impossible for government to grant to citizens the right to honor and to a good reputation, although it would be possible for government to provide safeguards—far better than they now exist—in the form of effective laws against slander and libel. It is not an abstract guarantee, either on the part of government or of Scripture, that establishes your rights; the limitations on my arbitrary exercise of the powers of violence, deceit, seduction, and false witness create your rights to life, property, family integrity, and personal honor (the Sixth, Seventh, Eighth, Ninth, and Tenth Commandments in the Jewish numbering).

ANOTHER IMPORTANT DISTINCTION: PROPERTY AND POSSESSIONS

The establishment of meaningful rights depends on setting certain limits on what we demand. Thus, just as we cannot reasonably or effectively demand a right to good health, we can demand and provide a moderate right to access to good health care. We cannot guarantee the right to ownership in the abstract (what, where, and how much should each person be guaranteed, and who is to produce what is guaranteed?), but we can protect existing and future ownership from encroachment by others. An absolute right to own property, goods, and money might seem to be incompatible with taxation, that quasidivine "staff of life" of government. In the attempt to secure the right to property, we must note that not everything that one may possess ought to be called property.

When contemporary Americans speak of property rights, they usually mean much more than we have in mind, namely, the absolute right to all that one can possess, and the right to do with it exactly as one pleases. Such a right would be inherently unenforceable; in addition it goes beyond any biblical warrant. Borrowing a Roman legal concept is useful: Property is to be distinguished from possessions because property consists of *res non in commertio* (things not in commerce), things that one is unable or unwilling to sell or trade, but that in the normal course of events will be handed down to the next generation.

We sometimes hear it said that a particularly possessive, patriarchal husband regards his wife and children as property, and that this is a dreadful thing. The phenomenon is dreadful, of course, but they really should not be called property. The man who tyrannizes his wife and children, even to the extent of selling them as slaves, is precisely *not* treating them as *property*— something intimately pertaining to him. *Possessions—chattels* in the old terminology—more accurately describes what they are in that situation.

The English word "property" is derived from the Latin *proprius* and means something that is intimately identified with one. In this sense a wife ought to be her husband's property and the husband the property of his wife. This is an implication of the "one flesh" concept of marriage (see Gen. 2:24; Matt. 19:5-6). Property in the classical sense was to be distinguished from possessions in that property was always *res non in commertio,* something not "in trade." Possessions might be bought, sold, and exchanged, but property could or should not be alienated other than by inheritance. There were two principal types of property, which we can designate as "real" property (real estate, which is what common parlance means by property) and "heirloom" property (things that so intimately belong to an individual or a family that they will not be sold or traded, but will be scrupulously handed down to a cherished heir).

We are all familiar with real estate as property. Biblically and traditionally, societies have a strong tendency to try to keep such property in the family. The story of Ahab and Naboth's vineyard is an apt illustration (see 1 Kings 21:1-19). Significantly, a foreigner conceived and staged the murder that permitted Ahab to expropriate the property that Naboth quite properly had been unwilling to sell or to trade, namely, Ahab's foreign queen, Jezebel. Heirloom property has been important, from antiquity right up to our own days, particularly for the aristocratic and patrician elements of society, but also for almost all others as well. Monarchs have crown jewels to hand down, and possession of the jewels has symbolized royal legitimacy. This is the principle, conscious or unconscious, behind the repeated demands of the Communist government of Hungary for the Crown of St. Stephen, in United States' custody since World War II, and the distress of Hungarian nationalists when President Carter ordered that it be returned to Hungary's foreign-installed Communist masters. Monarchs had crowns, and nobility suits of armor. But even the poorest families usually have something: a weapon, such as a sword or more recently perhaps a shotgun, family tableware, or an ancient cradle.

Both heirloom property and real estate have suffered terrible attrition in the modern world. World War II spread mass destruction, and revolutions and civil war have swept away the souvenirs of ancestry in many lands. Inflation has raised the price of genuine antiques and curios so that their traditional owners are greatly tempted to sell them, and mass production gives the impression that equally useful, "more modern" articles can be had for a price that permits the heirloom owners great profits, at least in paper money. But the heirlooms, once sold, are gone forever, and with them the memory and tradition they represented.

Real property has suffered as well. As Hannah Arendt so trenchantly observes, all modern governments expropriate, that is, alienate property and destroy its meaning.[6] Communist dictatorships do it out of hand, by fiat, while bourgeois governments operate more slowly and gently, but equally effectively, by a combination of taxation and inflation. Inflation accentuates the paper value of property, "justifying" tax increases, and the increased taxes can be paid for only by selling the real estate. This leads to a profit, often an apparently great one, and thus permits the former owners to amass currency, commercial paper, and the products of mass production, but they have lost their property and perhaps their family history.

Is it proper (or rather, "correct"), biblically speaking, to think of things, whether of real estate or of heirlooms, as being intimately associated with persons? Does not the Scripture tell us that we are "strangers and pilgrims" on earth itself and we seek "a better country" (Heb. 11:13-16, KJV)? Does not Jesus warn us that a man's life does not consist in the abundance of his possessions (see Luke 12:15)? Indeed they do. Therefore, we do not mean what Paul Tillich (an often helpful coiner of concepts, if a very unreliable spiritual guide) calls our "ultimate concern," namely, the "better country" of Hebrews 11, the "life" of which Jesus speaks. For this reason (as well as for others), it would be wrong to absolutize property or to think in terms of an *absolute right* to it. Biblically speaking, rights to property ownership exist, but they never exist in a vacuum. They are always tempered and conditioned by the responsibilities of stewardship and of charity. This does not mean, however, that such rights have only a tenuous and unreal existence. As a matter of fact, the very stewardship and charity responsibilities to which Scripture holds us can be met only if we have the right to own and to use property. Without at least some form of private ownership, we may theoretically be free to "do good and to share what [we] have" (Heb. 13:16, RSV), but we lack the ability, because we do not actually have anything to share or with which to work.

Even the casual reader of the Old Testament can see that property rights were important to God for His people. The Second Table of the Decalogue, which deals with our duties to our fellow human beings, creates a number of rights, most of which, alas, are recognized more by way of being destroyed than by being guaranteed or enforceable. The Fifth Commandment, "Honor thy father and thy mother," gives to parents the right to be honored by their children. The Sixth Commandment, "Thou shalt not kill," clearly conveys a general right to life, and the Seventh, "Thou shalt not commit adultery," the right to security in the marriage relationship. The Eighth, "Thou shalt not steal," conveys a right to tranquil possession of goods and property, and this right is reiterated in the Tenth, which forbids even desiring the expropriation or dispossession of what belongs to one's neighbor.

The Eighth Commandment does not distinguish between property and possessions, but simply forbids stealing. As this applies to mere possessions, it clearly applies *a fortiori* to what we mean by property, *res non in commertio*. It is apparent from the laws relating to the land in Israel that the right to own real property was given by God in His gracious disposition for the life of the people of Israel. The land itself has tremendous significance in God's covenant with Israel. Unconditionally promised to Abraham and his descendants (see Gen. 17:8), it has recently been recovered by the Jews. Without delving into the prophetic implications of the return of the Jews to modern Israel, I think I can safely say that it reemphasizes the importance of real estate to the people of God.

The land of Israel is evidently "proper" to the Jewish people in a deep sense; others can come between the people and the land, as others can come between a husband and his wife, and yet Israel is far more "proper" to the Jews than to any of the other nations that have occupied territory during repeated Jewish captivities and dispersions.

Not only was the land of Israel important to the people, but the individual parcels were meaningful to the families that owned them. The principle of the Year of Jubilee (see Lev. 25), which guarantees that real estate is to remain in the family, constitutes an unusual reaffirmation of the sense that "property" *non in commertio* is significant.

PROPERTY AND THE FALL

How are we to perceive familiar human institutions, such as civil government, that are explicitly ordained of God? Do they represent part of God's original purpose or only a divine concession to man's fallen condition? It is possible to speculate about what form human society might have taken apart from the Fall and original sin, and theologians have done so, but it is not possible to know the answer. Adam and Eve were naked in Eden, but were they also poor? The "creation mandate" to subdue the earth *precedes* the

Fall, as does Adam's stewardship over the garden. In the judgment of Genesis 3:16-19, several aspects of the human condition are presented as part of the curse, but property ownership is not one of them. It is certainly possible, if we imagine mankind as unfallen, to speculate that men and women might have held all things in common and that children would never have said, "Gimme it! That's *mine!*" Unfortunately, man is fallen, and perhaps fortunately, there is no way to know what social and economic structures might have been established in an unfallen world—fortunately, because otherwise we would doubtless try to establish them with our fallen abilities, fallen intellects, and fallen appetites. Indeed, as Thomas Molnar has shown, utopia is "the perennial heresy,"[7] an effort to imagine and to restore pre-Fall conditions without benefit of the work of Christ, and even without benefit of human repentance.

Of human institutions, the Church as a redemptive community is clearly God's provision for fallen man. But would there have been no "congregation of the saints" without the Fall? Government is a post-Fall provision, but unfallen mankind would presumably have had some kind of structure. The family is a pre-Fall ordinance, one that is endangered by the Fall, but clearly necessary after the Fall. Property ownership lies somewhere between government and the family; it is not self-evidently a pre-Fall ordinance, yet it is important after the Fall. Perhaps we can take a hint from the Marxist dream (or illusion). The Communist revolution, according to its advocates, was to result in the abolition of private property and in the "withering away" of the state—a return to Eden without repentance or divine renewal. In reality it has created the leviathan state—what the late General DeGaulle called "la pire des tyrannies jamais concue par l'homme" ("the worst of tyrannies ever conceived by man"). The dream of the total abolition of property also will prove incapable of bringing us back to Eden, but in the effort may well create "la pire des economies jamais concue par l'homme" ("the worst of economies ever conceived by man").

Private property, in short, is somewhat better than crutches for us, and somewhat less than a flying carpet—rather more like a bicycle. Like the bicycle, it cannot take us everywhere, certainly not to Eden, but it certainly beats walking on crutches.

EDITOR'S REFLECTIONS

Dr. Brown has set before us two simple but very profound insights. The quantitative and qualitative distinctions between wealth and property profoundly influence our attitudes toward property. Wealth is the quantitative and measurable market value assigned to property and reflects the value of aggregate exchange the wealth holder possesses. In our society, wealth is generally reduced to a single common denominator, *dollars*. Shares of common stock, acres of land, number of cattle, and other categories of wealth, including the value of labor, are equated or standardized by converting them all to a dollar value. The shifting of values, especially the value of labor, toward a common monetary value deeply concerned Karl Marx. He believed this would eventually result in a pecuniary world view where money would become the standard measure of everything and laborers would soon derive their identity from their wages, not their craft or skill, which would result in their alienation from their work. He concluded from this and other considerations that all private property should be abolished to help prevent these events. Thus, the abolition of private property became a cornerstone of Marxism. As Dr. Brown pointed out, though, such a concept is antithetical to the biblical view of property and its relationship to our need for freedom of choice if we are to mature in the image of God.

Wealth in the above sense then comes to symbolize the power to exchange and acquire other denominated forms of wealth—sell stock, receive cash, and buy a boat. A barter system merely excludes the common denominator of cash as the intermediate and common value—trade one sheep for three bushels of corn without the involvement of money. The Bible, however, focuses on the perverted attitudes that can so easily be stimulated by wealth; Scripture reveals no interest, per se, in the abstract concepts of wealth. This is one reason why the Apostle Paul's statement to the Philippians is so illuminating:

I have learned to be *content* in whatever circumstances I am. I know how to get along with humble means, and I also know how to live in prosperity; in any and every circumstance I have learned the secret of being filled and going hungry, both of having abundance and suffering need. (Phil. 4:11-12, emphasis added)

What Paul had learned provided him with a real *contentment* that guarded his heart from greed and covetousness, a real concern of God. It is obvious from Paul's letter that his contentment did not emanate from his wealth or lack of it. He was content when suffering a need or when prospering. This point is extremely significant because greed and covetousness are attitudes that emanate from desires or felt needs that people believe can be satisfied by acquiring the particular item(s) of wealth for which they long. However, such felt needs can only be temporarily salved by their material satisfaction.

Paul's contentment came from his relationship with Christ and his trust in Christ's sufficiency for all his true and eternal needs. When a person looks to wealth to satisfy desires for security, control (power), proof of success, or similar psychological longings, the needs will normally prove insatiable. This does not mean, though, that the psychologically hungry person will automatically and compulsively seek to gratify inner longings in a wrong way, but it does mean the person will lack contentment.

Property, on the other hand, is a much broader concept and is not biblically confined to quantitative terms; it can appropriately be thought of in terms of the quality or psychological attitude with which possessions are held. This explains why Paul could be content, no matter the circumstance. He wrote that "if we have food and covering, with these we shall be content" (1 Tim. 6:8). And Christ was certainly concerned about man's attitudes toward earthly and heavenly treasures (see Matt. 6:19-34; Mark 8:36).

As soon as wealth becomes an end, or a means to another perverted end, it is a dangerous snare. An inappropriate focus on wealth easily degenerates into idolatry. Property, though being broad enough to include wealth, is biblically understood as a means to other and better ends, such as service, a stimulus to recall memories of God's former blessings (a family heirloom), a call for thanksgiving and praise, an opportunity to share, and a host of other good ends.

Dr. Brown's second insight is absolutely central to the purpose of this series of books. We are seeking God's mind on matters pertaining to economic justice and all that this implies. Dr. Brown's assertion that property, in its biblical context, is essential if personal freedom is to exist as God intended it is a profound thing to contemplate. If individuals are not free to be stewards of property, neither will they be free to pursue positive temporal self-interests, to strive for economic profits, and to create and accumulate material wealth that will allow them to make the moral choices so necessary for human maturity. The very opportunities to share the benefits derived from property are drastically reduced when property is controlled by a few people, private or public. We are essentially dehumanized when the opportunities to manage private property are denied.

The biblical admonitions to clothe the naked, feed the hungry, and do other acts of personal charity presume our economic ability to do these things. Paul's collection of a monetary gift for the saints in Jerusalem came from the sacrificial giving of the believers elsewhere. Paul's letter to the church at Ephesus assumed people had the freedom to labor, save, and give when he wrote, "Let him who steals steal no longer; but rather let him labor, performing with his own hands what is good, *in order that he may have something to share with him who has need*" (Eph. 4:28, emphasis added).

Dr. Brown has clearly stated that many biblical propositions strongly advocate and undergird the concept of private property, which must exist if freedom of choice and economic freedom, prerequisites for economic justice and human development, are to exist. There is, however, the equally true and relevant reality that we have a fallen nature by which we create many problems, not the least of which are the many economic injustices discovered in every economic system. Although private property is the foundational concept of property in the biblical development of stewardship, the responsibilities associated with stewardship extend to the care of other individuals and the community at large. (Richard Pierard pointed to some of these needs and failures in chapter 3.) We will now consider the work of Richard Mouw, who reminds us that we are "doing business" in a fallen world where some people fail, for whatever reasons, to achieve their potential in the economic arenas, and that they and we, as individuals and as a community, have mutually interdependent responsibilities toward one another.

In Richard Mouw's chapter you will perceive the struggles of a sensitive man. Though in almost complete agreement with the other authors who point toward our obligation to seek as much freedom in the marketplace as practical, he is uncomfortable with letting the case rest there. He correctly insists that a biblically expressed concern for everyone in the economic community must involve us all in an effort to provide for the afflicted and needy in the community while leaving intact the concepts of private property and individual freedom in the marketplace.

Dr. Mouw also points out that, in his opinion, Christians will not necessarily be better economists than nonChristians, but he does think that Christians have several distinct contributions to bring to any economic discussion. He maintains (the editor agrees completely) that Christians have (1) "the [biblical] resources for keeping economic issues in perspective"; (2) "the strength available . . . to sustain a long-range commitment to doing good in the economic sphere"; and (3) "a community support system available . . . for gaining insight and inspiration for our efforts at responsible stewardship."

CHAPTER 7

OF HOUSEHOLDS AND ECONOMIES
Richard J. Mouw

Richard J. Mouw is Professor of Christian Philosophy and Ethics at Fuller Theological Seminary. Prior to joining the Fuller faculty in 1985, he taught for seventeen years in the philosophy department at Calvin College. He received the Ph.D. degree from the University of Chicago and has been a postdoctoral fellow at Princeton University. He has also been a visiting professor at a number of institutions, including Juniata College and the Free University of Amsterdam. Richard is an editor of The Reformed Journal, and he serves on the boards of both the Institute for Ecumenical and Cultural Research at St. John's University and the Skirball Institute of the American Jewish Committee. He is the author of five books and of articles and essays in dozens of periodicals.

The term we translate in English as "economy"—as we all should have learned at our parents' knees—comes from a Greek word that refers to the management of a household. The Greeks used this word *oikonomia* to indicate at least two different but closely related things: the office or position of managing a household, and the patterns by which that managing occurs.

Needless to say, we must not restrict the contemporary application of a term to the meaning associated with its ancient origins. (Many of us who are involved in "pedagogy," for example, do not literally lead children around.) But there is something instructive about remembering the original use of the word *economy*. It suggests that economics has to do with an office of sorts, an assigned task; it also suggests that that task involves ordering and arranging things. And, of course, it points to the importance of the context, the household, in which all of this takes place.

I want to argue that Christians should keep each item in mind as we think about the economic patterns of our contemporary world—and about the study *of* those patterns. And I also want to argue that when we do keep these matters in mind, we will operate with very different economic assumptions and attitudes from the ones shaping much of economic thought and practice today. But first I must clarify a few matters so that I am not misunderstood at the very outset.

* * *

Many people who have a strong interest in the subject of economics would be very nervous about applying the image of a household to economic life. Households are intimate places in which human relationships are tended to in very conscious and intentional ways. It is very misleading, they would argue, to give the impression that this is the kind of stuff of which economic patterns and relationships are made.

The line of argument I have briefly indicated in these few sentences would be endorsed by economic theorists who would otherwise agree with one another about very little. For example, both free market defenders and Marxists would assent to it.

The free market theorists would insist that the picture of a wise person actively managing the affairs of the household with a conscious commitment to making things work out well for all the dwellers is a very dangerous way of depicting the economic situation. The last thing in the world we need is for economic decision makers to think of their activity in these cozy terms. There is no real matchup in economic affairs between micro intentions and macro results. The market system has a life of its own, which operates in accordance with rules and patterns that have virtually nothing to do with any of our efforts to make things turn out in a certain way. Indeed, when we do try to "manage" economic affairs, aiming at imposed solutions for what we view as structural problems, we inevitably make things worse.

Those who look favorably on free markets get very nervous when we use the language of intimate relationships—quite fitting in familial households—to describe economic reality. The arena of buying, selling, saving, trading, wheeling and dealing, and hiring and firing isn't really the sort of context wherein it is appropriate to talk about love and care and obligation. Markets are markets—they aren't families. To recognize the market situation for what it is means that we need not feel guilty about wanting to produce in order to make a profit.

For somewhat different reasons, the Marxists also insist that economics has a life of its own that has little to do with the conscious intentions we bring to economic activity. In the present world that is tainted by capitalist structures, as the Marxists view things, individual intentions at best serve as a smokescreen hiding the brutalities of economic interaction from our immediate awareness. Systemic reality operates in accordance with a macro logic that aims at keeping the "haves" having and the "have-nots" having-not. And even in that workers' paradise toward which history is inevitably (if painfully) moving, the experienced harmony that will bind individuals together in communal solidarity will not *cause* good things to happen economically—it will be the *effect* of the revolutionary transformation of the economic order.

These two rival camps, then, issue a common plea: Let economics be itself; don't impose upon it norms and values and rules of behavior that belong to some other realm, like that of familial or ecclesial life. And this plea would be echoed by economic thinkers and practitioners who do not identify with either the free market or the Marxist cause.

I need to say here that I agree with this plea as stated. And I think that people who care about developing a consistently Christian perspective on economic matters need to see that this plea is, in its unadorned terms, a legitimate one. In my own consideration of the basic issues of economic thought, I draw heavily on the teachings associated with two Christian attempts to depict the proper relationships among various spheres of human interaction, one a Roman Catholic one and the other a Calvinist: the "principle of subsidiarity" as it has been set forth in various magisterial documents of Catholicism in the modern era, and the "sphere sovereignty" doctrine of Abraham Kuyper and his Dutch colleagues in the nineteenth-century antirevolutionary movement. These two perspectives are grounded in different philosophical-theological traditions; hence, they are not identical. But they have much in common on a functional level.

The principle of subsidiarity, appealed to several times in the American bishops' recent economic pastoral, pictures society as including a hierarchy of institutionalized strata or spheres of social interaction: Church, state, corporations, schools, families, and so forth. The Church is primarily concerned with "supernatural" affairs; the state, as the agency entrusted with the direct supervision of the common good of society, is the highest "natural" institution. Corporations are lower on the scale, but their subsidiary status does not mean that they are to be directly supervised or managed by the state. Subsidiarity in this scheme carries with it a large measure of functional independence; lower institutions are to pursue their aims without interference from higher ones to the extent that doing so is not detrimental to the common good.[1]

The sphere sovereignty doctrine is also designed to mark out patterns whereby various societal spheres remain relatively free from the direct control of the state. Kuyper insisted that God created the world in such a way that the creation was rich with cultural possibilities. Human beings were given a "cultural mandate" in Genesis 1, which meant that the Lord assigned them the task of cultural development and formation. The command to "fill the earth" was not limited to the making of babies. It instructed human beings to tend the garden in such a way that it would become a city, a place filled with cultural patterns and products: technology, language, disciplined labor, leisure time activities, worship, nurture, and so on.[2]

The Creator, on Kuyper's reading of the biblical text, is very interested in cultural diversity. God wants cultural life to flourish in manifold splendor: family, industry, agriculture, recreation, art. And the introduction of sin into the created order has not canceled out that divine interest in cultural formation. In each sphere of life, Kuyper insisted repeatedly, we live before the face of God. God wants the redeemed community to honor the creating design by searching out the proper patterns of obedience in various spheres of human interaction. Thus, true religion is not just a matter of Sunday worship and private devotions and personal evangelism. It is a "showing forth" of the rule of Jesus Christ over all dimensions of human life.[3]

* * *

It should be obvious that each of these Christian perspectives is motivated by a concern shared in common with those viewpoints, already mentioned, insisting that we allow economics to be itself. Both the Catholics and the Calvinists—at least the ones holding to these two perspectives—want to promote respect for the economic dimension of life as having its own integrity. The production and exchange of goods is a part of the good creation. God made people with the ability to engage in such activities, and God wants them to be good at it—something that will happen only if production and exchange is recognized as a distinct and valuable part of human life.

One way of putting the point being emphasized here is saying that we must respect the autonomy of economic life. And that is a perfectly reasonable way to formulate the point. But Christians ought not to get too carried away with using the word *autonomy* without first being clear what they mean by it.

There is obviously a very bad sense in which people might think of economic activity as autonomous. They could understand this to mean that human beings are on their own when they engage in economic transactions. This would be a very literal reading of *autonomy* as "self-law"; human beings would be treated as functioning as their own legislators in negotiating their way through the economic business of life.

This understanding of the term has been very influential in the modern era. The two prominent camps mentioned earlier—the free market perspective and Marxism—are heavily populated with people who celebrate this brand of autonomy. Secularist free marketeers often assume that individual economic agents are laws unto themselves; any rules or principles that are binding upon them in the economic sphere are ones that people choose out of purely self-serving motives—rules of thumb that help us make our way through an area of life for which the most appropriate metaphors are ones like "a hardball world," "the jungle," and "dog-eat-dog."

Secularist free marketeers strongly emphasize *individual* autonomy. For the Marxist, the self who "self-legislates" is a *collective* consciousness. The ultimate solutions to our economic problems will come from heeding the dictates of the right kind of people—for Marx, that meant the proletariat; for Lenin, the Communist party; for Fidel Castro, it is Fidel Castro.

But however these two camps may disagree about the size of the self that is to do the legislating of the norms governing economic activity, they agree that we are not to look to the revealed will of God. And this is, of course, the crucial issue for Christians. For us, there is only one true Legislator in the universe, and that is the Lawgiver who spoke to Moses on Mount Sinai and who many years later spoke in the Person of Jesus on yet another mountain.

The pagan philosopher Rousseau stumbled onto the basic truth of the matter in his idiosyncratic way in *The Social Contract* when he set out to describe the proper task of the political legislator:

> The task of discovering the best laws, i.e., those that are most salutary for each nation, calls for a mind of the highest order. This mind would have insight into each and every passion, and yet be affected by none. It would be superhuman, and yet understand human nature through and through. It would be willing to concern itself with our happiness, but would seek its own outside us. It would content itself with fame far off in the future; i.e., it would be capable of laboring in one century and reaping its reward in the next.[4]

This list of qualifications is rather demanding. And Rousseau is aware of the list of characteristics it would take to fill the job. He immediately adds,

"Law-giving is a task for gods not men."[5]

Rousseau was not announcing his conversion to Christianity in making his admission. But he was insisting that, strictly speaking, it would take a deity to provide us with the kinds of laws that we can genuinely rely on in guiding our lives. Once you come to this conclusion, you must still decide, of course, what you are going to do about it. If you don't believe that there is a God—which was Rousseau's posture—you can deal with that regrettable fact either by facing up to despair or by muddling along with hunches that are less than fully reliable. But if you do believe that there is a God who has revealed eternal wisdom to us, you would do well to treat that revelation with utter seriousness.

Christian believers can never settle for the kind of claim about autonomy that encourages us to restrict our attention to laws and rules of our own making. That is what the Devil wants us to do. The serpent's challenge to Eve was in effect an invitation to view herself as autonomous in this sense: "You shall be as God." Whether we think of autonomy as exercised individually or collectively, whether we locate our capacity for autonomous decision making in our powers of reason or in our arbitrary volitions or in our "go with the flow" affections, the autonomous project will get us into deep trouble.

Ultimately, it leads to "death."

* * *

But we do not have to throw out the word *autonomy*. There is a legitimate sense in which economic activity may be thought of as autonomous, and Christians would do well to call attention to this sense, even if we must also be careful not to give the impression that we support the "be your own god" type of autonomy.

Instead of saying that economic agents are laws unto themselves, we can say that the economic sphere of life has its own unique laws. "Laws" here need not be taken in a literal sense. What is intended is the observation that economic activity has its own "business," with unique norms, values, and goals.

Consider an analogy. Suppose we are playing checkers with a child for whom the game is a very new challenge. Most of us would approach that situation with a desire to be kind. The moves we make would be designed more for letting the child know how it is done than for displaying brilliance in the playing of checkers. We might even knowingly "make mistakes," letting the child "win" so that she can get the hang of what the game is all about.

This is a very unnatural way of playing checkers, and few of us would be able to sustain an interest in playing the game for very long if that was all there was to it. Playing checkers is not pedagogy or charity or "I-thou" relating. It is a game that is properly played with a desire to plan carefully, maneuver skillfully, and seek certain rewards within the framework of rules of fair play. In this sense it is an autonomous activity—it is not merely a disguised version, or a branch, of some other sort of activity.

And the same thing holds for economics. The production and exchange of goods has its own integrity. It requires planning, skillful maneuvering, and the seeking of certain rewards within the framework of rules of fair play. The talents and skills and rules that pertain to economic life are different from those involved in, say, politics or baseball or counseling. These other activities may have an economic side to them, just as production and exchange may regularly intersect with politics and baseball and counseling. But economic activity has a unique character.

It must also be said that the character of economics is complicated. We live in a world of vast and intricate networks of production and exchange. Much about this area of reality will remain invisible to us if we focus only on individuals and their actual intentions and plans and goals. Economic reality is *structural* in nature, which means that it must be studied carefully and systematically. In regard to issues of poverty, for example, it is not enough to ask economic agents about the intended goals of their actions and policies. Often the actual outcomes are very different from those that people intend. Policies formulated by people who deliberately set out to help the poor may be detrimental to those who suffer from poverty. And policies that have no intentional links to lessening economic hardship may actually do much to achieve that goal.

* * *

But back to the "household" image. What does this discussion about the legitimate sense in which we may think of economics as autonomous have to say about the appropriateness of the household metaphor?

Obviously, it means that if we are going to use the household image, we must do so with care. We must not use it to give the impression that economic activity is nothing more than a way in which family members promote and nurture intimate relationships. Why preserve the image at all, then? For one thing, it points to a kind of unity in which economic activity must find its place. In saying this, am I taking back much of what I have said previously about autonomy? Not at all. To say that economics is autonomous is not to imply that it is completely blocked off from the rest of what human beings do.

It isn't as if—to keep the household image going—the economy is one of the rooms in the house, and with a locked door at that!

Economics is an autonomous dimension of human life. We must let it be itself, but we must also think about how it can properly occupy its unique place in the larger context in which it necessarily finds itself. Playing games is also an autonomous activity—not exactly like anything else that we do. (Some people, of course, make sex into a game. Others make a game out of raising children or going to church. But this, too, is a confusion of "spheres.") When the way in which we play games, though, crowds out or distorts other relationships, things go bad. It is always relevant to ask how an autonomous activity is being *integrated* into the larger picture.

Thinking of economics as having to do with a household, then, is a way of focusing on the larger picture. And Christians should be very interested in promoting this concern.

The need to keep looking at the way in which economics fits into the larger picture is nicely laid out by Daniel Bell in his 1976 book *The Cultural Contradictions of Capitalism*. Bell distinguishes three aspects or layers of a society: its social structure, its polity, and its culture. The social structure is, roughly, the economy of a society—here Bell links society's technological patterns and its occupational system to the ways in which it produces and exchanges goods. The polity is the way in which a society structures its means of decision making and conflict resolution. And the culture has to do with the way the society expresses and symbolizes its "meanings" about the ultimate issues of human existence.[6]

In Bell's view, these three aspects of societal interaction have significant connections. Marxist societies are usually composed of a socialist economy, a totalitarian polity, and a secularist-atheist culture. The traditional conception of how the United States ought to be patterned blends three very different components: capitalism, democracy, and a value system grounded in theism (or at least deism).[7]

In spite of the impression one might get from his book's title, Bell is no foe of capitalism. But he does worry that modern capitalism has been dislodged from its traditional cultural foundations, which included the "Protestant work ethic" associated with Puritanism. The traditional Christian notions of accountability for our habits of stewardship, the call to responsible labor, the emphasis on charity, and the dangers of greed—all those themes provided the right sort of ethical context for an economic system that encouraged the accumulation of wealth and property. It is becoming very clear, Bell thinks, that this traditional system of meanings is quickly being replaced by a hedonistic outlook. This hedonism will destroy us if it continues to dominate the cultural landscape. Our only hope is for some "new reformation" in which a cultural outlook based on the recognition of "public goods" replaces "the pursuit of bourgeois wants." Bell's choice of an image at this point is relevant to our discussion: What we need, he says, is a new sense of "the public household."[8]

Unfortunately, Bell has little to offer as a *vision* for the human household. He has no clear conception of human nature, nor does he have any inclination to look to divine revelation for guidance. In the final analysis, as Bernard Zylstra has demonstrated, Bell's vision is that of classical liberalism in which one accepts the fact of private interests but hopes that people will somehow permit these interests to stand in a creative tension with a general notion of the common good.[9]

But lest we be inclined to set Bell's analysis aside as not being beneficial to Christian inquiry, we should be very clear about the importance of the issues he has raised. There is a crisis today with regard to holding the societal household together. And Bell's case provides evidence that one need not be a critic of capitalism as such to be troubled by modern capitalist society's loss of cultural moorings. In 1978 Irving Kristol issued a similar warning in his *Two Cheers for Capitalism*. He worries openly about an American drift toward moral nihilism, and he is especially disturbed because this nihilism has become just one more marketable commodity in the marketplace. We need, Kristol insists, a recovery of the older "Protestant-bourgeois" awareness of the human capacity for vice.[10]

* * *

Both Bell and Kristol are concerned about our sense of community and our understanding of the kinds of beings we are as we establish the conditions for human interaction in modern society. These are crucial matters. How shall we address them as people who have heard the good news of Jesus Christ?

For the Christian, it is not enough to posit a tension between private wants and public goods in attempting to account for the problems that affect economic life. A more basic concern is the challenge of honoring God's creating purposes in the world—including the economic sphere—while acknowledging the complex realities that human sin has introduced into the creation.

Needless to say, it is all too easy to fall back on "life is complex" as a cliche that excuses our lack of clarity on vital issues. But it may be good for Christians to admit that we do have a sense of life's complexities—not only for our own sakes, but also for the benefit of others. NonChristians often imply that people embrace the Christian faith because they want simple answers to the issues of life. And we Christians sometimes reinforce this impression by the facility with which we toss out our "Christ Is the Answer" slogans.

There is a profound sense in which an acceptance of biblical revelation complicates the quest for easy answers. This point struck home for me once when I was reading a book about political theory by a well-known academic. He began his discussion by asking, "Why are human beings political?" and then he went on to say something about how our human selfishness requires a coercive state to keep us in line. As I thought about why I was uneasy with his discussion, I realized that both his question and his answer were too simple for me.

As a Christian, I have problems asking why human beings are political without immediately introducing some nuances into the very question I am asking. If I am going to talk about the need for a coercive government, it is because I am focusing on human beings in their fallenness. But the Bible gives me glimpses of other manifestations of humanness: I look at our present fallenness against the background of the scriptural portrait of human beings as God originally created them. And I also live with the confidence that sin is not the final word about the human condition; God has provided a way of salvation for all who accept Christ—a redemption that will not be complete until "we shall be like him, for we shall see him as he is" (1 John 3:2). The biblical narrative about our humanness has, as it were, four chapters: creation, fall, redemption, and glorification. To recognize this is to insist that the human drama is more complicated than many nonChristians think that it is. And it also means that we must always introduce the appropriate nuances when we are talking about how this or that factor fits into human affairs as such.

This has important implications for the way in which we look at the human household that we are attempting to manage by means of (among other things) our economic activities. Each of the four chapters of the biblical narrative is about the household; we have not properly understood the human community in which we live until we think of it as a created household, a fallen household, a household that is in the process of being redeemed, and a household that will someday be glorified.

To some Christians—but not to all—my purpose will be obvious in putting the case in this manner. So I must try to be clear about some basics. When we say that in the beginning God created the human household, we come close to what very traditional theologians have meant by the teaching that Adam and Eve were "federal heads" of the human race. The story about the creation of the first human pair is not simply an account of the making of two isolated individuals. Adam and Eve were created as the beginnings of a community, a race—a human household. In a mysterious but very reliable sense, the story of their creation is the story of our creation. Their God-given assignments are our assignments. Their rebellion is our rebellion.

The first three chapters of Genesis, with their account of the creation and fall of our first parents, are a crucial introduction to the rest of the biblical message. When God sets out to redeem us, His intention is to remove the cursedness of our condition so that we can once again be what we were originally meant to be. Redemption is, as some theologians are fond of putting it, the restoration of creation. And the new creation described in the last two chapters of the Bible is the blossoming of that creating and redeeming project. The household that was originally created to exhibit God's glory will someday be renewed so that the divine splendor will finally shine forth again through all the works of God's hands.

Economics has a significant place in these "good" stages of creation-redemption-glorification. God created us with the plan that we would be producers. Not *only* producers, to be sure—God wants us also to be beings who worship and rest and play and hug and smell the roses. But we are also designed to engage in the business of producing goods. Harry Kuitert states that one of the central ways in which we are to image the God who made us is to be "covenant partners."[11] This nice combination of words points to two things. First, we are to *do* something. Partners form partnerships, which in turn expedite tasks. A vital element in our assigned tasks as people created in God's likeness is to work in the garden, shaping the raw material of nature into human handiwork.

The second thing is that we are to perform this task *together.* We are *covenant* partners, bonded together in a cooperative effort requiring us to manifest fidelity and trust and mutual upbuilding as we work together in God's creation. This is what we lost at the Fall, and this is what Christ restores us to when we are incorporated into His redeemed body—we become a community of covenant partners who are equipped by grace to do all things to the honor and glory of God.

But the final restoration has not yet come about. We have not yet been made perfect, and we certainly do not live in a perfect world. The household, and the management of that household in all its relationships and activities, has been badly damaged by sin. Economics is not in good shape; it is not functioning as it was meant to function.

Many people are living out their rebellion against God in the economic arena. And since we are not yet fully glorified, we share to some degree in keeping that cursed situation going. What are some marks of this economic rebellion? Well, for one thing, sin shows up in people's personal attitudes. We are envious and aggressively competitive. We covet things that others have, and we desire more than our share of the earth's riches.

Some Christians will get very nervous about my characterizations here. Am I suggesting that all competition is bad? Do I mean to imply that it is wrong to possess a strong motivation to acquire things? My answer to each question is basically negative. My guess is that something like a sense of competition and a motive to acquire are part and parcel of economic activity—and since I believe that economics is built into the creation, I suggest that these things can be very healthy parts of our psychic equipment.

I am, to be sure, hedging a bit in the way I put my point here. Something *like* competition might be a very good thing; the desire to acquire things *can* be a component of a healthy psyche. I am tentative because the competition and acquisitiveness familiar to us in this sinful age are often very harmful to human relationships, so I am reluctant to endorse them, even in qualified ways. But I do think that the competition and acquisitiveness that we experience under present conditions are distortions of something that can also function in a healthy manner. There is nothing intrinsically evil about admiring another person's talents and skills and productions and treating such things as a standard against which we will measure ourselves and set goals for our work. For all I know, Adam and Eve may have played something like checkers before the Fall—and if they did, they undoubtedly operated with a sanctified version of the desire to win. But we cannot use this fact— even if we could be sure that it is a fact—to justify all that gets done in the present world under the rubric of "just trying to win."

But sin touches more than our individual psyches. It weaves itself into the structures, the patternedness, of our economic lives, establishing the varieties of injustice. As an evangelical Christian who takes very seriously the biblical account of the Fall, I believe that sin begins in the individual heart. But it also spills over into the corporate dimensions of our lives. In the economic context this means there are ways in which our very *systems* of economic planning, decision making, production, job distribution, buying, and selling have become seriously bruised by human sinfulness.

Irving Kristol is right to encourage us to promote the kind of "Protestant-bourgeois tradition" of capitalism that—unlike what he calls "the secular, 'libertarian'" version of capitalism—is not limited in its imagination in dealing with the possibilities of human vice.[12] We human beings have not lacked skill at establishing injustice as we have carried out our sinful projects in the economic sphere. The biblical writers were quick to identify our evil practices: We have ignored the needs of the widow and the orphan; we have exacted unnecessarily high prices from the poor; we have taken advantage of the vulnerability of the sojourner; and we have cheated the field laborers of the wages due them for their toils. And in modern times we have continued and expanded these patterns of injustice, discriminating against women and persons of color while winking at—and even at times making heroes of— corporate leaders who have flagrantly violated the public trust.

* * *

I have just drawn a gloomy picture of our economic fallenness. Does this mean that there is nothing left of the household in our sinful world?

Not really. The household image is still a helpful one, even as a way of depicting life in our rebellious age. For one thing, it points us to the very real *unity* that still characterizes the complex social reality in which we live. The human race has not become a mere scattering of isolated units bound together only by those links we forge for purposes of our own convenience. We are still creatures of God, offspring of the parents whom God placed in the garden.

To be sure, we conservative Protestants are not altogether comfortable with romantic talk about "the human family." And for some good reasons. An important line of division has been drawn through the human race: the line between those who have heard the joyful sound of the gospel and have received Jesus as Savior and Lord and those who continue to live as rebels before God. We must never lose sight of this division—if for no other reason than that we must ever be mindful of the compelling need to invite others to come to the Cross for the forgiveness that will bring them new life.

Nonetheless, some ties bind us all together, saved and unsaved. The Bible points to these ties, and it does so sometimes in direct application to economic matters. For example, there are ties associated with the basic fact of economic interdependence. In Joshua's last recorded speech to Israel he reminded the people of their daily dependence on the labors of others who had gone before them. The Lord has given you, Joshua told them, "a land on which you had not labored, and cities which you had not built, and you dwell therein; you eat the fruit of vineyards and oliveyards which you did not plant" (Josh. 24:13). Amos later warned the people that if they continued in their patterns of injustice, the Lord would take their possessions away from them to give to others. His words also serve as a reminder of our economic bonds to future generations: "You have built houses of hewn stone, but you shall not dwell in them; you have planted pleasant vineyards, but you shall not drink their wine" (Amos 5:11).

We are not isolated from one another economically. The boast that "what I got, I got on my own" is deceptive. We are linked to the past labors of others, and others will experience the future effects of our present activities. The rich man of Jesus' parable (see Luke 12:16-20) who thought that his building up and his tearing down were his private business really *was* a fool!

But we are also tied to one another by virtue of our having common obligations before God. However we choose to spell out the intricacies of a "natural law" or a "common grace" perspective, we must at least be clear that God has not left fallen human beings without some sense of right and wrong. In the economic realm we can proceed with the assurance that it is worth our time to appeal to a person's sense of justice and fair play, whether or not that person is a believer.

For the Christian, this sense of economic right and wrong is grounded in the awareness of the Creator's purposes. John Locke has often been praised and blamed for having provided a strong philosophical undergirding for the notion of private property. But Locke was actually very explicit that human beings can claim ownership of things only in a relative sense. In the most straightforward sense of ownership, Locke insisted, God alone is the true owner of all that exists. We are not sovereign lords over the goods that we possess; rather, we are stewards of those goods, accountable to the one and only Sovereign Lord who in turn calls us to recognize our interdependence with our fellow creatures.[13]

This notion of stewardship points to another feature of the household image, one mentioned when we introduced the original meaning of the word from which *economy* comes: the notion of *office*. God created our first parents to be caretakers of the garden, and that creational assignment extends to all their descendants. Not that we should interpret this creation mandate in purely economic terms. One danger of "the Protestant ethic" is that it seems to foster the idea that we should be working all the time. To be good stewards of the creation is to be more than producers, earners, and exchangers. We must respect the proper rhythms of life by resting and worshiping and playing and telling stories and hugging one another. Economic work is only one of these rhythms. But again it is a vital one.

* * *

Closely related to the idea of stewardly office is the imposing of a *proper order* by means of our economic activity. Stewards manage the affairs of the household so that the household should run more smoothly and harmoniously if they do their job right. As we pursue our economic tasks, we are not free to do any old thing we want. We must obey a normative pattern, ordering life in accordance with God's revealed will.

It is not possible to lay out the requirements of this normative pattern in simple formulas. We certainly cannot do it merely by listing biblical prooftexts. Nor are we likely to arrive at a consensus simply by examining our individual consciences, even our sanctified consciences. But it is possible, I think, to get some idea of the considerations God wants us to operate with in our economic deliberations and activities.

In his book *Christians in the Crisis* Gerald Vandezande provided a helpful list of the considerations that seem to me to be the relevant ones. Even though his list is formulated primarily with an eye to investment policies, it contains matters that have implications for a much broader range of economic concerns. Christians, Vandezande says, must attempt the following: first, to be *gentle* in the way we treat the environment; second, *just* in the way we treat our fellow workers; third, *wise* in the use of the creation's resources; fourth, *sensitive* to the needs of our neighbors as they pursue their vocations and tasks; fifth, *careful* in the way we use technology so that we do not idolize technological knowhow but use it as a way of serving legitimate human goals; sixth, *frugal* in our patterns of energy consumption so that we do not waste the building blocks of the good life; seventh, *vigilant* in the prevention of waste; eighth, *fair* in the determination of prices; ninth, *honest* in the way we promote the sales of our products; and tenth, *equitable* in the earning of profit.[14]

Again, these seem to be the right sorts of considerations to keep in mind in economic decision making. They certainly are not hard and fast rules to be imposed on economic agents in a legalistic manner. Indeed, they are not really rules at all. They are not even, strictly speaking, considerations—even though I have been using that term to introduce them. Vandezande's list is more like a set of economic *virtues*—the dispositions to operate with certain attitudes and to keep certain factors in mind.

Some people—primarily folks who are inclined to offer strong free market defenses—might worry that these stipulated dispositions smack too much of the "liberal do-gooder" kind of thing. Two responses are in order in anticipation of this possible line of criticism.

The first response is that there is nothing intrinsically wrong with a do-gooder orientation in economic life. We Christians should want to insist that God *does* call us to do good in our economic dealings, as in all our activities. The question is not *whether* we should do good in economics but *how*.

Which leads to the second response. Vandezande's list of virtues is not biased in favor of a liberal or a socialist economic system. Whether these dispositions are easier to develop and pursue in those systems rather than in a capitalist context is a matter that has to be decided on empirical grounds. My inclinations in this regard are similar to those recently expressed by Max Stackhouse. He confesses, in his *Public Theology and Political Economy,* that he has "preached and taught" that "modern technological economies have solved the problem of production, and that the only remaining problems are the inequities of distribution"—inequities that "are compounded by the fact that today we are caught up in a demonic consumerism into which we are driven by corporations' seductive manipulation of desire."[15]

Stackhouse goes on to report, however, that he has come to doubt the truth of this way of depicting the situation. Those anticapitalist sentiments drove him during the past decade and a half

> to spend every study leave and sabbatical plus several summers either in Third World countries or in the socialist lands of eastern Europe, where significantly different modes of production are in operation. I found that I was substantially in error. Not only do traditional and socialistic economic systems enhance those social forces that inhibit the development of democracy, but in them problems of maldistribution and rampant consumerism are at least as dramatic, if not more striking than they are in the West. When either traditional or state-capitalist economies are examined, it appears that the evils of inequitable distribution and gluttonous consumerism are not rooted only in the modern Western structures of production.[16]

When Stackhouse gives his version of the proper normative framework for economic life, then, he does not mean to suggest that it is somehow unsuitable for a capitalist market system. And his framework has a very similar feel to the one Vandezande offered. The world of the productive corporation is functioning on its healthiest level, Stackhouse argues, when these five factors are encouraged: (1) economic activities manifest a sense of *vocation*; (2) *moral law* is recognized—as in, for example, a respect for human rights; (3) people experience the *liberation* that draws them into responsible economic involvement; (4) the influence of *sin* is not ignored; and (5) economic relations are bounded by *covenant*.[17]

In each case—the discussions of Vandezande and Stackhouse—the normative frameworks are meant to enhance responsible economic planning and action. They are not alien values designed to inhibit and restrict entrepreneurial activity. The proposed norms are ways of patterning and structuring production and exchange so that they bring out the best in the economic sphere.

Nor is it the obvious intention of either formulation to impose an artificial "equality" on the economic realm. There is no suggestion here that all individuals have to end up with the same amount of money or goods. Rather, the emphasis is on the active pursuit of economic goals in respectful and fair ways.

This is an important point. Debates about Christian obligations to the poor often get caught up in a polarization between those who think that we ought to see to it that the inequities between rich and poor get equalized via redistribution and those who think that all persons ought to be encouraged to produce for themselves. This kind of dispute is premised on an oversimplification. There are indeed some economically deprived persons whose only hope for a decent life hangs on the willingness of others to provide for their well-being. In biblical terms, these are the widows and the orphans — persons who are without normal familial support systems.

But there are other subcategories of the poor. And in spite of liberationist rhetoric, not all of the poor are also rightly described as the oppressed. For at least some have-nots, the lack of the means of support is due to their own laziness. These are the biblical sluggards who deserve to be admonished for their indolence. Other groups of the poor are made up of people, such as slaves and the workers in the field of James 5, who work hard but are not paid a fair wage. Still others are poor because of structural barriers that they face in their attempts to work; this is often the plight of the biblical sojourner — and in our day those people who suffer from racial and ethnic discrimination.

The Bible does not seem to support the notion that we can simply lump all these subgroups together and treat them as the proper beneficiaries of a grand scheme of economic redistribution. For most of the subgroups mentioned, the solution is to call them to engage in responsible production. If genuine barriers exist that limit their ability to respond to that call, we must remove those barriers in the name of justice. If some people refuse to work, we must preach to them about responsible labor. And if some are physically or psychologically incapable of engaging in the exercise of dominion, we must see to it that their basic economic needs are met.

The basic reference point in this biblical perspective on dealing with poverty, as I have outlined it, is God's call to human beings to engage in accountable dominion under the divine rule. Only those who are seriously incapacitated with regard to economic activity qualify as legitimate long-term "welfare" cases. The overall strategy is to enlist all capable persons for involvement in the decisions and activities necessary for their economic well-being. And this is precisely the kind of strategy that the norms laid out by both Vandezande and Stackhouse are meant to expedite. In each case the primary focus is on the enhancing of economic responsibility in a working environment characterized by integrity and dignity.

* * *

I have been arguing that biblical revelation provides us with a perspective on the economic dimensions of our life in the human household. Does all of this mean, then, that we Christians have a clear edge over others in negotiating our way through the ins and outs of economic activity? Are Christians better equipped for economic decision making, even for *leadership* in economic decision making, than nonChristians?

It would be wrong, I think, to claim that a commitment to the gospel gives us an inside track in dealing with economic matters. Economic leadership requires a combination of factors: skills, knowledge, perspective, sensitivities, and so on. There is no reason to think that Christians put the combinations together in their persons in a manner that always distinguishes them from nonChristians. Even if we might want to argue that—given the obvious superiority of a Christian perspective over its nonChristian rivals— we should expect Christians generally to function better than nonChristians, we would still have to take the actual dynamics of the human condition into account. The fact is, as Abraham Kuyper was fond of observing, that the unbelieving community regularly performs in a better way than our theology leads us to predict, and the Church regularly performs more poorly than it should.

But we should not ignore the genuine strengths the Christian community brings to economic life. Several of them are worth mentioning here.

First, we have the resources for keeping economic issues in perspective. We know that economics is not all of life, nor is it the most important part of life. It is one significant aspect of human functioning—an area that God cares deeply about. Christians have a marvelous opportunity to put together a way of life in which economics has its unique place without choking out the other essential things that go into living a full and responsible life before God. We have the motivation to keep reminding ourselves that economics must be seen against the background of the larger picture.

Second, we have the strength available to us to sustain a long-range commitment to doing good in the economic sphere. Our lives are in the hands of God. We know that we are pilgrims journeying toward God's new day. We are capable of thinking in terms of the long haul. We have no compulsive need for quick fixes or overnight solutions. Furthermore, we know that ultimately the real "fixing" is not ours to accomplish. We are not messiahs; we are servants of the only worthy Messiah. He, Jesus, will make it right in the end. Our assignment is to be responsible stewards in the ways in which the Lord makes it possible for us to understand and exercise our economic stewardship.

Third, we have a community support system available to us for gaining insight and inspiration for our efforts at responsible stewardship. Not that the visible Body of Christ is our only source of economic knowhow—we would be irresponsible indeed if we did not treat the larger economic dialogue with utter seriousness. But the Christian community is an important resource for sensitivities and concerns that we must bring with us to that larger dialogue. In economic life, as in all other areas of human interaction, we must test the spirits to discern which of those are of God and which are not. The Church of Jesus Christ is a crucial context for being equipped, on a continual basis, for this much-needed discernment. Even the airing of our disagreements as Christians is valuable to our maturation as disciples called to economic stewardship. The opportunity to argue together about how best we can show forth the mind and heart of Jesus in the economic realm may well be the most important gift we can cultivate in this regard.

Our community support system as Christians is of great economic value. Taking seriously our life together as disciples of Jesus Christ is one way in which we can show the larger human community that we are dedicated to living as interdependent persons. As Christian people who are committed to one another, and committed to working together to serve God and our neighbors—especially those neighbors whose lives have been brutalized by suffering and oppression—we can engage in some very necessary economic modeling.

In *Habits of the Heart,* Robert Bellah and his associates insisted that if we are to stem the tide of individualism in our North American culture, we must form intentional "communities of memory" in which we keep older modes of cultural discourse alive. The churches and synagogues, they argued, are the most likely places in which these memories can be kept alive.[18]

These are days in which it is urgent that Christians function as a community of *economic* memory. We must keep alive the older perspectives whereby people had a clear understanding—the understanding that is rapidly becoming a scarce resource in our time—of their mandate from God to serve as stewards in the human household. This could be one of the most important services that we can perform in the contemporary economic *milieu*: to remind our fellow humans about whose creatures they really are and about what best contributes to our true profit.

EDITOR'S PERSPECTIVE

The twelve scholars who had gathered for the presentation and discussion of these chapters were excited by the substance and balance of Richard Mouw's paper. There seemed to be a sense of relief when once again the tensions that necessarily accompany a biblically responsible discussion about our individ- ual and collective obligations toward one another were brought to the surface for discussion. Along with the excitement, however, there simultaneously emerged a need to discuss and acknowledge that the determination of what is a perfectly balanced relationship between our individual responsibilities and those of the community is beyond our doing. It is wonderful to be able to conceive of the perfect, but it can be demoralizing and demotivating, at the same time, to realize that it is unobtainable by human effort.

As maturing Christians, we should not allow the awareness of our inabilities to either deter or depress us. Our inability to achieve a perfect balance between our personal responsibilities and those of the community should stimulate us instead to contemplate three other essential aspects of our truly finite and dependent nature. First, and most important, our inability to create and bring about those attitudes and behavior in the community that manifest God's concerns for both the individual and the community should stimulate us to seek His face and implore Him to bring about the kind of balance and economic justice that will best achieve His eternal purposes. We know that God's greatest "end" for us is our salvation, but we know at the same time that He favors human choice and private property in our economic affairs, as a general principle. We do not know His broader purposes in allowing people to violate His expressed desires in these matters. The ends of His common grace are not revealed beyond the fact of Scripture's declaration

159

that He is absolutely sovereign in every affair and that every act and consequence will eventually resound to His glory and to the good of His children.

The Spirit of God is capable of moving people's hearts so that they will be willing to give everything they own to care for their neighbors (see Acts 2:44-45; 4:32-35) and of allowing people to be so hard and selfish that they will even refuse to share with people who have been kind to and protective of them (see 1 Sam. 25:2-13). Neither condition of the heart, however, is offered in Scripture as a normative goal for God's people. No one can comprehend or untangle the interrelated truths pertaining to God's sovereignty and mankind's responsibility, but Scripture attests to the absolute reality of both. We are not in control of our destinies; God is. We plan our ways, but God directs our steps (see Prov. 16:9).

The second thing we are to realize and do is to set our face in the direction that we are to go and labor to foster those things that will create genuine opportunities for people to make responsible choices and to own private property. The Christian community is not responsible for the successes or failures we may experience as we labor for God in these matters so long as what we are doing is in keeping with His expressed purposes. We are responsible for our labor, not its final achievements (see Ezek. 33:1-9). This is one reason why the work of Joe Brown is so significant. He, like Ron Nash, has pointed us in the right direction.

Udo Middelmann called us, in the first book, to understand and acknowledge that God created us to be moral decision makers. Ron Nash called us to foster freedom of choice in the marketplace. Now Joe Brown has enunciated the role of personal property in the maturing of our moral nature and the place of personal freedom and private property in our moral development. Personal property, the created capacity for moral choice, and the freedom of exchange are intricately tied together and are vital for the full nurturing of God's image bearers. God's design calls for freedom of choice and private property as a means to a greater end—being fully mature in Christ.

Just as surely as we can recognize mental and physical retardation in people when their handicaps are severe enough to impair normal patterns of speech and conduct, people who are denied the opportunities associated with the stewardship of personal property are also simultaneously stripped of many opportunities to exercise their God-given right to make moral choices that are inherently associated with the stewardship of property. These choices include the freedom to keep, alter, exchange, or consume what has been entrusted to them. Denying people such opportunities in the temporal realm must of necessity stunt their moral development. So the right to hold property for the purpose of sharing, re-creating, exchanging, or enjoying it is important in God's economy.

How are we to reconcile that (1) we are absolutely unable to guarantee that the biblical principles associated with freedom of choice and private property will be maintained or established in any society, for only God has such an ability, and (2) we are to labor to bring about freedom of choice and to expand the realization of private property? We can acknowledge their truth, but we cannot reconcile them. We must learn to relax and be secure in God's absolute sovereignty while we simultaneously work in a godly way, as hard as we can, to achieve His revealed and normative will as if the outcome completely depended on us, with the knowledge that only He can accomplish it. This is not a cop-out; this is reality!

Putting it another way, we are to pray and pray as if everything totally depended on God's work; we are to then get off our knees and work with all our strength, as unto the Lord, as if the outcome is our responsibility; and when the results are discernible, we are to praise God and give Him the full credit. We must understand that we absolutely depend on God for everything, even our next breath, yet we must be fully responsible for our every thought and action. Of course, this whole concept of God's sovereignty and man's responsibility is beyond our full comprehension. It is, nevertheless, true, which is why so much of what we can know about God's truth is correct, though it is beyond our ability to bring about a positive change (see Matt. 6:27).

Finally, as we acknowledge our personal inability to do anything substantial to bring about an ability in the populace to balance individual and community responsibilities, we are not to think of ourselves as insignificant or to think that it is useless to try. If God is sovereign—and He is—it is also true that He has ordained to use mankind's efforts in His behalf to bring about much change in society. What we do as individuals to balance our individual, family, church, and community responsibilities is extremely significant in God's plan. And modeling—living out what we profess—is an integral part of God's long-term plan.

The way we approach our stewardship responsibilities affects everyone associated with us. One of the most indelible impressions of my youth was of my parents' concern for persons who were willing to work but who were unemployed during the 1930s. We lived in a small rural town where two major railroads came together, and the complex switching and crossing of the tracks required trains to go slowly through the area, allowing those who "rode the freights" to get off near town. A number of those men came to our back door looking for food and clothing.

My dad told Mom that no one in need of food or clothing was to be turned away, but that no one was to receive anything without first working for it so that he might maintain self-respect. Mom had a "feeding table" set up on the back porch, and the only worry I remember her having was over the kind of chore she could find for the next person who would ask for food. She managed to find something for them all to do, but it was not always easy.

God used that experience, and later Scripture, to impress on me the responsibilities I have when I encounter genuine need. What we model in life does count in our families. We count as individuals in our businesses and churches. Churches count in our communities. Our communities count in our nation. Our nation counts in the world. We must all do what we can as individuals, for the community is a synergistic aggregation of individuals, nothing more.

Many biblical principles are coming into focus now as we approach the halfway point in this book. We can summarize them as follows:

1. God's character and behavior establish and manifest the standards by which we are to evaluate the conduct and performance of our economic systems.
2. Human nature must also be carefully considered in the establishment of any system of production and distribution, because everyone has both a positive and a negative capacity to do right and wrong as a result of the Fall, and these must be set free or held in check.
3. The land was cursed at the time of the Fall, and now our labor is difficult as we seek to release the earth's richest benefits.
4. Economic progress depends on short-run material sacrifices.
5. The economic pie is not fixed in size; therefore, one person's gain is not at the expense of someone else.
6. God has provided a multitude of biblical principles to guide us as we seek His will regarding our attitudes and conduct in the economic arena.
7. These guiding principles are as helpful and operative in our modern and technically oriented culture as they were when first given.
8. God's precepts call us to be economically self-reliant and to be generous and compassionate toward those who are unable, for whatever reason, to immediately help themselves.
9. As a means of realizing an abundance of economic benefits and for the sake of the development of our greatest human potential,

our ability to choose and our consequent need for opportunities to exercise freedom of choice were established by God at the time of creation and should be protected and nurtured in the marketplace.

10. God encourages a good form of temporal self-interest in the marketplace.
11. The good of gainful employment is biblically advocated.
12. The good of profits is affirmed in Scripture.
13. The good of material wealth is set forth in God's Word.
14. The holding of personal property is essential in the affairs of life if personal freedom is to exist and flower in the manner God intended.
15. We are not to conceive of personal freedoms as intended solely for personal or even family ends; they are to be used also for the good of the community and to aid those in need.
16. The balance between our need for true individuality and our need to be responsible members of a community can be balanced and harmonized only through the work of God in our lives, for our fallen nature has perverted our ability to achieve and maintain such a balance on our own.

These biblical understandings establish a definitive direction for Christians to move in economically.

BIBLICAL INCENTIVES AND THE FORCES OF ECONOMIC SYSTEMS

Secular social scientists have devoted much time to developing and studying theories of motivation during the past four decades, and businesses have spent huge sums of money on training programs designed to implement these theories in an effort to increase employees' productivity and the corporation's profits. Deterministic theories of motivation claim that our drives are largely programed by our previous experiences. Cognitive theories suggest that our drives are learned through observation, and genetic theories hold that motivated parents will have children with above-average levels of motivation. Motivational theorists hypothesize that basic, inherent needs—to have self-esteem, to be in control, to be secure, to satisfy special interests—and a host of other psychological drives propel human activity. Abraham Maslow believed our needs were hierarchical. Frederick Herzberg talked of "dissatisfiers" and "satisfiers" as a means of understanding human motivation. For example, experiencing poor working conditions might be a "dissatisfier," while working for a company that offered employees quality daycare facilities for their children might be a "satisfier."

But what does Scripture have to say about incentives and motivation? While it certainly is not silent about motivation, it does not talk about the subject in the language of modern psychology. Furthermore, the Bible does not treat motivation as if it were primarily psychological or spontaneous. Scripture treats it as if it were tied directly to our intellect and will, regardless of our feelings and impulses. This distinction means that from the perspective of Scripture we are personally responsible for our actions, regardless of our felt desires or drives. Nonbiblical theories of motivation seem to make the subject a subset of our feelings and deep psychological impulses, for which we have little responsibility or control. In contrast, the Bible elevates motivation to the level of the intellect and human will. These differences are profound.

We want to do several things in this section: (1) identify the external incentives the Bible sets before us as motivators so we can understand them and incorporate them in our thinking when we choose and advocate the maintenance of a particular economic system; (2) see which contemporary economic system is most compatible with the biblically identified incentives—which ones are not and why; and (3) consider what the Bible has to say about our internal attitudes and drives as they relate to our personal conduct in the marketplace.

The pattern we have followed so far of having two authors present the different perspectives on each topic has not been followed in this section. Instead, E. Calvin Beisner has written both chapters. He discerns and articulates clearly the differences set forth in Scripture between the external incentives God puts before His image bearers (both in the natural order and through special revelation) and the internal attitudes and drives contained in our fallen nature, with which we engage God's external incentives.

Christians must learn to distinguish between (1) the forces at work in the market and the synergistic fallout from the operation of a particular economic system where the collective consequences of the actions of the entire community can be observed and (2) the consequences and effects our fallen nature has on our personal attitudes and behavior in a particular economic system. Market forces and structures cannot change human nature. Structures are channels of opportunity for expressing our nature, but our nature stands independent of any economic structure. Two great flaws in the thinking of Karl Marx were his failure to believe that mankind had a fallen nature and his belief that human nature was materialistically determined and could, therefore, be reshaped by altering the external political and economic systems.

Cal Beisner's first chapter helps us examine the first issue and is very thought-provoking. You may find yourself resisting the magnetism of his presentation, however, because the analysis may be unfamiliar for the very reason that Scripture's treatment of external motivators is frequently antithetical to the world's discussion of them. The world, by and large, uses psychological categories for discussing motivation theory and speaks of internal motives and forces. Scripture, while not denying the presence of such felt needs, sets before us two primary incentives that are external to our being and beyond our control—*rewards* and *punishments*.

One's first reaction to such a simple enumeration of incentives and to the very idea that God's incentives are primarily external may be a hesitancy to accept such a view. Do not sell Cal Beisner's insights short, though. They are deep; they are biblically sound. The study of motivational theory is simply one of those many places where, because the biblical perspective has not been explored, presented, and popularized in the Christian community like the works of Maslow and Herzberg, we may have been more influenced by the world than we have been transformed by Scripture.

Cal Beisner has gone one step further, though, by tying the biblical concept of rewards to the marketplace notion of competition. He has not done this to glorify competition but to point out boldly that as people seek the rewards available in a free market system, where personal choices prevail, they are merely responding to the rewards that God has built into the natural order. Thus, Cal concludes that competition should be understood as a positive dimension of the natural order. In the world, where the things of the Spirit are not discerned or obeyed, the notion of being motivated by the love of God, or of working "heartily, as for the Lord rather than for men" (Col. 3:23), is of no benefit to those who do not truly know and love Christ because when God's loving rewards are out of mind, they cannot serve as motivators. In their stead God has provided, by common grace, the possibility for physical and psychological rewards in the work environment. Scripture refers to competition as "rivalry" and declares it to be vanity from an eternal perspective because it is a substitute for God's best incentives and rewards (see Eccles. 4:4), but this does not negate the fact that competition has an overall salutary effect of fostering business conduct that provides the best economic outcomes for the most people in a fallen world.

CHAPTER 8

BIBLICAL INCENTIVES AND ECONOMIC SYSTEMS

E. Calvin Beisner

E. Calvin Beisner is a professional writer and speaker in the fields of Christian ethics, economic ethics, and apologetics. He is the author of Prosperity and Poverty: The Compassionate Use of Resources in a World of Scarcity *(Crossway, 1988),* Psalms of Promise: Exploring the Majesty and Faithfulness of God *(NavPress, 1988),* Answers for Atheists *(Campus Crusade for Christ/Northstar, 1988),* God in Three Persons *(Tyndale House, 1984),* The Teachings of Witness Lee and the Local Church *and* Is Baptism Necessary for Salvation? *(Christian Research Institute, 1978, 1977), and of many articles in Christian periodicals. Presently he is working on a book on the Christian understanding of the development and conservation of natural resources, economic growth and development, and environmental concerns (Crossway, projected fall, 1989). He is a former editor of* Discipleship Journal *and a former newspaper editor and publisher. He has twice been named a Literary Fellow of the Marguerite Eyer Wilbur Foundation (1983 and 1987) and is national chairman of the economics committee of the evangelical Coalition on Revival. He holds the M.A. in Society, with a specialization in economic ethics, from International College, and the B.A. in Religion and Philosophy from the University of Southern California.*

INTRODUCTION

I have been asked to defend the thesis, "Biblical incentives are compatible with the driving forces of world economic systems." Alas, I cannot, for it is false. But I can defend the thesis, "Biblically legitimate incentives are generally compatible with the dominant driving forces of one of the world's major, mutually exclusive economic systems and generally incompatible with the dominant driving forces of the other."

First, we must carefully define some key terms. This endeavor may not seem exciting, but it can prevent or reduce needless misunderstanding and conflict.

Definitions—First, an *incentive* is "that which influences or encourages to action; motive; spur; stimulus."[1] The clear implication is that many things can serve as incentives, a fact undercutting the careless assumption that only material wealth can do so—an assumption common to many uninformed discussions of economics. Shortly we will observe a wide variety of incentives drawn from biblical examples and prescriptions.

Second, two definitions of *system* are relevant to economics: (1) "a set or arrangement of things so related or connected as to form a unity or organic whole" and, closely related to this idea, "a regular, orderly way of doing something; order; method; regularity"; and (2) "a set of facts, principles, rules, etc. classified or arranged in regular, orderly form so as to show a logical plan linking the various parts."[2] The second definition treats a system as an ordered set of ideas; the first, as an orderly working arrangement of various things (including people). The second definition is ideal; the first, real. Because we are discussing incentives that do *in fact* drive world economic systems, not incentives that philosophers and ideologues *wish* drove them, we will use the first definition—of real, working arrangements among real things and people.

What makes a system *economic*? It must facilitate economic activity. And what is economic activity? It is choosing among various alternative, mutually exclusive ways of allocating scarce resources for the production, distribution, and consumption of wealth in households, private businesses and associations (including churches), communities, and civil governments.[3]

This definition is heavily laden with practical implications. When we choose to allocate our time—a scarce resource—to writing books, we forgo all incompatible allocations; we cannot simultaneously hang glide, play the violin in a symphonic performance, or witness to winos on skid row. Similarly, the energy we choose to use throwing a temper tantrum we cannot use to build a car or a boat or to preach the gospel on a street corner. The money we choose to spend on a new book we cannot give to a missionary, and the amount we give to a missionary we cannot spend on food for the needy family next door. Corn used to feed cattle cannot be shipped to Ethiopia's starving people (except later in the more expensive, less efficient form of beef).[4] Every choice we make about the allocation of our time, therefore, is an economic choice.[5]

Economic incentives, then, are the spurs or motives (whether internal or external) that influence our choices among alternative, incompatible uses of scarce resources for the production, distribution, and consumption of wealth, and wealth is simply anything that people value—whether time, money, power, food, clothing, shelter, knowledge, relationships, or other material or nonmaterial goods. Incentives lead us to choose one use of a resource over any other, to produce one sort of wealth instead of any other, to distribute wealth one way instead of any other, to consume one sort of wealth instead of any other. In addition, incentives influence our choice whether to use resources productively—that is, whether to invest our time, energy, ability, capital, raw materials, and intelligence one way or another, productively or unproductively.

Third, an incentive is *biblically legitimate* if it is modeled or prescribed in Scripture as worthy or permissible in God's sight.

Fourth, what does it mean for a biblically legitimate incentive to be compatible with the dominant incentives driving a given world economic system? The dominant incentives inherent to the system in question are, in principle and in application, consistent with those approved in Scripture. If, for instance, Scripture approved of the desire to gain material wealth as an incentive, and that incentive were a dominant driving force in one economic system, we would conclude that that biblical incentive was compatible with that economic system. If Scripture disapproved of the desire to gain wealth as an incentive, and that incentive were a dominant driving force in one economic system, we would conclude that that dominant driving incentive was not compatible with Scripture.

The compatibility of one driving force, or others, in a given economic system with biblically legitimate incentives would not imply the compatibility of the whole system, or even of the majority of the driving forces of that system, with Scripture. It would mean the two were consistent only at that one point of comparison.

Fifth and finally, what incentives drive allocational choices in each of the two major world economic systems? Our answer hinges on our understanding of the nature of those two systems, a matter that we will discuss later, so we will postpone this point until then. Let it suffice for now to say that the same incentives are inherent to both economic systems, since incentives are bound up in human nature and human nature is the same in both systems. But one system, by its nature, tends to magnify some types of incentives while the other tends to magnify others; and the dominant incentives in one system tend to be applied appropriately while the dominant incentives in the other tend to be applied inappropriately.

Scriptural examples of incentives—Because all of life involves choices, it should be no surprise to find that incentives are pervasive. Even the most superficial reading of any historical or biographical material reveals, to those who have the subject in mind, a wide variety of incentives operative in the lives of those involved.

A quick survey of the first twenty-one chapters of Genesis reveals nearly fifty incentives at work in people's lives, including such things as biological reproduction, the desire for food, embarrassment, peer pressure, malevolence, gratitude, and obedience to God's command.[6] Obviously, some incentives are good, and some are bad. The Apostle Paul's descriptions of "the acts of the sinful nature" and "the fruit of the Spirit" include many of each kind. "Sexual immorality, impurity and debauchery; idolatry and witchcraft; hatred, discord, jealousy, fits of rage, selfish ambition, dissensions, factions and envy; drunkenness, orgies, and the like" are evil incentives; "love, joy, peace, patience, kindness, goodness, faithfulness, gentleness and self-control" are good ones (Gal. 5:19-23). But even these lists are not exhaustive. Incentives can be as varied as the facets of the richly varied human psyche, made in the glorious image of God, yet sadly corrupted.

The complexity of incentives and the subjective nature of economic value—The complexity of incentives is evident to modern economists, who understand economic value not as objective (inherent in the thing or act valued) but as subjective (attributed to a valued thing by the valuing person).[7] Because human psyches are so multifaceted, because every person differs from every other person, and because one person's needs and desires change constantly over time depending on his circumstances, economists recognize that incentives must also vary greatly from one person to another and over time. An incentive sufficient to elicit a certain action from one person might not elicit the same action from another, or even from the same person at a different time.[8]

Modern economists see all incentives as varieties of self-interest.[9] Many Christians think this means that economists approve of selfishness, but that misunderstands the term. *Self-interest*, in economics, refers simply to whatever a given person (self) is interested in doing or having done, getting or giving. The degree of sacrifice—the amount of energy, time, money, natural resources, etc.—that he is willing to invest to achieve his goal measures the value he places on that goal.[10] Because he values the spread of the gospel, someone who gives money to Bibles For the World to support its program of mailing Bibles to people in hard-to-reach lands is acting as much out of his own self-interest, as economists define the term, as someone who buys himself a new Corvette because he values the thrill of fast driving. Because he believes everyone deserves justice, a lawyer who takes on charity cases at no fee is acting as much out of self-interest as one who takes on no case in which he expects to earn less than $50,000.

Some self-interest, in other words, is directed toward others' benefit and some toward one's own. Normally, human nature being fallen, our self-interest takes both others' and our own benefit into account. At the very least we may say that even the most altruistic person rarely sacrifices something of great value to himself in order to confer on someone else something he knows the recipient values little.[11]

TWO TYPES OF ECONOMIC INCENTIVES

Biblical precept and example reveal two chief types of economic incentives: reward and punishment.[12] While we will isolate the two types here for theoretical purposes, we must remember that, given every person's varied needs and desires, his multifaceted relationships, and the corruption of man's heart, it is rare for anyone to do anything on the basis of only a single type of incentive; more frequently, motives are mixed. As Nobel Prize-winning economist James M. Buchanan points out, economists who see man as nothing more than a monetary profit-calculating machine grossly distort the real choosing process in man. "The elementary fact," writes Buchanan, "is . . . that *homo economicus* does exist in the human psyche, [but only] along with many other men and that behavior is a product of the continuing internal struggle among these."[13]

These two types of incentives, or motives, for economic action derive from outside the choosing person. That is, the promise of reward or threat of punishment comes from someone other than the actor himself, and he responds to the promise or threat based on his evaluation of each.[14] Thus, reward and punishment may be spoken of as *external* incentives, though they always appeal to *internal* value judgments.

That is why the same rewards—external incentives—will not always produce the same choices in different people. Our differing likes and dislikes result in differing responses to rewards and punishments. Someone might entice me to work for him by promising me a day of uninterrupted study in a library; he might prevent someone else's destroying his property by threatening the same thing.

Reward—The first type of incentive is *reward,* or the promise of reward, in return for specified actions. God frequently promises reward for obedience to His commands, and so uses reward as an incentive for man: "If you follow my decrees and are careful to obey my commands, I will send you rain in its season, and the ground will yield its crops and the trees of the field their fruit" (Lev. 26:3; cf. Deut. 6:1-3, 17-18, 24-25; 7:12-15; 8:1; 11:8-9, 13-15; 28:1-14). Sometimes rewards are to be enjoyed directly by the one to whom they are promised; at other times they are to be enjoyed by someone else for whom the choosing person cares. Thus, God urged Israel to keep His commandments not only "so that your days . . . may be many in the land," but also so that "the days of your children" may be (Deut. 11:21).

God offers people many kinds of rewards. Some are largely material, like those promised to Israel on its entry into Canaan, on condition of its obedience (see Deut. 28:3-8; Prov. 2:9-10). God even offers material rewards as incentives for pursuing moral virtue (see Matt. 6:33; Prov. 8:17-18). Sometimes the attainment and preservation of moral virtue are themselves rewards for attending to godly instruction (see Prov. 5:1-2).

One great reward is approval in God's sight, which is why the Lord Jesus warned,

> "Be careful not to do your 'acts of righteousness' before men, to be seen by them. If you do, you will have no reward from your Father in heaven. . . . But when you give to the needy, . . . [do it] in secret. Then your Father, who sees what is done in secret, will reward you. (Matt. 6:1-4)

Christ motivates us to self-denial in this life by appealing to our wish for self-preservation in the life to come: "For whoever wants to save his life will lose it, but whoever loses his life for me and for the gospel will save it. What good is it for a man to gain the whole world, yet forfeit his soul?" (Mark 8:35-36). Just so, the command of God that we believe in His Son is accompanied by a promise of eternal life to those who do (see John 3:16). Clearly self-interest, even in the simplest sense of seeking our own good, cannot be condemned in principle since God expressly appeals to it to motivate us to do what He wills. But when self-gain is sought *at the expense of others,* Scripture condemns it (see James 5:1-6).

The greatest reward of all, however, is God Himself. Asaph, after bemoaning the seemingly unmitigated wickedness around him, concluded, "Whom have I in heaven but you? And earth has nothing I desire besides you" (Ps. 73:25). Augustine's comment on this passage is profound:

He that seeks any other reward from God, and is willing to serve God for that reason, makes what he wants to receive more precious than God Himself, from whom he hopes to receive it. What then, is there no reward in seeking God? None except Himself. This [the godly man] loves, this he esteems; if he loves any other thing [as an end toward which he aims in loving God], his love is not chaste.[15]

Anyone who serves God solely to gain any reward—money, power, wisdom, even eternal life—other than God Himself is like the man who marries a woman for her money. God must be seen not as a means to an end, but always as the great End of all means, our All in all.

Rewards of many sorts, both spiritual and material, are considered legitimate incentives in Scripture. We may, in fact, pursue a wide variety of rewards without being selfish. We must, however, be prepared to sacrifice ourselves and our comforts, riches, and honor for the sake of Christ's service (see John 12:24-26).

Punishment—The second type of incentive is *punishment*, or the threat of punishment, in response to specified actions. God frequently threatens punishment for disobedience to His commands, and so uses punishment as an incentive for obedience (see Lev. 26:14-17; cf. Deut. 6:14-15; 7:25-26; 8:19-20; 11:16-17; 28:15-68).

Like rewards, punishment might be physical or spiritual. God threatened capital punishment to those who committed murder (see Gen. 9:6), and the New Testament confirms the state's authority to execute lawbreakers (see Rom. 13:4). Just as material prosperity may be the reward for wise and righteous living, so material poverty may be the punishment for foolish and wicked living (see Prov. 23:20-21). And just as God Himself is the greatest reward, so being cast eternally from God's presence is the greatest punishment (see Matt. 25:41-46; Mark 8:37-38).

Minimum standards and striving for excellence—Although rewards and punishments have important similarities, there are also significant differences beyond the simple fact that one offers something we desire and the other threatens something we loathe.

First, rewards better motivate people to make sacrifices (contract costs, expend effort) beyond the minimum than do punishments. Think simply of a time when you told your child to stay out of the kitchen, warning that he'd get spanked if he didn't. If he was like most children, his toe strayed little from the line that marked the beginning of the kitchen. He did the bare minimum to avoid a spanking. But whenever you promised him something he greatly valued—extra dessert, or a trip to the lake to feed the ducks—if he stayed in the play room and picked up his toys, the results, more often than not, were markedly different. Punishments restrict behavior to certain minimum standards; rewards motivate people to reach beyond minimum standards, to go as far as they can.

People readily expend great effort, even at great personal sacrifice, to gain rewards—whether fame, fortune, power, moral satisfaction, or treasure in Heaven—because they know the magnitude of the reward depends partly on the magnitude of the achievement, which in turn depends partly on the magnitude of the investment of knowledge, time, labor, capital, and natural resources. But avoiding punishment requires no great sacrifice; one merely refrains from doing what is wrong. Thus, the threat of punishment as an incentive is inherently limited in its effects, while the promise of reward is inherently expansive in its effects.

Second, rewards are granted for behavior beyond the call of basic duty; punishments are exacted for behavior contrary to duty. That is why Scripture prescribes civil punishments for violating others' rights but not for failing to love them. Civil government rightly may punish for theft, not for stinginess. And rewards go not to those who simply refrain from beating people up but to those who risk life and limb to save innocent victims from angry mobs. Rewards, in other words, serve as incentives to go beyond the minimal standard of basic justice and to rise to the standard of self-sacrificial service.

The unfairly maligned moral philosopher Adam Smith[16] distinguished thus between justice and beneficence when he wrote,

> Actions of a beneficent tendency, which proceed from proper motives, seem alone to require a reward; because such alone are the approved objects of gratitude, or excite the sympathetic gratitude of the spectator.[17]
>
> Actions of a hurtful tendency, which proceed from improper motives, seem alone to deserve punishment; because such alone are the approved objects of resentment, or excite the sympathetic resentment of the spectator.
>
> Beneficence is always free, it cannot be extorted by force, the mere want of it exposes to no punishment; because the mere want of beneficence tends to do no real positive evil.[18]

This distinction between beneficence, which deserves rewards, and simple justice, which may only claim exemption from punishment but may not claim reward, is fundamental to any understanding of society. It forms the limits of *coercion*, the awful good that distinguishes civil government from private persons. Paul tells us that governing authorities, established by God, may promote goodness only by commending it, not by punishing its absence, but must resist evil by punishing it (see Rom. 13:1-4). That is why, when they function as God ordained, "rulers hold no terror for those who do right, but for those who do wrong" (v. 3).[19]

Smith again made this distinction clear:

> Society may subsist among different men, as among different merchants, from a sense of its utility, without any mutual love or affection; and though no man in it should owe any obligation, or be bound in gratitude to any other, it may still be upheld by a mercenary exchange of good offices according to an agreed valuation.
>
> Society, however, cannot subsist among those who are at all times ready to hurt and injure one another. . . . If there is any society among robbers and murderers, they must at least, according to the trite observation, abstain from robbing and murdering one another. Beneficence, therefore, is less essential to the existence of society than justice. Society may subsist, though not in the most comfortable state, without beneficence; but the prevalence of injustice most utterly destroy it.
>
> Though nature, therefore, exhorts mankind to acts of *beneficence*, by the pleasing consciousness of deserved reward, she has not thought it necessary to guard and enforce the practice of it by the terrors of merited punishment in case it should be neglected. It is the ornament which embellishes, not the foundation which supports the building, and which it was, therefore, sufficient to recommend, but by no means necessary to impose. *Justice*, on the contrary, is the main pillar that upholds the whole edifice. If it is removed, the great, the immense fabric of human society . . . must in a moment crumble into atoms. In order to enforce the observation of justice, therefore, nature has implanted in the human breast that consciousness of ill desert, those terrors of merited punishment, which attend upon its violation, as the great safeguards of the association of mankind, to protect the weak, to curb the violent, and to chastise the guilty.[20]

The threat of punishment, then, is used properly only to motivate people to live up to the minimum standard of human relations, namely, not to violate one another's rights. It should not be used to motivate people beyond that minimum standard. The appropriate incentive for motivating behavior beyond the minimum standard is reward.

The role of competition in economies—Rewards and punishments, then, are closely tied to the roles of *competition* and *compulsion* in economic activity, for competition occurs, normally, in the pursuit of rewards, and compulsion occurs (at least properly) in the administration or threat of punishment. Competition for rewards, therefore, is essential to a productive economy, meaning that the condemnation or prohibition of competition is economically counterproductive.

Idealists sometimes wish that society could survive and prosper based on pure altruism without regard to external incentives, primarily because the pursuit of rewards creates competition, something they consider innately evil. But society is made up of fallen human beings, and so it seems hardly likely that such a utopia will ever develop. In his book *The American Cause*, Russell Kirk states,

> If a society is deprived of competition, it is forced to rely either upon altruism, the unselfish efforts of men and women who work without reward; or upon compulsion, force employed to make people work without reward. Now the number of utterly unselfish men and women always is very small—insufficient to provide for the wants of the mass of society. And the use of compulsion to enforce work and a semblance of industry, thrift, honesty, and ingeniousness is slavery—incompatible with a free society and the concept of the dignity of man. Therefore a society without economic competition either falls into a dismal decay, because there are not enough unselfish people to do the world's work; or else it falls into slavery, the degradation of human nature and civilization.
>
> . . . In essence, it is not competition which is ruthless; rather, it is the lack of competition that makes a society ruthless; because in a competitive economy people work voluntarily for decent rewards, while in a non-competitive economy a few harsh masters employ the stick to get the world's work done.[21]

TWO CHIEF ECONOMIC SYSTEMS

We are ready now to look at the two chief economic systems and how they work. Then we will be prepared to compare how well their dominant driving forces comport with biblically legitimate incentives.

The misnomer of capitalism—The two chief economic systems are the controlled economy and the free market. Though the free market often is called capitalism, *capitalism* is a distinctly unfortunate term for the system; it focuses on only one of several essential factors of economic production and ignores completely the two chief factors that distinguish the free market from the controlled economy. Regardless of the sort of economic system under consideration, capital (money, tools, buildings, transportation and communication systems, etc.) becomes a factor of production only when combined with labor (including the application of knowledge in management, design, and entrepreneurship) and natural resources. These three factors of production must exist and be used in *any* economic system in order for production to occur. Thus, controlled economies are as much "capitalist" as are free enterprise economies in that they depend as much on capital.[22]

An earlier theoretical definition of capitalism emphasized the relationship between capitalists—people who owned and could invest capital for production (not theoreticians of capitalism)—and laborers, a relationship alleged by Karl Marx to be exploitative. A nineteenth-century edition of the *Encyclopedia Britannica,* for instance, explained,

> The characteristic feature of the capitalistic system of production is that industry is controlled by capitalists employing free wage-labour; that is, while the capitalist owns and controls the means of production, the free labourer has lost all ownership in land and capital and has nothing to depend on but his wage.[23]

This explanation depends heavily on Marx's mistaken notion of economic history. Marx thought that prior to the rise of what he called "capitalism" most laborers owned their own land and tools and so possessed a degree of economic self-determination impossible once they found their only employment working for others with tools that didn't belong to them. In reality, under feudalism—the dominant economic system before "capitalism"—most laborers worked as peasants on land owned by nobility, used tools owned by nobility, and did tasks assigned by nobility. They were legally bound to their lords and so were far less free than workers who, under "capitalism," were free to auction their labor to the highest bidders. Far from enslaving workers by divorcing them from their tools, then, "capitalism" actually increased their freedom.

Not only that, but "capitalism" increased the rate at which workers owned means of production—not in terms of individual tools, since much work shifted from cottage industries to factories and to the use of tools far too of corporations. The capital-labor distinction is not the sharp line presupposed by Marxist ideology. Most investors of capital work hard, and many laborers under "capitalism" own significant shares of capital in the form of savings and checking accounts, insurance policies, pension plans, stocks, bonds, mutual funds, certificates of deposit, and so on. Furthermore, even though wages in the factories of the early decades of "capitalism" were abysmally low by modern standards, they were significantly higher than those earlier generations, employed primarily in agriculture, received—a fact evidenced partly by the voluntary movement of workers from agriculture and cottage industries to factory employment. And the falling costs of living brought on by improved productivity meant that wages, almost for the first time in history, provided more than the basic necessities of life for which earlier generations had been accustomed to scrape and scrounge.[24]

In contrast, modern communism best fits Marx's description of "capitalism" as a system in which "the people who control capital are able to force the mass of men and women to work for them at wages which barely keep the working people alive." Kirk elaborates,

> There is capital in Russia. . . . And there are capitalists in Russia—
> that is, persons who control that capital. But the Communist capitalists are a much smaller class than American capitalists, and infinitely more powerful as a class. The Soviet Russian capitalists are the commissars and Communist party officials who control Soviet industry and agriculture. These Communist capitalists are supreme: there is no check upon their authority, from government or labor unions or political parties. They can, and do, force the peoples of Soviet states to work under whatever conditions they prescribe, for as small wages as they like. And those conditions often are wretched, and those wages usually are very small, because the masters of the Soviet system choose to spend most of the industrial surplus upon armaments and "Five Year Plans" and other grand state designs. . . .
>
> None of the exaggerated charges of Marx and Engels against nineteenth-century capitalism accuse the private capitalists of such methods as are now employed daily by the Communist-capitalists of the Soviet states. The exploitation of the worker which Marx and his followers predicted would be carried out by the private capitalist of the future, now is executed, instead, by the disciples of Marx.[25]

The two chief distinguishing factors between the free market economy and the controlled economy are not the different relationships between capital and labor but the different conditions under which capital, labor, and resources are brought together and allocated to one or another of various alternative uses. Those conditions may be understood under the headings of the two key words *free* and *market*, both of which stand opposed to the one word *controlled*.

Under the free market economy, people can choose for themselves how to employ their capital, labor, and resources, and toward what ends. Their private, uncoerced choices as consumers in the market determine prices, which in turn determine profits (rewards), which in turn determine how producers allocate capital, labor, and natural resources for production. That is, consumers control the direction of the economy by exerting demand (offers of reward) for desired products, and producers respond to consumers' demands by allocating the factors of production toward meeting their demands.

The functional terms are *free* and *market*, and it behooves us to define these carefully to avoid misunderstanding.

The meaning of freedom—When we speak of a *free* market economy, we mean not that things are available at no cost (economics by definition deals with choices of allocation of scarce, and hence costly, resources), but that the agents in the market—consumers and producers, investors and managers and laborers—choose what to produce, buy and sell apart from the threat of arbitrary force (punishment).[26] This definition is particularly important because the concept of freedom often is confused with three other concepts: (1) political self-determination (the ability of a national population to select, through some form of elections, those who rule); (2) the ability to do whatever one chooses without regard to natural or economic restraints; and (3) the absence of moral restraints and their enforcement.

The Teutonic root of the English word *free* described "a protected member of the community"; it distinguished between those who were enslaved to others and those who were their own masters. The Latin *liber* (from which "liberty" derives) and the Greek *eleutheros* referred to the same distinction between slave and freeman.[27] Properly understood, then, the *freedom* of the free market is not that of political self-determination (free market economies can thrive under monarchies as well as in representative democracies, and some representative democracies have fairly strictly controlled economies), the ability to do whatever one chooses (that is, the absence of natural and economic restraints on human action), or the absence of moral restraints and their enforcement (Paul argues in Rom. 6 that real freedom is freedom from sin and slavery to righteousness); it is freedom from arbitrary coercion by others. Ludwig von Mises described it this way:

This, then, is freedom in the external [note the importance of this qualifier] life of man—that he is independent of the arbitrary power of his fellows. Such freedom . . . did not exist under primitive conditions. It arose in the process of social development and its final completion is the work of mature Capitalism. The man of pre-capitalistic days was subject to a "gracious lord" whose favour he had to acquire. Capitalism recognizes no such relation. It no longer divides society into despotic rulers and rightless serfs. All [economic] relations are material and impersonal, calculable and capable of substitution. With capitalistic money calculations freedom descends from the sphere of dreams to reality.[28]

Under feudalism, freedom was strictly limited in part because the serf (the word comes from the Latin *servus*, a slave) could own no production property but was bound in feudal servitude to his master's land and was transferred with the land when a new lord took possession of it. The growth of towns, peopled by men and women who belonged to no feudal lord but who earned their livings by trade instead of by agriculture, paved the way for the recognition that with ownership of productive property came freedom from servitude (serfdom). Thus, freedom and property are closely linked, so much so that in the Fifth Amendment to the United States Constitution they are bound together as two of three fundamental rights (the third is life) that cannot be taken by the state apart from due process of law.[29] The Marxist claim that freedom comes with the abolition of private ownership of capital is nothing more than an appeal for the resurrection of feudalism. It is precisely through private ownership of capital that serfdom ends.[30]

This proper definition of freedom is critical in light of such modern movements as liberation theology, which confuses economic freedom with both political self-determination and the ability to fulfill one's wishes.[31] Because of this confusion, liberation theology trades real economic freedom for economic slavery in hopes of obtaining political self-determination and increased prosperity. In practice it gains neither of its goals and loses the one sense of freedom with which it begins, for as Kirk points out,

In the modern industrial world, it really is not possible to buy economic security at the price of liberty. It is possible only to surrender freedom in exchange for total planning—which relieves most people of the necessity for making their own choices in life, but also relieves them of their prosperity and their birthright as human beings.[32]

The importance of the market—When we speak of a free *market* economy, we mean an economy in which the market—the vast set of relationships among freely choosing buyers and sellers of producer goods, consumer goods, labor, information, capital, etc.—guides the direction of economic activity rather than governmental planners backed up by the threat of force.

Because the market effectively processes information about people's subjective valuations of various alternative goods and services, it provides essential information about the most efficient allocations of resources. By communicating this information to producers, the market enables consumers' choices to guide the whole action of the free market economy. Under a free market economy, producers know that they must meet consumers' demands if they are to earn profits (rewards). Thus, the market facilitates people's choosing freely to serve others.

The loss of freedom and markets—The controlled economy stands in stark contrast to the free market economy on both essential factors.

First, under the controlled economy, planners employed by the civil government instruct people how to bring capital, resources, and labor together, and toward what ends. Their plans are based on their assumptions about people's wants and needs, as well as on the goals of the government they represent—goals that do not by any means necessarily coincide with the best interests of the population. Those who refuse to comply with the planners' instructions face sanctions (punishment). Thus, the controlled economy seriously curtails freedom, while the market economy both presupposes and enhances it. Also, the controlled economy misuses the biblical incentive of punishment by applying it to actions not prohibited by biblical justice.

Second, under the controlled economy, planners determine prices based on their computations of costs of production or on their predetermined goals, which might be to redistribute income from one part of the economy to another, to build a powerful military force, to increase exports, to increase the nation's supply of hard money (the goal of mercantilism), among other possible goals.

Determining prices on the basis of presumed costs of production is exactly opposite the method of the free market, in which consumers' expression of subjective economic values in the form of willingness to purchase at certain prices and unwillingness to purchase at other prices determines price and so determines the costs producers are willing to incur in meeting consumers' demands. The controlled economy's adoption of prices higher than those most consumers are willing to pay necessarily causes surpluses of the goods and services affected; the higher prices crowd marginal consumers out of the market, and some of the goods and services go unsold. Its adoption of prices lower than most producers' costs of production necessarily causes shortages of goods and services by driving marginal producers out of the market.[33] It also contributes to inflexibility and lack of innovation since it removes incentive to find less costly methods of production.

Determining prices based on national goals sacrifices people's needs and desires to those of the bureaucratic apparatus and easily leads to widespread slavery. It also fails to take seriously the inability of finite human beings to predict the future adequately to set nationwide goals that will seem as worthwhile in retrospect as they did in prospect, whether they're achieved or not.

The controlled economy is, therefore, inherently inefficient and incapable of the fundamental task of economic calculation.[34]

CONCLUSION

Our brief discussion of the two chief types of biblically legitimate incentives and of the two chief kinds of economic systems leads us to some definite conclusions.

First, the two types of incentives properly apply to very different types of behavior. Reward applies to behavior that surpasses the minimum standard of justice; punishment applies to behavior that transgresses (or fails to achieve) that minimum standard. Rewarding injustice and punishing people for anything but injustice are both condemned in Scripture (see, for example, Ezek. 18).

Second, the two types of incentives have very different effects on human action. Rewards elicit behavior beyond minimum standards; punishments elicit behavior that barely meets them. Rewards, then, are more conducive to the production of wealth beyond the level of subsistence than are punishments.

Third, because the free market emphasizes rewards (incentives best suited to eliciting behavior beyond minimum standards), it facilitates the production of goods and services of greater value to consumers than does the controlled market, which emphasizes punishments (incentives best suited to eliciting behavior barely conforming to minimum standards).

Fourth, the free market is more consistent with the biblical principle of human freedom (essentially the reservation of coercion solely to enforcing justice rather than to forcing behavior conforming to the arbitrary whims of a ruling class) than is the controlled economy.[35]

Fifth, the free market processes price information—that is, information about the subjective values of consumers—more efficiently than does the controlled economy, and so more efficiently meets consumers' demands through more efficient allocation of resources. The controlled economy's attempt to do away with the market pricing mechanism results in misallocation of resources and more unmet consumer demands than occurs in the free market.

Sixth, the free market economy relies primarily on rewards to influence economic behavior, reserving its resort to punishment only to actions that violate the minimum standard of justice. As such, the dominant driving force of the free market economy is consistent with biblically legitimate incentives.

Seventh, the controlled economy relies primarily on punishments to influence economic behavior. Insofar as it resorts to rewards at all, those generally are offered not for exceptional service to consumers in terms of their preferences, but for exceptional service to the state—whatever that service might be, even if it involves violating others' rights. As Leon Trotsky put it in one of his more candid moments, "In a country where the sole employer is the State, opposition means death by slow starvation. The old principle: who does not work shall not eat, has been replaced by a new one: who does not obey shall not eat."[36] The dominant driving force of the controlled economy, then, is inconsistent with biblically legitimate incentives.

Scripture permits the state to use its monopoly of force only to prohibit, prevent, and punish violations of human rights by transgression of the Sixth, Seventh, Eighth, and Ninth Commandments; to provide such public goods as are requisite to that function (e.g., the building, regulation, and maintenance of a system of roads, or the provision of streetlights as security against crime); and to collect such taxes as are necessary to the performance of such duties. Any use of coercion by the state for other purposes violates biblical limits on the state and thus violates the human rights protected in the very commandments the state is ordained to enforce. A state, therefore, that allows market freedom within the constraints of moral law is, in that respect, functioning according to biblical prescription; one that controls the economy beyond those bounds functions contrary to biblical prescription.[37]

Admittedly, in the real world no absolutely free market and no absolutely controlled market exist. The latter is impossible granted the essential limits of man's knowledge and power; the former, whether possible or not,[38] has never yet been achieved, in part because confusions about such fundamental concepts as justice, freedom, and economic value have led people to restrict economic freedom far more than appears necessary given biblical ethics. Nonetheless, real economies do occupy places on a continuum from most controlled to least controlled. The more an economy tends toward one end of the continuum or the other, the more it tends to use rewards and punishments correctly or incorrectly. The more an economy tends to use rewards as incentives for economic achievement, the more productive it tends to be. Conversely, the more an economy tends to use punishments as incentives for economic achievement and to minimize rewards, the less productive it tends to be.

A third way? An objection to this entire analysis might be that I have falsely dichotomized free market and controlled economies, forgetting that there is a third way—the "mixed" or "interventionist" or "guided" market economy.[39] Might such an economy properly use biblically legitimate incentives?

Though thorough treatment of the question would take more space than is available here, the answer must, ultimately, be no. As Ludwig von Mises argues demonstratively in his *Planned Chaos*, interventionism leads logically and, in practice, almost inevitably to ever-increasing control of the economy by civil government. Interventionism negates the essential pricing and allocating functions of the market, causing increasing economic chaos. Historically, this normally has led to the institution of dictatorship as the only apparent remedy. The only means of avoiding that result is reducing or, preferably, abandoning interventionism.

The logical and historical progression from the mixed economy toward total control occurs because every intervention of civil government into the free market other than to prohibit, prevent, and punish violations of God-ordained rights is necessarily self-defeating, occasioning more problems to which interventionists respond with more intervention. The self-defeating nature of interventionism may be demonstrated either inductively or deductively. *Inductively*, we can observe the effects of actual interventions and see that they invariably have exacerbated rather than diminished the problems they were intended to solve. *Deductively*, we can argue either (1) that interventions, with the exceptions noted above, violate God-given ethical principles, and that because moral and physical reality are one, a violation of moral principles must have deleterious physical effects; or (2) that the interventions necessarily change the variables involved in equations of marginal utility and so change economic behavior in unpredictable ways that vitiate the end intended by the designers of the interventionist policies.[40]

Most pertinent to the subject of this chapter, however, is that every state intervention in the economy involves the threat of punishment (the minimizing incentive) for those who violate it.[41] This coercive activity most signally distinguishes the driving force of a mixed economy from that of a free market economy; and it is precisely the same as the driving force of the controlled economy, from which it differs in practice only by degree and in principle not at all. The driving force of the mixed economy, therefore, is not compatible with the legitimate applications of biblically legitimate incentives.

The choice is not between a chaotic, unplanned free market economy and an orderly, planned economy. That false dichotomy stems from the failure of critics of the free market to recognize that there is nothing automatic about it. It, too, is planned—but planned piecemeal and by private individuals whose only means of influencing others are persuasion and reward, rather than wholesale and by government bureaucrats whose chief means of influencing others is the threat of punishment. Von Mises wrote,

> The dilemma is not between automatic forces and planned action. It is between the democratic process of the market in which every individual has his share and the exclusive rule of a dictatorial body. Whatever people do in the market economy, is the execution of their own plans. In this sense every human action means planning. What those calling themselves planners advocate is not the substitution of planned action for letting things go. It is the substitution of the planner's own plan for the plans of his fellowmen. The planner is a potential dictator who wants to deprive all other people of the power to plan and act according to their own plans. He aims at one thing only: the exclusive absolute preeminence of his own plan.[42]

EDITOR'S REFLECTIONS

"The greatest reward of all, however, is God Himself." Cal Beisner has drawn our attention to this truth, which goes to the heart of the whole subject of biblical incentives. Oh, that Christians would seek to *experience this truth* in their life in Christ! While it is true that the standards of our faith are the truths of Scripture given to us in propositional (not existential) form, it is just as true that this central truth comes to life in us through the work of the Holy Spirit, who enables us to respond to Christ in loving obedience, a prerequisite for us to "see" Him and truly know Him. Christ wants us to have fellowship with Him and truly know Him, not merely to know *about* Him (see John 14:15-24; 2 Cor. 13:14; Eph. 1:15-18). Indeed, truly to know Him is to have eternal life (see John 17:3), and to know Him is to desire and love Him, *the most godly and powerful motivator on earth* (see Ps. 16:2, 5; 73:25-28). To recognize that God does not exist to serve us, but that we exist for His glory and that He Himself, not anything else, is the true end and ultimate satisfier of all our needs, desires, and longings for love, contentment, competency, success, and fellowship, is to come to the truth that all reality has its final meaning and fulfillment in God the Father, God the Son, and God the Holy Spirit.

Job discovered this truth when he finally "saw" God with the eyes of his heart. Then his suffering and all the questions related to it became insignificant and were immediately resolved to his complete satisfaction (see Job 42:1-6). Jacob, however, like so many of us, was slow to be weaned from his perception that God existed to satisfy his personal desires (see Gen. 28:20-21) and was slow to grow to the mature understanding that God Himself was his sufficiency. It would seem that Jacob came to the end of his

187

own strength and resources and completely trusted God only when he was an old man (see Gen. 43:14; 46:1-7).

Fallen people always seek to satisfy their deepest drives and identity needs by relating to people, things, or their own accomplishments in the temporal realm because their identity is of necessity attached to such things when they are alienated from God. For example, they seek acceptance by doing things to please other people, or they strive for wealth, power, success, and other worldly symbols that speak of their personal competency in an effort to bolster their self-esteem. Persons without Christ are self-condemned to a false identity in this life.

Christians, on the other hand, are undergoing an "identity transplant" where their most basic psychological needs are being slowly detached from the world and rooted in God. This is one significant meaning contained in the reality of our being *in* Christ (see Eph. 1:3-14 where this concept appears ten times). Even relatively mature Christians may discover, however, that their approach to God sometimes reflects a "gimme, gimme" attitude where God is still treated as a "means" to care for their continuing worldly desires instead of their learning to be content in Christ, no matter their condition (see Phil. 4:11-13). The Holy Spirit will not leave God's children in such an immature state indefinitely. Instead, because we are God's children, He will transplant our identity into Himself.

Closely interrelated with the transfer of our identity from the world to Christ is our growing ability to have a loving response (obedience) to the clearly expressed will of God. Christ reveals Himself to His children by degrees and over time as we *respond* to His teachings and follow Him. This is embodied in Christ's statement:

> "If you love Me, you will keep My commandments. And I will ask the Father, and He will give you another Helper, that He may be with you *forever*; that is the Spirit of truth, *whom . . . you know . . .* because He abides with you, and will be in you. I will not leave you as orphans; *I will come to you . . .* He who has My commandments and keeps them, he it is who loves Me; and he who loves Me shall be loved by My Father, and I will love him, *and will disclose Myself to him.*" (John 14:15-18, 21, emphasis added)

Scripture is filled with the relationship between *love* and an *obedient response,* both of which are acts of our volition, not merely emotional responses. Our lives are certainly not devoid of many rich emotional experiences, but the test of our real faith or the evidence of our true conversion is found in our obedient and loving response to Christ's call in every area of life, not in how we feel emotionally about a particular circumstance or demand.

Cal Beisner is on target when he identifies *rewards* and *punishments* as the basic incentives God puts before His image bearers in the Scripture. While it is necessary for the rebellious, the untaught, the naive, and the fallen to be taught that negative consequences (punishments) justly flow from inappropriate conduct, it is just as true that rewards work better as a motivator than does the threat of punishment. This is precisely why a fundamentally free market economic system is so superior in the natural order to a highly regulated and controlled system. The hoped-for rewards are powerful motivators, even when they represent intermediate or incomplete ends to satisfy our identity needs.

Because Cal Beisner so thoroughly understands both mankind's fallen nature and that there are so many people in the world who do not love God and respond obediently to His will, he was also invited to write the second chapter in this section. Here he discusses the attitudes and inner drives that are available to Christians (and desperately needed) through the work of the Holy Spirit. In doing this, Cal faced a choice. He could have discussed the "fruits of the flesh," which are so predominant in the world, and talked about mankind's selfishness and its deleterious effects. But he rejected this approach, writing to the editor:

> I was convinced that it wouldn't be of much value simply to compare the sorts of incentives in business and the workplace that we readily think of as immoral with the biblically legitimate counterparts— greed versus generosity, selfishness versus service, and so on. Many Christians, especially those in business, I think, would find that sophomoric; they're acquainted with such motives in their own hearts and know the difference. Those who don't know the difference, I think, wouldn't likely be swayed by the enumeration of the contrasts. Instead, they need to see a positive, constructive case made for proper biblical incentives, and in the light of that they'll be prepared to recognize and reject improper incentives.

It would be next to impossible to set forth a more positive and clear discourse on the proper biblical incentives for the individual than what Cal Beisner has written in the next chapter. He not only lays bare the biblical incentives, but also reveals the great gulf separating the typical thinking of the nonChristian with regard to business ethics and the Scriptures' straightforward declaration about what is essential for a godly appraisal of ethics. The typical businessperson simply assumes that if an economic act provides a positive outcome, it is morally good. (Sounds good, doesn't it?) Scripture makes it clear, though, that God always looks upon the inner intent and motives of the heart, along with the outward conduct, and that the inner, hidden root of the act is of first importance to God (see 1 Cor. 4:5; 2 Cor. 5:12). This truth is one of the things that makes the next chapter so profound. It deals with the *internal* attitudes and incentives that must be present in our lives if our conduct is to be considered godly.

CHAPTER 9

BIBLICAL INCENTIVES AND AN INDIVIDUAL'S ECONOMIC CHOICES

E. Calvin Beisner

INTRODUCTION

The assignment for this chapter was to argue for "the incompatibility of biblical incentives with the driving forces of world economic systems." We saw in the previous chapter, however, that biblically legitimate incentives are more compatible with one of the world's two chief economic systems (the free market) than with the other (the controlled economy). Thus, at the same time that we saw the compatibility of biblical incentives with one of the world's chief economic systems, we saw the incompatibility with the other.

This being the case, we will explore here some of the more important biblical ethical standards of motive and behavior and compare them with incentives to economic action in everyday life.[1] Our focus changes from overall economic systems to individual economic choices and from the two chief categories of incentives—rewards and punishments—to the specific, complex, and often manifold motives underlying those choices.

At this level, the question largely disappears as to whether one economic system or another is more compatible with biblical incentives. At least in respect to moral nature, people are fundamentally the same whether they work, buy, sell, spend, save, consume, and invest in a free market or in a controlled economy. The Apostle Paul wrote, "There is no difference, for all have sinned and fall short of the glory of God" (Rom. 3:22-23). Neither the free market nor the controlled economy can change the fundamental fact of fallen human nature. The "new Communist man," free of greed, covetousness, and the will to power, will never arise from the Communist system; but neither will a fundamentally righteous, self-sacrificing man arise from the free market. Neither private nor state enterprise exempts anyone from depravity.[2] Liberation from the sinful nature is a gift of God, a mighty work of His grace through spiritual regeneration (see Rom. 6; 2 Cor. 5:17). It requires a radical change of nature that no outward circumstances can effect.

In the previous chapter we saw that there are scores of different incentives, or motives (words that, for the purposes of this chapter, we will use interchangeably), some good and some bad. Considering each in any depth is impossible in short compass.[3] Instead, we will group them in categories, view biblically sanctioned motives first, and then look at corruptions of those motives that often sully human thought and behavior in the marketplace. Before looking at specific motives, we must do three other tasks.

First, we must distinguish carefully between motive and sanction. A *motive*, or incentive, is the "subjective reason" for doing something; it "can be traced to the personal preferences of the moral agent." But a *sanction* is "an objective consideration . . . which enforces a moral imperative upon the agent from outside him. That which validates the moral judgment and thereby objectively incites to moral action is a sanction; motives are inner impulsions or inducements to action."[4] A sanction justifies a choice as morally right; an incentive energizes a person's choice, whether right or wrong. It should go without saying, of course, that good motives are no justification for wrong actions. Nonetheless, we deal here with incentives (or motives), not with sanctions.

Second, we must note that identical acts can arise from widely varying motives, some laudable and some damnable, as Carl F. H. Henry points out:

> The vegetable clerk in a supermart always packages exactly five pounds of potatoes for customer convenience. If he is asked why, he may reply: (1) he wishes to establish a reputation for trustworthiness with his employer, so his job will be secure; (2) he believes that honesty is the best policy as a rule of success in business; (3) he has cheated in the past, and wishes now to placate a guilty conscience by rigorous honesty; (4) he intends to cheat his customers in the future, but first wishes to establish a reputation for integrity; (5) he practices honesty as part of a "salvation by works" philosophy; (6) he desires, as a partaker of God's redemption from sin and its consequences, thankfully to glorify God in his deeds, and he knows that he reflects the character of God when he gives what he promises.[5]

A good act may be done with good motives or bad, just as a bad act may be done with bad motives or good. The effect on others will always be the same, however, and one of the tests of an economic system is its ability to induce even those with bad motives to do good acts. It is better for everyone concerned that good acts should be done with bad motives than that bad acts should be done at all.[6]

Third, we must distinguish between the motive for an action, on the one hand, and the action and its results, on the other. Christian ethics requires not only that we do the right thing but also that we do it for the right motives. Henry comments,

> The underlying contention of Christian ethics is that every want of conformity to God is sinful and wicked. This includes both lack of conformity in action and in motive and affection. The deepest recess of the heart is judged equally with any external deed.[7]

An insight of free market economics—that the necessity of trading for mutual advantage to some degree mitigates the *effects* of man's innate selfishness—must not be misunderstood as an argument that somehow the free market makes selfishness good. The insight, rooted in eighteenth-century moral philosopher Adam Smith's doctrine of the "invisible hand"—which was for him not a mere rhetorical device but an affirmation of the real providence of God in turning evil intents to the common good—relates solely to the objective outcome, not to the subjective intentions, in economic relationships.[8] Smith never intended this doctrine to be used as a justification of selfishness. Echoing the ancient stoics and Romans 8:28, he believed

> that as the world was governed by the all-ruling providence of a wise, powerful, and good God, every single event ought to be regarded as making a necessary part of the plan of the universe, and as tending to promote the general order and happiness of the whole: that the vices and follies of mankind, therefore, made as necessary a part of this plan as their wisdom or their virtue; and by that eternal art which reduces good from ill, were made to tend equally to the prosperity and perfection of the great system of nature. No speculation of this kind, however, how deeply soever it might be rooted in the mind, could diminish our natural abhorrence for vice, whose immediate effects are so destructive,and whose remote ones are too distant to be traced by the imagination.[9]

Smith was clearly not a utilitarian but rested the goodness of any act in its intrinsic nature instead of its ultimate effects. Indeed, he denied man's capacity even to know ultimate effects of any acts, hence making illegitimate any appeal to ends to justify means.

Far from Smith's justifying selfishness, he condemned it, holding that the properly formed conscience could approve of nothing less than self-denial for the sake of others:

> And hence it is, that to feel much for others, and little for ourselves, that to restrain our selfish, and to indulge our benevolent, affections, constitutes the perfection of human nature; and can alone produce among mankind that harmony of sentiments and passions in which consists their whole grace and propriety. As to love our neighbor as we love ourselves is the great law of Christianity, so it is the great precept of nature to love ourselves only as we love our neighbor, or, what comes to the same thing, as our neighbour is capable of loving us.[10]

While, for Smith, the "invisible hand" could effect a just, peaceful society of mutual benefit using solely men's motives for personal gain, a society of "grace and propriety" could come about only through self-denying love.

One final remark before we consider incentives directly. I find it increasingly difficult, as I study both economics and biblical ethics, to distinguish at all between economic and noneconomic activity. Every minute of our lives we choose among various alternative, mutually exclusive ways of allocating scarce resources—time, energy, attention, material possessions, and so on. And that is the very definition of economic activity, as we saw in the previous chapter. I therefore find it difficult, if not impossible, to confine my considerations here to our incentives and actions solely in the workplace or the marketplace.

From the Christian perspective, *all* life is the workplace: the workplace of the servant of God. Neither the temptations that assail us nor the opportunities that present themselves to us on the job, during a sales call, or in any of the other situations normally thought of as "economic," are truly distinct from those we encounter elsewhere. Perhaps this will make what follows seem less specifically helpful to persons who struggle with ethical questions about incentives in "economic" activity. But perhaps, instead, it will make what follows helpful to a broader audience, and ultimately, more broadly helpful even to the narrower audience, if it encourages the latter to view paid work, buying, and selling as simply facets of service to God rather than isolated, "economic" aspects of life that operate under rules different from those for "noneconomic" life.

CATEGORIES OF INCENTIVES

Incentives may be categorized in several ways. The previous chapter identified two chief sorts, reward and punishment. Adam Smith, in *The Theory of Moral Sentiments*, used three classifications: prudence ("concerned with the achievement of the necessary conditions for preservation"), justice ("the observance of a set of legal rules by which each person's freedom is reasonably secured and coercion is outlawed"), and benevolence or beneficence (the highest motive of human behavior, always voluntary and discretionary, a self-denying concern for others).[11] Wheaton College economics professor Jim Halteman, in *Market Capitalism and Christianity*, names five categories of incentives: material reward, social and psychological benefit to the worker, political pressure to produce, the desire to serve the needy, and the desire to witness the gospel.[12]

Carl Henry, in *Christian Personal Ethics*, writes of eight categories of motive for the Christian. (He does not present them as if they comprise an exhaustive list.) Highest of all is gratitude for God's grace imparted by the atoning work of Christ.[13] "Gratitude," observes Henry, "is the wellspring from which arises the response of love to love." It is "the connecting link between justification and sanctification."[14] Love for God and then for man is the second and consequent motive. To these Henry adds (not in order of importance) trust in Christ's atonement, admiration and emulation of the examples of Christ and the apostles, fidelity to the will of God, desire for reward, fear of chastening (but not of condemnation, since there is none to the child of God), and the pursuit of happiness.[15]

Gratitude, love, and service—The *Heidelberg Catechism* (1563) "sums up all Christian ethics under this heading—'Gratitude.'"[16] "Since, then, we are redeemed from our misery by grace through Christ, without any merit of ours, why must we do good works?" the *Catechism* asks. And it answers,

> Because Christ, having redeemed us by his blood, renews us also by his Holy Spirit after his own image, that with our whole life we may *show ourselves thankful* to God for his blessing, and that he may be glorified through us; then, also, that we ourselves may be assured of our faith by the fruits thereof, and by our godly walk may win our neighbors also to Christ. (question 86; emphasis added)

The emphasis on gratitude reflects the setting in which God gave the Ten Commandments. He introduced them with a reminder of His saving work for

Israel, for which He expected Israel to respond in grateful obedience: "I am the LORD your God, who brought you out of Egypt, out of the land of slavery" (Exod. 20:2; Deut. 5:6). The New Testament, too, presents gratitude as the foundation of Christian service: "Therefore, since we are receiving a kingdom that cannot be shaken, *let us be thankful,* and so worship [Greek *latreuomen,* lit., serve[17]] God acceptably with reverence and awe" (Heb. 12:28, emphasis added). Even love itself is the response of gratitude to God, not a primary—that is, underived—motive in the human heart: "We love because he first loved us" (1 John 4:19).

Love that springs from gratitude to God is neither undefined nor autonomous, but defined and Law-directed. It is defined by the moral Law revealed in the Ten Commandments, of which it is the complete summary and fulfillment (see Matt. 22:37-39; Rom. 13:8-10). It works itself out in generous giving in mimicry of the grace that excites the gratitude from which it springs (see 2 Cor. 9:6-10; cf. 8:8). And it replicates itself in its beneficiaries, in whom it engenders a new generation of love-producing gratitude to God (see 2 Cor. 9:11-15). Thus, grateful love inspires gracious service by which the Kingdom of God grows as more and more people experience the King's love and respond in grateful, loving service.

It should be clear from this that gratitude to one's fellowmen is a pure and good motive for reciprocal service. In some circles it is popular to denigrate reciprocation of benefits as somehow demeaning, intended merely to "balance the score" or, worse, to place the initial giver in debt to the respondent. Occasionally, concrete expressions of gratitude are withheld for fear of implying that we think our benefactors served us only to evoke gratitude and *quid pro quo.* Both reasons for rejecting gratitude as an appropriate motive for service are inadequate; the first presumes that it is impossible for gratitude, and the second that it is impossible for generosity, to be genuine. Both presume that anything less than a perfectly unmixed good motive is to be rejected, a presumption that makes all good motives unacceptable in a world of fallen, depraved humanity. On the contrary, Scripture approves of our returning favors in gratitude. It was partly that motive for which Paul was confident that the people of Corinth and Rome would give to the poor in Jerusalem. The saints in Jerusalem had served them through the gospel; they should return the service through material provision (see 2 Cor. 8:13-15; Rom. 15:27).

The distinction between gratitude and service makes apparent a difference in outlook between responsive and prospective motives. Gratitude is responsive: It focuses on the past, on benefits received. Service is prospective: It focuses on the future, on benefits to be bestowed on others, and particularly on the growth of God's Kingdom. Between and uniting the two stands love, which is both responsive and prospective: It expresses gratitude and looks for ways to pass on to others the benefits that gave it rise.

Seeking first the Kingdom—The growth of God's Kingdom, and by it the glorification of God, is the great aim of all Christian activity (see Matt. 6:33). Grateful love in response to God's grace produces a service wholly consumed by passion for the glory of God displayed in the increasing breadth and intensity of His reign in and over and through men and women everywhere. The overriding concern of the grateful Christian is that God's Kingdom should come, that His will should be done, on earth as it is in Heaven (see Matt. 6:10).

Thus, furthering God's Kingdom, and by that glorifying Him, is the highest prospective incentive for Christian service. It is a covenantal activity, undertaken in grateful response to the King for deliverance from bondage and bestowal of privileges.[18] As such, it is rooted in the two primary relationships of the redeemed to the King: sonship and priesthood. These two facets of Christians' identity and of our relationship with God should shape all our activities. To the extent that we understand them and act them out rightly, we will act with right motives; to the extent that we misunderstand them and act them out wrongly, we will act with wrong motives.

Let's look, then, at how sonship and priesthood should shape our activities in furthering the Kingdom of God, and consider how the motives and actions that grow from them can be corrupted, particularly in our jobs and other environments typically thought of as economic.

Dominion: the exercise of sonship—The redeemed of God are, by our new birth, adopted as sons of God. Our sonship, in which we are made "heirs of God and co-heirs with Christ," replaces a spirit of fearful slavery with a spirit of royalty that promises a share in the glory of the Redeemer (see Rom. 8:14-17).

In Christ Jesus, God is restoring and perfecting the rule over the earth that He gave to Adam but that Adam corrupted in the Fall (see Gen. 1:26-30; 3:17-19; Ps. 8:3-8). This rule was intended to be exercised in humble submission to God, and Christians are reborn to this humble submission. We are intended to share in this restoration of proper rule to the Second Adam and His brothers.

All our acquisitive activities should be undertaken from the perspective of participating in and advancing this godly rule, or dominion. Our desires to get wealth, power, or honor should be harnessed to this underlying motive: the expansion of the Kingdom of God and the extension of its benefits to more and more people. So long as these desires are so harnessed, they will seek only godly ways of fulfillment. Thus, for instance, Paul condemns stealing as a means of acquiring wealth, but commends acquiring wealth if it is done for the purpose of serving others: "He who has been stealing must steal no longer, but must work, doing something useful with his own hands, that he may have something to share with those in need" (Eph. 4:28). Similarly, the *Westminster Shorter Catechism* (1647) says, in explaining the positive implications of the Eighth Commandment ("Thou shalt not steal"), "The eighth commandment requireth the lawful procuring and furthering the wealth and outward estate of ourselves and others."

Refraining from violating a neighbor's property and lawfully producing and acquiring our own property to be used for our own and others' benefit are biblically proper. The Christian who works hard and wisely to provide goods and services economically to others and is rewarded for this service with wealth should be looked upon not as greedy but as effectively fulfilling his calling as a steward of God's household (see Matt. 25:14-30; cf. Luke 19:12-27). God presents it as a matter of course that He will enhance the prosperity of faithful stewards.

The desire for wealth, then, must not be condemned in itself. Whether it is laudable or damnable in a specific individual depends on the purpose for which the wealth is desired and on the means by which he is willing to get it. If he seeks wealth for the sake of self-aggrandizement and luxurious living, his desire is wrong; if he seeks it as a means of serving others, his desire is right. If he seeks wealth by taking advantage of others, his desire is wrong; if he seeks it by serving others, his desire is right. Frequently man, who looks on the outside but cannot see the heart, is a poor judge of another's true motives. Often enough it is more than sufficient challenge for us to ascertain and control our own motives without judging others'.

Neither should it be assumed—though it often is—that greed and opportunism are vices solely of the rich. Outward circumstances do not determine inner moral condition. Cupidity is as often a vice of the poor and others who would like to become rich—the persons Paul had specifically in mind when he wrote the oft-quoted words, "For the love of money is a root of all kinds of evil. Some people, eager for money, have wandered from the faith and pierced themselves with many griefs" (1 Tim. 6:10).[19] Many rich people know better the futility of trusting in riches than do many poor and middle-class people who have never had the chance to learn the lesson by experience.

How might an individual assess his motives in his attempts to get wealth? Clearly, any violation of others' trust and property betrays moral rottenness. Not only outright theft violates the Eighth Commandment, but

> also all wicked tricks and devices whereby we seek to draw to ourselves our neighbor's goods, whether by force or with show [i.e., pretense] of right, such as unjust weights, ells,[20] measures, wares, coins, usury,[21] or any means forbidden of God; so, moreover, all covetousness, and all useless waste of his gifts.[22]

St. Francis de Sales, in his *Introduction to the Devout Life,* suggested this test of our motives toward possessions:

> You are truly avaricious if you longingly, ardently, anxiously desire to possess goods that you do not have, even though you say that you would not want to acquire them by unjust means. A man shows that he has a fever if he longingly, ardently, and anxiously desires to drink, even though he wants to drink nothing but water. . . . If you are strongly attached to the goods you possess, are too solicitous about them, set your heart on them, always have them in your thoughts, and fear losing them with a strong, anxious fear, then, believe me, you are still subject to such fever. When feverish men are given water they drink it with a certain eagerness, concentration, and satisfaction that the healthy are not accustomed to have. . . . If you find your heart very desolated and afflicted at the loss of property, believe me, Philothea, you love it too much.[23]

"Where your treasure is," said Jesus, "there your heart will be also" (Matt. 6:21). If our efforts always are directed toward ourselves, our hearts are self-centered. No wonder financial counselor Larry Burkett frequently says he can tell a great deal about a person's spiritual maturity by looking at his income tax return to see the extent of his charitable giving! To paraphrase what Jesus said about another issue, it is not what goes into a man's estate that defiles him, but whether it stays there to rot or is used to serve others. Certainly anyone whose giving falls below 10 percent of his net income should consider carefully whether he is serving God or mammon.[24]

In economic affairs, then, each of us must ask constantly, "Am I doing this for my own benefit alone, or also—even predominantly—for the benefit of others?" Ruthless honesty alone can answer adequately, and more often than not it will drive us to confession and repentance, humbly asking God to forgive us for self-centeredness and cause us to know and emulate "the grace of our Lord Jesus Christ, [who] though he was rich, yet for [our] sakes he became poor, so that [we] through his poverty might become rich" (2 Cor. 8:9).

Service: the exercise of priesthood—In Christ, believers are made not only children of God but also priests—a "royal priesthood" (1 Pet. 2:9), "a kingdom and priests to serve our God, and . . . reign on the earth" (Rev. 5:10). As priests we are called to a mediatorial function, bringing the grace and blessings of God to others. This we do through service.

Yet service has its own danger, for the more effectively we serve, the more likely we are to be rewarded with honor, position, and property. The comment of the master in the parable of the talents, "Well done, good and faithful servant! You have been faithful with a few things; I will put you in charge of many things" (Matt. 25:21, 23), is no fabrication of Christ's. It reflects not only God's response to faithful spiritual service but also the world's response to faithful material service. Good workers rise through the ranks; bad ones don't.

Not that it's dangerous to be rewarded with honor, position, and property. No, the danger is that we will make those, not gratitude and love, the driving motives behind our service. That way lies sycophancy, fawning, toadyism. The difference between servanthood and servility is more than a matter of spelling. Whoever serves for the sake of preferment makes himself vulnerable to every temptation to forsake right to get might, to abandon the good for the sake of the goods, to behave dishonorably to gain honor. Christian servants must remember that our priesthood is royal and so must do nothing unbecoming the royalty displayed in Christ's service.

This doesn't mean, however, that we should do no service on which the world looks with contempt. Jesus made foot washing—a task of the lowliest household servant—the pattern for our servanthood (see John 13:1-17). The motive underlying our service, not necessarily the act itself, makes the difference. A Fortune 500 corporation's president is guilty of sycophancy if he runs his company solely with the aim of currying favor with the board of directors, while the janitor cleaning a gymnasium's restrooms is performing royal service if he does it "with sincerity of heart, . . . not only to win [his employers'] favor when their eye is on [him], but like [a slave] of Christ, doing the will of God from [his] heart" (Eph. 6:5-6).

There is no obvious and foolproof way to discern, by looking at outward actions, whether our motives are right or wrong. The same deeds may flow from diverse incentives. Christians must pursue economic (and all other) goals not as ends in themselves but as means of fulfilling our calling as sons and priests of God, a calling to lead through service.

When the world's systems call us to pursue wealth, power, or honor as an end in itself rather than a means of bringing more of this world into submission to God's gracious rule or of acquiring more tools with which to serve others, they tempt us to abuse our princely calling as sons of God. When they call us to serve for the sake of personal advancement rather than as a grateful, loving response to God's grace or as a means of bestowing grace on others, they tempt us to abuse our calling to serve as priests.

Our gratitude for God's grace should fuel in us a love for others that reaches out to them in selfless service. Ultimately, quietly examining our hearts in prayer will be of more use to us in the world of God's business than reading any number of books on success or attending any number of motivational seminars. We do well to heed the wisdom of these words: "Whoever wants to become great among you must be your servant, and whoever wants to be first must be your slave" (Matt. 20:26-27).

EDITOR'S PERSPECTIVE

The first chapter of this section concerned itself with God's external incentives—rewards and punishments—which are clearly set forth in Scripture. Their natural benefits are easily discerned in the world where comparisons are made between those economic systems that employ these incentives properly and those that do not. That incentives need to be external when one is not spiritually discerning should make good sense to those of us who understand things of the Spirit, because the natural (fallen and unregenerate) man can focus on and discern only those things that appeal to the flesh and temporal appetites (see 1 Cor. 2:14). All managing and governing authorities must approach their followers in a way that allows them to understand and respond to directives. We can call for certain behavior and offer rewards for appropriate responses, but we cannot, at will, call into being specific attitudes and motives.

For example, the Law was given at Mount Sinai as a body of commandments that could be understood as calling for specific external behavior and that were to be administered under a reward-and-punishment system (which many people soon limited to the letters on the stone tablets—"letter of the law"), but the commands could not be required to be spiritually understood so that persons would automatically respond to them according to the "spirit of the law"—the law written on our hearts by the Spirit. Christ's Sermon on the Mount makes it very clear that the letter and the spirit of the law can be made into something very different from each other, which was never God's intent. Furthermore, a nation of people is a mixed group, with some possessing an old "fleshly" nature and some a new "spiritual" nature, so the common denominator by which everybody must be approached is through the external demands, embodying rewards and punishments.

Cal Beisner insists that a free market economic system must be allowed to operate, even with its many imperfections that result from our finitude and sin nature, because those who govern cannot accomplish in their small numbers what the entire group can for the greatest benefit of all precisely because they have innate limitations. He rejects the idea that people should foster controlled economic systems, and he also rejects the presumed wisdom in developing a mixed market economy where there is a kind of partnership between the private and the public sectors. The problem with the latter notion is, he says, that those who govern have an inherent power advantage that will eventually dominate and bring forth a controlled economy—apart from God's restraining grace. He does, however, correctly acknowledge that the state has the only biblically authorized monopoly on the use of force to prohibit, prevent, and punish persons who violate human rights by transgressing the Sixth, Seventh, Eighth, and Ninth Commandments (murder, adultery, stealing, and bearing false witness). He further asserts that the government can use its power to tax and provide for public goods and services like highways, streetlights, and other public protection and safety concerns that flow from Exodus 20:13, 22:6, and Deuteronomy 22:8, but apart from actions like these, Beisner would exclude government intervention in the marketplace altogether.

Yet even people with world views that are compatible with Cal Beisner's do not agree on how far government should go in regulating health and safety measures (e.g., the high tech chemical industry) in an effort to avoid any long-run violations of the Sixth Commandment regarding the taking of life. Scripture not only gives us the prohibition concerning murder, but it also calls for the elders (state) to redress even unintended but, nevertheless, real injury to innocent parties. So where on the continuum of prohibition and prevention should the government be allowed to operate in regulating industrial standards pertaining to health and safety? Is it only right for the state to act after someone is injured, or should it act in a preventive manner by establishing certain regulations?

Chapter 9, which is devoted to a discussion of the individual's attitudes and motives, deals beautifully with the Scripture's discourse on the inner man and the internal drives and responses we all find in ourselves. All Christians, being mildly schizophrenic as we struggle to control our old nature and allow our new nature to dominate, should have little trouble identifying with the content of this chapter. Our author points out what everyone in Christ longs to have created by God in himself or herself: the ability to respond in perfect love to Christ's will, manifesting a godly attitude and spirit. As His children we long to be more Christlike.

These two chapters strike a marvelous balance in portraying the biblical tension that exists when discussing external incentives and internal motivations, and when seeking to understand which kind of incentive is necessary for the operation of a biblically consonant economic system and what kind of inner attitudes and motives the individual must ultimately come to grips with.

The editor wants to return now, though, to the thornier issue of how the government should relate to the economic system so that both are consonant with God's revealed will. The editor has arrived at a perspective on this issue that some people believe is *pragmatic*. For many Christians, the very concept of being pragmatic is antithetical to their notion of discovering and being guided by God's precepts and biblical principles, the very objective of this entire series of books. Pragmatism can smack of compromise and expediency and of being unprincipled to those who fix their eyes on the normative "ends" God establishes. The editor acknowledges this as a possible consequence (but not an automatic outcome) of pragmatism. Therefore, as we seek more godly economic, social, and political systems in a fallen world, neither compromise nor working for partial victories along the way is ruled out.

Christians are *never* to compromise for even a moment with sin in our character or personal behavior. We are to do battle with our sin nature whenever and wherever it emerges in our lives. This was the intent and force of Christ's teaching when He said,

> "If your right eye makes you stumble, tear it out, and throw it from you; for it is better for you that one of the parts of your body perish, than for your whole body to be thrown into hell. And if your right hand makes you stumble, cut it off, and throw it from you." (Matt. 5:29-30)

Sin in our personal character and behavior is to be treated as cancer of the soul and attacked with prayer and every other godly means of getting rid of it. Furthermore, Christians are *never* to put a stumbling block in front of a neighbor or intentionally tempt a neighbor to do anything ungodly.

But even when fully believing all these things, Christians are still required to work in a pluralistic world with people who have very different world views, and we have a responsibility to try to bring the institutions in our society into conformity with God's standards while we maintain our personal holiness. We are to work in the political and economic arenas with those who do not love and seek God's ends, and we are to do it in a manner that leads everybody in the community to higher ground by (1) appealing to their prudential self-interest in a way that is respectful of everyone's rights and carries with it the best long-term interest of the community so that we can move toward God's ultimate intentions *without* insisting that we must go to the "perfect end" in one step, or not at all; and (2) explaining things in a way that makes them both understandable and acceptable on mutually beneficial and prudential grounds to the pluralistic body.

This is not sinful or substandard Christian conduct. To the contrary! Proverbs teaches us that "the heart of the wise teaches his mouth, and adds persuasiveness to his lips" (16:23); "the tongue of the wise makes knowledge acceptable" (15:2); and "I, wisdom, dwell with prudence, and I find knowledge and discretion" (8:12). In this context, to be pragmatic means that we are to seek God's ends in the world by godly means and wisdom, but we can be willing to go forward one step at a time, accepting what can be gained, without apologizing for what cannot be immediately accomplished. It also means that we are to seek every opportunity to advance God's cause by speaking up for God's standards in a way that makes prudential self-interest what it is in the Bible—wisdom! There is an appropriate self-interest.

Whether we like it or not, we live in a mixed economy with a lot of freedom of choice at the point of consumption, somewhat less at the point of production, and considerable wealth redistribution. There is, though, a growing concern among the general population about the long-term impact of high technology on the environment and on human health and safety. The news media also often present us with illustrations of bad ethics in both the private and the public sectors. In addition, individuals frequently feel they are at an inherent disadvantage when trying to resolve differences between themselves and wealthy corporate entities. They believe they will fare better with an umpire. Who will see that equity prevails, or how will it prevail?

Then what is the solution as we seek a balance between the free choices of individuals and the need for constructive restraint in the marketplace so that the greater interests of everyone can be protected? There is no static or absolute solution per se. A solution implies a final resolution, and none will be available before Christ's second coming. But it does no violence to Scripture to take Christ's words to His disciples, "Behold, I send you out as sheep in the midst of wolves; therefore be *shrewd [wise, mindful, prudent]* as serpents, and innocent as doves" (Matt. 10:16, emphasis added), and say that we should apply this directive in the marketplace and in government. What can Christians do or support if we are to realistically advance a positive change in the political and economic environments so that government remains within its biblical bounds and those who work in the economic arena exercise more self-control?

We can revamp our thinking about personal accountability in the economic and political arenas because for over one hundred years we have allowed those who rule (manage and govern) to hide behind the legal and *personified* skirts of the corporate or public entities they lead or work for. To illustrate, persons who manage our very largest corporations have functioned with very little personal accountability for their personal decisions so long as the internal board of directors and the external financial community were content with the "bottom line." The corporations, not the managers, have traditionally been held financially and legally accountable for any harm the corporations may have caused, or laws they may have broken, even when such problems have emanated from incompetency and willful disobedience.

Holding a nonmoral entity legally, financially, and morally accountable for its actions seems rather strange. This insulation from personal consequential accountability has allowed managers (the true moral agents of these powerful economic entities) to act without the appropriate fear of personal culpability, and the financial community has had little incentive to worry about institutional conduct so long as the financial reports were healthy. The historic absence of personal consequential accountability in the corporate environment has only encouraged nonrestraint by many managers, and that has resulted, on many occasions, in the display of the worst aspects of our fallen nature.

The ideas expressed by our many authors that support a free market economy are biblically sound and point us in the *direction* we are to face and work for in the political and economic arenas, but *until there is a great deal more personal consequential accountability for every manager and every government leader, and their subordinates,* the ideal concept of maintaining a free marketplace with a healthy balance between those who manage and those who govern will remain an elusive goal.

SECTION E

WHO IS RESPONSIBLE FOR THE POOR?

Scripture is clear that we will have the poor with us always (see Matt. 26:11). It is also clear that we are not only responsible for our own lives but also subject to God's ordained duties regarding our neighbors. We need to remember at least four significant consequences of man's fall as we seriously consider our responsibilities toward the poor. First, we are fallen and therefore pervert, unintentionally and intentionally, God's expressed will in every facet of our lives. Second, God has established governments as instruments of His common grace for the sake of His children to constrain the growth of evil that so easily befalls those not governed by God. Government is better than anarchy. Third, corrupted aspects of our character reflecting our fallen nature foster insecurity, procrastination, sloth, and other debilitating habits that can materially affect our families, communities, and economic environment. These in turn give rise to both personal and institutional problems that can interfere with the creation of wealth and its fair distribution. Fourth, the imperfect allocation of wealth in a fallen world contributes to the establishment of a class of people known as the poor. But who are the poor? What causes poverty? What is the best way to address the plight of the poor? Who is responsible for helping them? These and similar questions are addressed in the next two chapters.

Many biblical passages focus on the poor, but Christians frequently do not understand their personal responsibilities toward them. And while conservative, evangelical Christians are often negative about governmental assumption of many responsibilities for the poor, the true nature of their concern is not always easy to discern. They have been quick to criticize the specific programs created by those who govern, but they have not always

207

offered concrete alternatives to alleviate the economic burdens of the poor. Such negativism can be construed as a cop-out for an uncaring heart. Surely the more Christians endorse the kind of thinking expounded by the scholars contributing to this series of books (such as the biblical truth regarding our need for opportunities to exercise free moral choice in the economic environment), the more we should conclude that we have some genuine responsibilities toward the poor.

The tension, however, between the correct role for individuals regarding the poor and the biblically sound role for those who govern remains an illusive balance to define and delineate. To help us with this issue, T. M. Moore and Joseph A. McKinney set before us two distinct approaches to helping the poor: "The Private Sector and the Poor," and "The Public Sector and the Poor."

In preparing his chapter, T. M. Moore added a note that so clearly presents his objectives, the editor decided to rescue it from the end notes and let the reader see firsthand what Moore desires to accomplish. He wrote,

> Readers looking to find in this paper a Biblical theology of the poor will be disappointed. This paper looks at the problem of poverty in our society from a problematic perspective, that is, from the viewpoint that poverty is something to which the Church must address itself in order to fulfill its mission of bringing Christ to the lost. If this paper were to take the form of a Biblical theology of the poor, it would probably follow an outline something like that suggested by the two Scriptural quotes and the citation from Ronald Nash with which the paper begins.
>
> Poverty is a problem inherent in the human situation, intimately linked to our condition as sinful creatures. Like all other conditions that human beings may suffer—misery, depression, fear, doubt, oppression, etc.—the presence of poverty must motivate the people of God to action in the name of Christ and His love for lost men and women in their sin. In the specific case of poverty, however, we must not hold out utopian expectations of ridding the world of this blight —any more than we would boast of eradicating fear and depression among men. This is the talk of politics, not of those who have a realistic Biblical world view.
>
> Yet we cannot ignore poverty, as Scripture makes abundantly clear. In seeking to overcome the effects of poverty, the Church must begin within its own household, caring for its own poor and destitute as a first priority in this kind of ministry. Yet, for the sake of the

Gospel, and to exemplify the love of Christ, the Church must make bold to follow His example and find ways of addressing the problem of poverty, beginning in its own Jerusalem and Judea, and reaching out even to the uttermost parts of the earth from there.

Mr. Moore never argues that Christians have responsibilities regarding the poor; he assumes this fact is so biblically evident that it does not need to be argued. So he carefully defines the differences between the "private" and the "public" sectors, and differentiates between the types of the poor. The type of poverty one experiences generally points to its cause, which tells us in large measure how we can help the poor help themselves to emerge from their plight. (The principle of "helping people help themselves" is fundamental to a biblical concept of economic help.) Mr. Moore then emphasizes ways to mobilize the Christian community to meet the needs of the poor.

Some readers may be troubled that Moore did not discuss the forms of unjust discrimination that have plagued our society and contributed to the pitiful situation of certain individuals, families, and larger groups. The editor would point out, though, that such an analysis would have been an excursion into a specific problem area that goes far beyond the scope of Mr. Moore's assignment. Such a discussion, while extremely profitable and appropriate in a broader and more comprehensive work, would have been a distraction in the context of this particular book—and the topic is to be covered in a later book. Furthermore, such a discussion would have absorbed too much of the space available for defining the types of poor and would have reduced Moore's effectiveness in focusing on what he considers to be the biggest problem related to the Christian community's involvement with the poor—finding ways to constructively mobilize Christians so they will be properly motivated and drawn into the work of caring for the poor.

T. M. Moore believes we need to carefully define *who* the poor are and identify the cause of their personal poverty. He also believes we need to determine *what* we should and can do to help the poor so that we are biblically wise as we provide help that does not enable those being helped to become inappropriately dependent on the helper. The big challenge, as Moore sees it, is not an intellectual one related to any lack of knowledge regarding our duty to help the poor, but a volitional problem of getting people to do what they know they ought to do. The editor agrees. It is almost always more difficult to get people to act righteously than it is to get them to understand righteous conduct.

Other readers may also note that neither author in this section points to or addresses any structural problem that might exist in our mixed economic system, or that would be present in a free market system, that can or does give rise to economic injustices. The editor perceives one such problem, which will be discussed in the "Editor's Perspective" following chapter 11.

CHAPTER 10

THE PRIVATE SECTOR AND THE POOR

T. M. Moore

T. M. Moore is President of Chesapeake Theological Seminary in Baltimore, Maryland. He is a graduate of the University of Wisconsin (B.A.) and Reformed Theological Seminary (M.Div., M.C.E.). He has pursued doctoral studies in systematic theology and educational leadership. He is an ordained minister in the Presbyterian Church in America, and is the author of four popular books, numerous scholarly articles, and a wide range of essays, editorials, and reviews. He writes and produces a daily radio editorial and is much in demand as a conference speaker and workshop leader.

"For the poor you have with you always." (Matt. 26:11)

However, there shall be no poor among you, since the LORD will surely bless you in the land which the LORD your God is giving you as an inheritance to possess, if only you listen obediently to the voice of the LORD your God, to observe carefully all this commandment which I am commanding you today. (Deut. 15:4-5)

One of the two sides of Christian social concern *is* the Christian's clear obligation to care and to be concerned about the poor and oppressed and to do what he can on their behalf. But the other dimension of Christian social concern adds the stipulation that if a Christian wishes to make pronouncements on complex social, economic and political issues, he also has a duty to become informed about those issues.[1]

INTRODUCTION

A biblical approach to economic matters will certainly scrutinize the issue of poverty. What are its causes? What forms does it take? How is it to be addressed in a just society?

In this chapter I examine the problem of poverty from the perspective of the private sector and its responsibility to the poor. My purpose is to try to understand the causes of poverty in a society and then to consider the role of one segment of the private sector in responding to this challenge.

This discussion is especially timely for at least three reasons. First, there is a growing sense that the programs implemented by governments at all levels in the name of the War on Poverty have, in fact, defected to the enemy and are only making matters worse. This claim, put forward most forcefully by Charles Murray,[2] is coming to be conceded even by those initially skeptical of Murray's conclusions and scornful of his methodology.[3] Myron Magnet aptly summarizes it as he observes,

> The underclass's entrenched culture of dependence, its inability from one generation to another to participate in the larger society, the stunted development of its human potential—all this was fostered by the welfare system and the War on Poverty.[4]

The growing lack of confidence in governmental efforts to eradicate poverty has spawned new investigations and publications addressing the possibilities for welfare reform. Thus, in the second place, the floor seems to have been opened for discussion, and new voices may have the opportunity to be heard in the process of deciding where, as a society, we are to go from here in seeking to resolve this critical issue. As one panel of scholars puts it, finding solutions to the problem of poverty "will require working together as a national community to increase the numbers of self-reliant citizens."[5]

In the third place, the numbers of the poor continue to increase. This is true of some sectors of the poor more than of others, to be sure; however, it is among the most vulnerable of the poor population that the ranks seem to be growing at alarming rates. Most notably, the rise in single-parent, female-headed households puts at risk a whole generation of children who may never know anything other than the experience of living in poverty.[6]

This is why this chapter's subject is so important. What is the responsibility of the private sector to the poor? Are there obligations incumbent on it? Has a door of meaningful opportunity been opened? How shall we understand this question, and in what directions shall we proceed if the private sector is to make a meaningful contribution to the resolution of this crisis?

Particularly, it would seem, the current debate over what to do about the poor presents an unprecedented opportunity to one segment of the private sector, namely, the evangelical Christian community. In many ways we have become a community without a mission. We have proven inept and relatively ineffectual in the political arena. The nationally publicized scandals surrounding certain sectors of the evangelical community have reflected adversely on us all. For over a generation now, we have exhausted ourselves in new programs, new buildings, new and enormously expensive media ventures, new experiences of the reality of our faith, new sorties into such cultural fields as education and music, and new hopes of revival in our nation and under our leadership only to watch as our society has continued its downward slide into materialism, relativism, and ethical uncertainty. Our credibility and our self-image have suffered.[7] And it may well be that the current discussions about the poor can lead to our rediscovering our mission and reasserting our presence in society in a way that can have long-term, beneficial results for us all.

I want to address the question before us in three stages. First, I will examine some definitions of the relevant terms—the private sector, the poor, and the notion of responsibility. This section will narrow the focus of my discussion. Next, I will concentrate on the biblical teaching concerning the Christian community's responsibility for the poor. Much of this section will be on the order of summaries of the work of others since several very thorough and convincing treatises have been produced by members of the evangelical community in recent years. Finally, I will consider how to mobilize the Christian community to undertake its God-given responsibility for the poor. This section will take more of the form of a strategy for getting started and developing a workable plan than of describing in great detail the models, programs, and paradigms on which others have elaborated so fully.

My general conclusion is that the time is right for every member, every family, and every church in the evangelical community to undertake some responsibility for the poor—if only in their immediate locale. The main problems to overcome are motivational, educational, and organizational in nature. As such, they can be surmounted, though not without vision, patience, determination, and grace.

DEFINITIONS

First, what do we mean by *the private sector*? The private sector can perhaps be best understood in contrast to the public, or governmental, sector. It is the segment of society that undertakes its affairs on the basis of private initiative, as opposed to the coercion of legal strictures or mandates. The private sector is motivated by things other than legal requirements, governmental constraints, or bureaucratic regulations. It is comprised of free persons acting individually or in free association with other free persons through a wide range of vehicles. These might include churches, social and service organizations, voluntary societies, charitable and educational organizations, and businesses and corporations.

Clearly, the private sector as I have described it is much too large a subject to deal with effectively as it relates to its responsibility to the poor, at least within the scope of this brief study. We must narrow our focus to arrive at some meaningful conclusions for a particular segment of the private sector in the hope that what we discover may also have some relevance for other segments. For our purposes, we will limit our discussion to the evangelical Christian community, specifically, individual Christians of an evangelical persuasion, their families, and their churches.

Second, we need to specify who we have in mind when we discuss *the poor*. Conflicting studies and reports have arrived at differing conclusions about who the poor are, where they are to be found, and how many of them there are.

These studies do seem to agree, however, on the need to differentiate among the poor. That is, there are several categories of poor people, and they have arrived at their condition through a variety of causes.[8] Michael Harrington asserts, "There is no such thing as poverty; there are *poverties.*"[9] Without a clear differentiation of the kinds of poverty, it will be difficult to know exactly how to respond.[10]

One way to get at this task of differentiation is to examine some causes of poverty as they have been identified in the literature. These causes include (1) the psychological, such as one's outlook on life and the future;[11] (2) the physically disabled who cannot care for themselves; (3) the moral, reflecting such causes as (*a*) the lack of an adequate work ethic,[12] (*b*) the presence of oppression or injustice,[13] and (*c*) persistence in social behavior not conducive to personal or economic independence;[14] (4) the societal, which can include changes in a society's ethos[15] as well as in its economic structures;[16] and (5) the political, when poverty results from unwise or ill-conceived political and governmental strategies.[17]

Thus, any effort to define the poor that focuses only on an economic "bottom line," though it may be helpful in locating those people in our communities most in need of our assistance, can be misleading when it comes to prescribing solutions. Merely throwing money at the problem cannot solve it. Instead, a careful attempt should be made to identify the causes of the particular poverty to which an individual or a family has fallen victim. Only when this has been painstakingly researched and the cause carefully established can we begin to know how to treat the problem effectively. The individual who is poor because of a poor self-image will need a different kind of help from the one who is experiencing a temporary period of impoverishment due to the loss of a job. In the same way, the individual whose poverty is the result of a cavalier attitude toward work will need to be approached differently from the person who is suffering from a permanent physical disability. (We shall have more to say about defining the poor when we look at the biblical teaching concerning the kinds of poverties that we can expect to encounter.)

This brings us, in the third place, to the idea of *responsibility*. For our purposes it is particularly helpful to have narrowed the scope of our discussion to the evangelical Christian community; here we can reach a ready consensus concerning the idea of responsibility and how we may go about determining its parameters for the question at hand. We can do this precisely because the evangelical community recognizes the Bible as the authoritative and inspired Word of God, which speaks definitively on this and all other matters of human life and interest. Evangelicals understand personal and corporate responsibility, in all aspects of social and personal interaction, to have been delineated in the Bible. For evangelical Christians, therefore, responsibility is what the Bible describes as our duty before God—as servants of one another, stewards over our resources and opportunities, witnesses to the truth of God, and equippers of others for the work to which God calls us.

Evangelical Christians should expect the Bible to instruct and guide them in discerning how they should respond to the problem of poverty in their communities, their nation, and the world. This being true, therefore, we turn now to consider what the Bible has to say about the poor and how the members of the evangelical community are to address the problem of poverty.

BIBLICAL TEACHING ABOUT
OUR RESPONSIBILITY FOR THE POOR

George Grant tells us, "According to Scripture, the poor are divided between the 'oppressed' and the 'sluggardly.'" The oppressed, he says, "are the objects of God's special care," and "the sluggardly are the objects of His special condemnation."[18]

But who are these oppressed? How shall we recognize them, and what distinguishes them from the sluggardly as objects of our special care and attention? David Chilton groups those most vulnerable to oppression in two classes, widows and orphans.[19] Under the former category Chilton refers to immigrants and aliens who, having just arrived in our communities, often do not possess sufficient resources to make it on their own. Under the latter category Chilton refers to those who, bereft of the basic support and provision mechanisms that the family can supply, are found to be in want and, thus, in need of assistance.

At least two other categories of oppressed people may be identified. For example, some individuals are poor because of disease or other physical ailment. The Gerasene demoniac and the woman with the flow of blood would be two examples of people impoverished physically, the one because of spiritual oppression, the other because of illness (see Mark 5:1-15, 21-34). Moreover, some people are subjected to poverty because of political or economic oppression (see Amos 2:6-8). These biblical categories fit rather nicely with several of those cited above as having been identified in the contemporary literature on our subject.

Then there are the ones Grant calls the sluggardly. Chilton considers this group "irresponsible" and correctly observes that "biblical charity . . . *never subsidizes irresponsibility.*"[20] This category may correspond to that described above as persons having become poor because of some moral deficiency or change in the social ethos.

Thus, bringing our biblical categories of the poor together with those identified by the literature on the subject, we may propose two headings as follows:

CAUSES OF POVERTY

Oppression	Sluggardliness
Psychological or spiritual	Moral deficiency
Physical	Societal
Societal	
Political	

Before we proceed, we should observe that the Bible clearly indicates that the poor have a responsibility for themselves, especially those who are not hampered by some form of oppression. Both Grant and Chilton agree in discerning this responsibility of the poor for themselves in their discussions of gleaning.[21] Grant enumerates three principles deriving from the biblical story of Ruth that concern the role of the poor in taking responsibility for their own deliverance.[22] He observes, in the first place, that "recipients of Biblical charity must be diligent workers, unless entirely disabled." The privilege of gleaning unharvested segments of a farmer's field also entailed the responsibility of making the effort to provide for oneself by the labor of one's hands. Related to this is the second principle: "Biblical charity is privately dispensed by the landowners, not by an over-arching state institution." Although segments of each farmer's land were to be left unharvested by mandate of the Law of God, the produce of those lands remained the possession of the farmers until diligent gleaners reaped it. Thus, the third principle is "that Biblical charity is discriminatory." It comes only to individuals who are willing to accept responsibility for their plight and to labor in an effort to improve themselves.

This concept has its modern parallels, as Grant points out, in such organizations as Goodwill Industries, the Salvation Army, and other such groups that "collect discarded commodities and then repair them for sale by using unemployed and handicapped workers."[23] Thus, we must not allow the agricultural context of the original setting to obscure the concept's possible applications today. To the extent that evangelical churches can help to support and further such works in their communities, they will be taking an important step in helping the poor begin to assume their responsibility for overcoming their impoverished condition.

We must now look more closely at the particular responsibility of the evangelical community for the poor. Evangelical churches have faithfully attended to this role in the past, beginning with the care of their own poor and extending to the larger community thereafter.[24] Grant summarizes the biblical teaching on our responsibility by saying,

As Christians, we are commanded to show charity and to exercise compassion to both the oppressed poor and the sluggardly poor—to both the temporarily dispossessed and the chronically dispossessed. It is not enough simply to acknowledge their existence. It is not enough to be able to make distinctions between them. It is not enough to compare government studies and Bible verses. We must respond. We must respond charitably.[25]

In addition to the concept of gleaning, Chilton cites three other ways in which Christians may undertake to help the poor: through the tithe, through lending for investment, and through slavery.[26] This last item will no doubt raise serious concerns, and Chilton is careful to define what he understands the Bible to mean by this term. A close examination of his conclusions would be instructive, although it is beyond the scope of this present study.

Grant does not mention slavery, but he does have a great deal to say about how individual Christians, Christian families, and Christian churches can use their tithes and other resources to reach out to the poor. This order of beginning to reach out to the poor coincides well with Moynihan's recommendation for strengthening American families as a means of addressing the problem of poverty. He remarks,

> A credible family policy will insist that responsibility begins with the individual, then the family, and only then the community, and in the first instance the smaller and nearer rather than the greater and more distant community.[27]

Grant believes that the mandate for helping the poor in the name of Jesus Christ begins with individuals:

> The testimony of Scripture is clear: all of us who are called by His Name must walk in love (Ephesians 5:2). We must exercise compassion (2 Corinthians 1:3-4). We must struggle for justice and secure mercy, comfort, and liberty for men, women, and children everywhere (Zechariah 7:8-10).[28]

This will involve making our time, energies, and resources available on a more determined basis to address the problems of poverty in our communities. Grant's book offers many helpful ideas about how we may begin.[29] The variety of activities and projects that may be undertaken by Christian families and their churches is limited only by their imaginations, and a growing body of reports, news accounts, and analyses should ensure that those imaginations continue to be stimulated.[30]

At the same time the Christian community should bear in mind that other segments of the private sector can and must join in the struggle to help the poor. For example, American corporations donated $4.5 billion to private charities in 1985. One report observes, "In fields as diverse as education, hunger, housing and youth employment, there are scores of successful examples of corporate participation in problem solving."[31] Christians can and should enlist the aid of local businesses. Since local businesses have a vested interest in an economically strong community, it is to their advantage to work toward long-term solutions to the problem of poverty among persons in their area.

Finally, the Christian community—as well as the rest of the private sector—must labor to see that government does not exceed its bounds in attempting to care for the poor. The controversy over the success of existing government programs of development and relief warrants caution in arguing for more such programs. In addition, government economic policies—such as exorbitant taxation, unreasonable regulations. and other forms of intervention in the marketplace—can contribute to the increase of poverty.[32] Thus, the Christian community must exercise vigilance so that unwise or ill-conceived government activities do not exacerbate the problem of poverty in the name of attempting to alleviate it.

George Grant has aptly summarized the responsibility of the Christian community to the poor:

> Charity to the oppressed involves loosening "the bonds of wicked-ness," undoing "the bonds of the yoke," and letting "the captives go free" (Isaiah 58:6). It involves dividing bread with the hungry, bring-ing the homeless poor into safe shelter and covering the naked (Isaiah 58:7). It involves transforming poverty into productivity by any and every means at our disposal.
>
> Charity to the sluggardly, on the other hand, involves *admoni-tion* and *reproof* (2 Thessalonians 3:15; Proverbs 13:18). It involves a reorientation to reality through the preaching of the Gospel (John 8:32). The compassionate and loving response to a sluggard is to *warn* him. . . .Charity to the sluggardly equips and enables him to move *beyond* dependency, beyond entitlement.
>
> Christians have the responsibility—the inescapable respon-sibility—to exercise both kinds of charity with all diligence and zeal.[33]

I turn now to the question of how to mobilize the Christian community to carry out that responsibility as a vital part of its mission in the world.

MOBILIZING THE CHRISTIAN COMMUNITY

Through many means, individual Christians, Christian families, and evan-gelical Christian churches can carry out their God-given responsibility to meet the needs of the poor. To attempt to describe and analyze all the programs, vehicles, models, and other activities that have proved effective in this effort would take more time than this study can allow and would merely rehearse briefly what others have explained in great detail in their works.

For our purposes the point is not so much *what* we shall do to carry out our responsibility to the poor, but *how* we shall begin to draw the members of the evangelical Christian community into this work. With so much to do and so many opportunities and proven approaches available to us, it would seem that, if only we could find some way of motivating and educating the saints to their responsibility, getting them organized for effective action would be the least of our concerns. Because so few churches seem to have taken caring for the poor as a priority for their local ministries, I believe that the motivational and educational gap has yet to be effectively bridged for most members of the evangelical community. It is to this challenge that I shall primarily address myself in this concluding section.

In the first place, having a vision for this labor as central to their mission in the world seems to be essential to involving Christians, their families, and their local churches in the work of caring for the poor. Throughout the Bible, the Lord led His people in acts of courageous obedience by means of a vision of how their obedience fit into the larger scenario of His plan for their lives. In the Old Testament, Jehovah continuously spread before His people a vision replete with promises and the hope of a new and more glorious day. In the New Testament the Lord Jesus Christ exhorted His disciples to faith and obedience by means of the vision of the Kingdom of God. The purpose of each vision was to provide the people of God with a context for their obedience that transcended space and time, was larger than themselves individually or corporately, and would catch them up in a work of permanence that had God's enduring blessing. Something like this kind of vision needs to be projected for the people of God today when it comes to the work with the poor.

The secular literature on our subject would seem to be in agreement, albeit from a different point of view. The Working Seminar of the American Enterprise Institute has observed,

> *The battle against poverty is a long one.* . . . An effort to reduce poverty is not a twenty-year task; it is never ending. It must go on steadily, constantly relying on and appealing to the capacity of free persons to make successful choices.[34]

Concerning this matter George Grant comments, "Change will come when we are faithful in motivating others to right action through right thinking. We must instill vision in those who see no future."[35] This would be true for the poor in their distress as well as for the people of God in their frustration over the way to take effective action on behalf of the poor. And if, as Rev. Eugene Boutilier is quoted as saying, "our motivation is not just to provide three hots and a cot, but to change lives,"[36] we must articulate a vision for this work that will affect the lives of those who are to be served and those who must serve. David Chilton, writing from a postmillennial perspective, attaches the "conquest of poverty" to the eschatological vision of Christianity becoming the universal religion and the Law of God holding sway in all the nations of the earth.[37]

But it is not necessary to be a postmillennialist to claim the promises and power of God for carrying out a work that has been so clearly and consistently assigned to the evangelical Church and so faithfully carried out by our forebears. Rather, it takes men and women, pastors and laypeople, committed to understanding the teaching of the Bible concerning our responsibility for the poor and then beginning to find ways to expound and explain that responsibility in meaningful and urgent terms to the rest of the members of our local churches. Unless concern for the poor makes itself felt in our preaching, our leading of Bible studies, our dinner conversations, our individual and corporate prayers, and all the other activities of the local church and its families, it is not likely that a vision for effectively addressing the needs and opportunities before us will ever come to light.

As part of that vision-projecting activity, we need to think in terms of some attainable goals for reaching out to the poor. Each church must attempt to define the results that it would hope to achieve through such activity, and each family and each individual must be willing to undertake some particular activity or activities toward meeting those goals.

One initial goal would be to create a working group to research the biblical and social parameters of the task and to initiate the organizational work of mobilizing the church. This step can be undertaken by a layperson or a pastor who perceives the importance of this effort as a result of his or her own growth and study. This working group could create several task forces: one to research the biblical teaching on our responsibility to the poor; one to visit the Christian bookstores and to write to theological libraries to discover the resources available for furthering this study; and one to contact local agencies to evaluate the extent of the problem in the local area and to determine what is being done already. Yet another task force could write to Christian relief agencies—such as World Vision or Samaritan's Purse—to find out how Christians in other parts of the world are meeting the needs of the poor.

From the findings of such a group a vision could emerge that would suggest additional goals for an ongoing ministry to involve every individual and each family of the church on behalf of the poor. Some goals might be educational—to include excerpts from Christian books or passages of

Scripture in the church newsletter or the weekly bulletin; to sponsor a Sunday school class on ministering to the poor; to purchase and make available through the church library books on the subject such as these mentioned in this study. Educational efforts should strive to motivate others in the church to share in the burden of the working group and to show them how they also might become involved in ministering to the poor. Along with these educational goals the working group could give encouragement and assistance to individuals and groups in the church as they put in place the various ministries and programs that will begin to reach the poor in their distress.

A second goal for such a working group could be to lead the church in working for a new community consensus on caring for the poor. For the most part the communities of our land have been content to let governmental and charitable agencies cope with the problems of the poor. There does not appear to be an overriding sense of individual responsibility for those in need among the population at large.

However, since the church is to function as salt and light in its community, it must believe that it can be used of God to effect a new consensus, if only at the local level, about the problems of the poor. A church can begin to do this by enlisting other churches in the effort to assist the poor and then, as an evangelical community, by calling on other local institutions to do their part in motivating and leading the citizenry to care for those who are in distress around them. It is clear that government, television, newspapers, universities, the schools, religious institutions, the cinema, popular singers, and neighborhood organizations do not leave the public unaffected by the behaviors they glamorize and the behaviors they mock. Such institutions shape the set of life stories, symbols, and images that teach a population the sorts of behaviors expected of them.[38]

If the local church can catalyze the rest of the evangelical community to reach out to such institutions, it may be able, over the long haul, to spark the whole community of which it is a part to take more responsibility for the poor among them. Beginning media campaigns, having personal meetings with corporate leaders, leading efforts to affect public school curricula and extracurricular activities, and undertaking more strategic involvement in service clubs would be a few examples. A speaker's bureau could be created and made available to local clubs and gatherings. Literature addressed to the needs and opportunities of the local community could be distributed. And community-wide projects could be initiated by evangelicals working with community leaders.

The forging of a new consensus on the poor might seem an impossible task. Yet it need not be so if we can see it as a generation-spanning, ongoing activity that must become a priority for evangelical churches if this part of their mission is ever to be realized. The American Enterprise Institute's Working Seminar noted,

> Social change has by no means come to an end, and since human beings are not helpless before inexorable forces of either "progress" or "decline," a determined generation can substantially affect the directions of social change.[39]

The remaining question is this: Is the evangelical community willing and able to become such "a determined generation"?

Undoubtedly the greatest contribution that the evangelical community could make to alleviate the distress of the poor would be to enlist them in the battle on their own behalf. The working group of a local church, committed to developing a vision and goals for leading the church in ministry to the poor, must have this as the third segment of its overall strategy, and several critical components may be involved.

First would be the work of evangelism. For the most part, the evangelism undertaken by evangelical churches today can be described as highly selective. Usually it is concentrated on bearing witness as a follow-up to those who have visited our churches or to those who occupy the life-spheres of our church members. The effect is to narrow the arena in which our witness goes forth. Yet Christ has called us to make all the nations—all the peoples of the world—His disciples. Thus, we cannot overlook any of the "people groups" in our communities who have not had the opportunity of hearing the gospel, including the poor.

We must find ways of reaching the poor on their turf. Perhaps the best way would be to make certain that those who become involved in caring for the poor are trained to proclaim the gospel as an integral part of their ministry. To this point we have taught people to evangelize without teaching them what is involved in the whole work of redemption and reconciliation. George Grant states,

> Our evangelism must include sociology as well as salvation; it must include reform and redemption, culture and conversion, a new social order as well as a new birth, a revolution as well as a regeneration. Any other kind of evangelism is short-sighted and woefully impotent. Any other kind of evangelism fails to live up to the high call of the Great Commission.[40]

At the same time, we must not motivate and equip people for ministry to the poor without also teaching them the importance of the gospel of the Kingdom as the only ongoing life context that can effect lasting change in men and women. We must insist that our ministries to the poor be in the name of Christ and be a means of declaring His good news to lost sinners. This we can do without manipulating or otherwise intimidating the poor to accept our ideals as they also accept our bread. Commitment to an evangelistic thrust in our ministries to the poor need not mean that true compassion will be any less in evidence in our work with those who reject the message of God's grace.

A second component of enlisting the poor to help themselves must be in the area of educating and training. This aspect of our outreach must be prepared to address everything from the problems of self-image and illiteracy to those of social protocol, job interviewing and application, and work skills.[41] Further, we must look for ways of giving leadership in ministries to the poor to those who have experienced poverty and who, through their own efforts and work with groups and activities such as those evangelicals will be sponsoring, have overcome their distress and found a new lease on life. Ken Auletta has shown the value of using such people in teaching and equipping roles in his study of the underclass in New York City.[42]

An effective vision and strategy for enlisting the poor will also find ways of incorporating them into the local churches of which we are a part. In the process of recovering from their poverty they will need ongoing support, encouragement, and assistance. If we cannot bring the poor into our midst, including into our homes when appropriate, we cannot expect to be credible to them or anyone else when we claim to be motivated by the love and compassion of Christ. John Miller has shown the power such a "welcoming church" can have in meeting the needs of others. His is a model that many more churches need to emulate.[43]

Finally, the working group must lead the church in a constant effort to monitor governmental activities related to the poor. We must remain mindful that government policies can exacerbate the problem of the poor, albeit quite unintentionally.[44] And although it is perhaps not prudent for a local church to mobilize in opposition to, say, taxation policies that impact negatively on the family and thus threaten to increase the ranks of the poor,[45] we can provide the saints with information and guidelines for making their *individual* concerns known to the appropriate public officials. At the same time, we will want to keep the people of God alert to legislation that promises to promote such things as greater individual responsibility by the poor for their condition.[46]

Evangelical churches that have a vision for mobilizing themselves and their communities on behalf of the poor can make a significant difference in helping the private sector to assume more responsibility for addressing this growing social issue. The failure of government programs over the past two decades has created a golden opportunity for evangelical churches to recapture their sense of mission, to begin to realize their calling to be salt and light in the world, and to regain some credibility for the message of God's grace in Jesus Christ that has been lost. It is my prayer that God might raise up a generation of men and women, laypeople and pastors, who will take upon themselves the responsibility of bringing this challenge and opportunity to the attention of their churches in the days to come.

EDITOR'S REFLECTIONS

Even though T. M. Moore has not attempted to write a biblical theology of the poor, nor held out a utopian idea that poverty can be completely eradicated, he does call the Christian community to obedience in response to God's expressed will concerning the care of persons in need: those who are willing to help themselves and those who cannot help themselves (not those who can but will not help themselves). Moore believes the biggest problems we encounter are motivational, educational, and organizational. Apathy regarding the poor, as he sees it, sends the message, "We don't care about you."

The editor knows that most Christians, even those of very modest means, occasionally wrestle with the question of what they ought to do personally in response to God's call to His children to minister to the poor. I remember doing that very thing some eighteen to twenty years ago. I concluded that I did not know anyone who was poor. (I thought I was isolated from such people because I did not live or work near them.) I was tempted to put the whole matter out of my mind because I saw no specific opportunities to minister open to me. I even wondered if my initial concern for the poor was just an abstract idea reflecting a psychological urge that might be attached to some latent guilt about my general apathy toward the poor. Or was it the prodding of the Spirit of God?

The thought came to me that I should give God the opportunity to speak more directly to me regarding the matter. So rather than merely think about the issue, I prayed! I asked God to show me a specific person to help if He had someone in mind. My prayer was answered so quickly that it practically took my breath away. I was presented with not just one person to help, or even one

226

family, but two. What was I to do? I actually became fearful. The poor, so long as they existed in theory and at a distance, were "safe" to think about, but being confronted with real people, with real needs, meant I had to face my apathetic heart and count the cost—commitment, time, and money.

I already knew the people rather well, but had not thought of them. Furthermore, they were my brothers and sisters in Christ. One was a hard-working janitor, a godly deacon in his church, who earned a minimum wage and had a wife with numerous health problems. He never complained or talked about himself or his family's situation, so I had been blind to his real need for financial counsel and help.

The second person was a widow in her early sixties who bore the full responsibility for the care of her severely retarded sister who was in her fifties. This lady was a paid nursery worker at the church where I was a deacon. I asked the deacons to consider helping her as a true widow (see 1 Tim. 5:3-10). The church treasurer was sent by himself to investigate her plight, and he returned with the report that she did not need help. I later learned that he did not investigate her financial condition but merely walked around in her house and concluded she was not destitute and was, therefore, able to care for herself and her sister. Her social security payments were minimal; she could not adequately meet her food and utility costs.

My wife and I accepted these two families as God's appointed oppor-tunities for us to minister to, pray with, and help financially. They and we have been blessed through the years—"He who gathered much did not have too much, and he who gathered little had no lack" (2 Cor. 8:15; see Exod. 16:18).

The editor would simply add a question at the end of T. M. Moore's chapter: Are we willing to pray and ask the Lord to show us the poor and oppressed that He would have us help? They are there!

Although Mr. Moore feels passionately about God's call to His people to minister to the poor, he does not categorically rule out all government involvement in doing this. In fact, the only comment he made in his paper about government involvement was that "the Christian community—as well as the rest of the private sector—must labor to see that government *does not exceed its bounds* in attempting to care for the poor" (emphasis added by the editor).

Does government have a legitimate role to play in addressing the plight of the poor? If so, what is its role? Should it directly intervene in the marketplace (require a minimum wage, demand certain levels and kinds of insurance coverage for employees, provide public housing, and so forth) or only provide incentives to the private sector to get persons there to act responsibly toward the poor (offer tax credits to employers for employing and training those who have been unemployed for a certain number of months, give incentives to locate plants in areas of urban blight and high unemployment, and so forth)?

Should the government become involved in conscious efforts to redistribute wealth through taxing the private sector and allocating its proceeds to the poor and disadvantaged by making transfer payments (social security payments, food stamps, child care payments, etc.) or providing entitlements to governmentally funded opportunities (education grants, retraining programs, legal assistance, etc.)? The questions are many and complex. It should be acknowledged, though, that the involvement of governments (federal and state) in the care of the poor came into existence because (1) a perceived need for help existed and the private sector had not responded to the need or had responded inadequately, and (2) those who governed and perceived the need were able to get the majority of those who governed with them to agree that the need was real and that it was appropriate for the public sector to act to address the need.

Dr. Joseph A. McKinney addresses the question of the legitimacy of the public sector's involvement in ministering to the needs of the poor. His approach is cautious and thought-provoking. He points out accurately that while most of the Old Testament directives were given to the individual members of the nation of Israel, they were nevertheless given to a *nation of people,* and the king was to care for the oppressed and downtrodden when the "private sector" failed to (see Ps. 72:12-13, a prayer for the king). Dr. McKinney acknowledges the difficulty in making a direct transfer of directives and precepts given to a theocratic state to a pluralistic state, but he correctly observes that those who rule are responsible for the well-being of those in the state.

Dr. McKinney makes the point that there are no "clear delineations in Scripture concerning individual responsibility versus societal responsibility in dealing with poverty," and he concludes that those who live in a community have both the freedom and the responsibility to decide how they should balance the private-public sector issues. He also asserts,

> In most societies the Christian Church cannot realistically be
> expected to bear the entire burden of poverty alleviation. Even if this
> were feasible, it would not be wise. Through the state all citizens can
> be required to pay their fair share in alleviating poverty so that the
> resources of the Christian Church can instead be focused on evangel-
> ization and other aspects of ministry.

CHAPTER 11

THE PUBLIC SECTOR AND THE POOR

Joseph A. McKinney

Joseph A. McKinney is Professor of Economics at Baylor University. He received the B.A. degree in Economics from Berea College, and the M.A. and Ph.D. degrees from Michigan State University. He has taught at the University of Virginia, Baylor University, and Seinan Gakuin University in Japan. His research has been primarily in the fields of international trade policy and the Japanese economy, but he has recently coauthored several articles in the field of business ethics. He is a member of the American Economic Association and a founding member of the Association of Christian Economists.

One of the more controversial economic issues among evangelical Christians is the state's proper role in preventing and alleviating poverty. God's concern for the poor and oppressed as a recurrent theme in both Old and New Testaments is generally acknowledged. At the same time there are strong disagreements, even among Christians holding similar views on theology and the authority of Scripture, concerning the Christian's appropriate response to the problem of poverty. Some are convinced that the poverty problem should be left to private charity alone, particularly to the Christian Church. Others believe just as strongly that Christians have an obligation to marshal the forces of society, through the political process, to address the problem.

That evangelical Christians should differ so strongly on this issue no doubt reflects that the Scriptures do not draw a clear dividing line between the realm of individual responsibility and the realm of public sector responsibility for poverty alleviation. Since the Bible does not speak directly to this point, its message must be inferred.

The lack of consensus among evangelical Christians on this subject may simply indicate our incomplete understanding of Scripture. On the other hand, the fact that the Bible is God's Word for all peoples, in all cultures, throughout all history, must be considered. Governmental structures, cultural values, and economic institutions have varied greatly from nation to nation and from time to time. They will surely continue to do so. Thus, the absence of clear delineations in Scripture concerning individual responsibility versus societal responsibility in dealing with poverty is not too surprising. This issue will probably have to be addressed by Christians in each society and era by drawing on transcendent principles in Scripture that are universally applicable but find different expression under different institutional circumstances.

SOME RELEVANT SCRIPTURAL TEACHINGS

The creation and fall of man—The biblical record of creation provides insight into economic matters. Man and woman were placed in the garden and were given work to do. God gave them dominion over the world, but this dominion was constrained. When the constraint was violated through disobedience, economic conditions became more difficult (see Gen. 3:17-19). When sin entered the world, all creation, including economic relationships, was affected. The material sufficiency that God intended for His creation was no longer assured.

The creation of man and woman in God's image also has implications for the poverty problem. Having been created in the image of God, human beings possess an inherent dignity and worth. The structures of society should encourage and enable each person to realize all the fullness and dignity associated with that unique condition. A powerful case is made for redistribution whenever some lack the material resources necessary for living a life of dignity and realizing their God-given potential while others possess great abundance of material wealth.

Mosaic laws—The most direct scriptural teachings concerning poverty prevention and alleviation are found in the Mosaic laws. Through them, God ordered the life of Israel with laws and institutions specific to the era and environment of Israel. The arrangements that God ordained in the Old Testament for dealing with poverty were given in the context of a theocracy, for the religious community and the state simultaneously. Therefore, they cannot necessarily be considered prescriptive in today's circumstances. But the principles upon which they were based are valid for all time.

The provisions of the Mosaic law indicate that the poor were intended to receive enough to meet sufficiently their basic needs. Money was to be lent without interest to those in need. If the money could not be paid back within a seven-year period, the lender was to forgive the remaining balance (see Exod. 22:25; Lev. 25:35-38; Deut. 15:1-11). Israelites who had become slaves because of inability to pay their debts had to be released at the end of six years if they had not been able to redeem themselves (see Exod. 21:1-11; Lev. 25:39-43, 47-53; Deut. 15:12-18). If land were sold to pay debts, the land was to be repurchased when the family had recovered financially enough to do so. If this could not be accomplished by the Year of Jubilee (which was to occur during the fiftieth year), at that time the land was to be returned to the family and any remaining debt written off (see Lev. 25:8-34).

In addition, there were provisions for the poor and aliens to benefit from the produce of the land. The workers in the fields and vineyards were not to harvest the edges of the fields nor to repeat their harvesting or picking a second time so that some would remain for gleaners to gather for their needs (see Lev. 19:9-10; 23:22; Deut. 24:19-21). Also, each field and vineyard was to be uncultivated every seventh year, with the natural growth left for the poor to harvest (see Exod. 23:10-11; Lev. 25:1-7). Finally, the third-year tithe was to be given to "the Levite, the alien, the fatherless and the widow, so that they may eat in your towns and be satisfied" (Deut. 26:12).[1]

After careful consideration of the biblical texts, the history of Israel, and the best biblical scholarship on this era, John Mason has concluded that at least some of these provisions for assistance to the poor would have been legally enforceable in Israel:

> The clear fact is that the provisions for the impoverished were part of the Mosaic legislation, as much as other laws such as those dealing with murder and theft. Since nothing in the text allows us to consider them as different, they must be presumed to have been legally enforceable.[2]

Thus, while these laws, for the most part, required individual response, this response was not strictly voluntary.

As Mason and other writers have pointed out, these provisions placed greater emphasis on preventing poverty than on alleviating it. The intention was to keep each family unit viable and maintain it as a contributing part of the community. If one family fell on hard times, the blow was cushioned and the family's economic viability restored through sacrifices by the larger community.

Psalms and wisdom literature—Many psalms are concerned with the poor, particularly with their oppression. God is portrayed as the protector of the poor and the defender of their rights. Psalm 72 views the righteous king as one who "will deliver the needy who cry out, the afflicted who have no one to help. He will take pity on the weak and the needy and save the needy from death" (vv. 12-13). As a messianic psalm, this passage looks beyond the king for whom it was originally composed to find its ultimate fulfillment in Christ.

In the book of Proverbs, respect for the poor and kindness toward them are depicted as pleasing to God. Proverbs also warns against laziness and dishonesty, whereas honest dealings, diligence, thrift, and hard work are held up as ways to avoid poverty and to be successful. The book of Ecclesiastes also extols the virtues of work but at the same time cautions against letting it dominate life or trying to find the ultimate meaning of life in it.

The prophets—The prophets of the Old Testament had much to say on the subject of the poor and oppressed. They repeatedly warned of God's judgment on insensitivity to the needs of the poor and oppressed. The prophets appealed to kings as well as to the nation at large to have due regard for the less fortunate. Numerous passages in Isaiah, Jeremiah, Ezekiel, Amos, and Micah develop this theme, which appears with less frequency in some of the other Prophets.

New Testament—While most of the direct biblical teaching on the poverty problem is found in the Old Testament, much of the New Testament testifies to God's concern for the poor and asserts proper Christian attitudes toward the poor. The theme is set in Luke 4:18-19 where Jesus applies to Himself the prophecy of Isaiah: "The Spirit of the Lord is on me, because he has anointed me to preach good news to the poor. He has sent me to proclaim freedom for the prisoners and recovery of sight for the blind, to release the oppressed, to proclaim the year of the Lord's favor." This theme is continued throughout Luke and Acts.

The seriousness with which God views our actions and attitudes toward those who are poor and oppressed is seen in the teachings of Jesus Christ on the Final Judgment (see Matt. 25:31-46) and the story of the beggar Lazarus and the rich man (see Luke 16:19-31). Both passages sternly warn against insensitivity toward those in need. In addition, passages related to the poverty problem appear in Hebrews, James, 1 John, Revelation, and almost all of Paul's Epistles.

THE CASE FOR PRIVATE CHARITY ALONE

Given the scriptural evidence of God's regard for the poor and oppressed, the question remains about the proper Christian response in light of this. As stated earlier, some are convinced that the poverty problem is to be dealt with by the Christian Church through private charity alone. According to this view, the Eighth Commandment ("You shall not steal") establishes property rights that cannot be encroached upon by the state for purposes of redistribution. Furthermore, the sole function of the state is said to be "to punish those who do wrong and to commend those who do right" (1 Pet. 2:14).[3]

Most Christian writers espousing this view are admittedly influenced by writers of the Austrian school of economics.[4] This school of economic thought, which is strongly libertarian and is adhered to by only a small minority of professional economists, tends to consider governmental interference in the market system as inherently counterproductive. There is also a tendency to perceive any limitations on economic freedom as a step leading inexorably toward totalitarianism. To those operating from such a frame of reference, virtually unfettered private enterprise is the only acceptable economic system. The role of the state is best confined to protecting and enforcing private property rights, including provision for the national defense.[5]

Although the Bible neither prescribes a particular economic system nor provides a detailed model of the state, its principles are consistent with a private enterprise economy. In particular, the Bible emphasizes human freedom, a prime characteristic of a private enterprise economy and a condition best preserved in such an environment. The Eighth Commandment's prohibition of stealing makes it clear that property rights are to be respected. About these matters most evangelical Christians can agree.

The disagreements arise in connection with the income distribution resulting from the functioning of a free market economy. This income distribution is based on the productivity of labor, or of assets owned by individuals, in producing those goods that society values most as measured by the monetary votes of consumers. The set of goods produced in a free market economy and the resulting income distribution are not uniquely determined, however. They depend on the income distribution in previous periods and also on the values of society, both of which determine what goods will be demanded.

An argument that the unrestricted operation of market forces yields a just distribution of income implicitly assumes that the income distributions of previous periods affecting the present distribution were also just. The income distribution that falls out of the functioning of a free market economy would have been different if either the distribution of income in previous periods had been different or the preferences of consumers (admittedly distorted by sin) had been different.

Those who make the case for private charity alone readily admit that some individuals are so impaired mentally, physically, or emotionally that they could not expect to earn even a subsistence level of income in a market economy from their productive efforts. However, because of the view that private property rights are absolutely protected by the Eighth Commandment, redistribution by the state is ruled out. The only legitimate reason for taxation is said to be for the maintenance of order in society and the punishment of wrongdoing. Those who so contend also frequently point to the ineffectiveness of the state's efforts to alleviate poverty as prima facie evidence that such efforts are contrary to Scripture. After all, if these efforts are carried out in opposition to God's plan for mankind, they are doomed to failure. It is no surprise that "in the War on Poverty, poverty won," for the battle plan was all wrong from the start. Studies such as Charles Murray's popular book *Losing Ground,* in which he purports to demonstrate that government efforts to alleviate poverty in the United States have actually increased the level of poverty, are cited in support of this view.[6]

THE CASE FOR GOVERNMENT INVOLVEMENT

To set forth the case for public sector involvement in the poverty problem, we must deal with two questions. First, is there anything in the Scriptures that would rule out such assistance? Second, is such assistance necessary?

The instructions in Scripture—With regard to the first question, the Scriptures nowhere explicitly forbid efforts of poverty prevention and alleviation by the state, even when redistribution is a part of these efforts. Jesus recognized the legitimacy of the state and of paying taxes when He said, "Give to Caesar what is Caesar's, and to God what is God's." Also, in Romans 13:1-7, Paul speaks of the state as ordained by God to maintain order and *to do good* ("For he [the one in authority] is God's servant to do you good" [v. 4]). Interpreting the Eighth Commandment as prohibiting the government from redistributing income is not the only possible interpretation, and probably is not the interpretation accepted by the majority of evangelical Christians.

Douglass North emphasizes that every society has chosen some form of the state in preference to anarchy. A primary function of the state is to enforce a system of efficient property rights promoting economic growth so that everyone is at least potentially better off.[7] If individual property rights were absolute, the Eighth Commandment would forbid the state's taking of income or property away from an individual for the common good. However, the Bible teaches that everything belongs to God, and that we are merely stewards of what He has entrusted to us. Given God's concern for the poor, is it inconceivable that society through the state could legitimately redistribute some of this property to alleviate the plight of the poor? I think not.

The Bible gives an account, with no apparent disapproval, of the coercive powers of the secular state being used for redistribution to the benefit of society at large. In communicating what God had revealed to him concerning Pharaoh's dream, Joseph offers the following advice:

> Let Pharaoh appoint commissioners over the land to take a fifth of the harvest of Egypt during the seven years of abundance. They should collect all the food of these good years that are coming and store up the grain under the authority of Pharaoh, to be kept in the cities for food. This food should be held in reserve for the country, to be used during the seven years of famine that will come upon Egypt, so that the country may not be ruined by the famine. (Gen. 41:34-36)

Because this advice was followed, much suffering was avoided.

The biblical text does not indicate that the grain taken by the Egyptian government was held and later returned precisely to those from whom it was taken. Instead it was sold to the Egyptians during the years of famine, and "all the countries came to Egypt to buy grain from Joseph, because the famine was severe in all the world" (Gen. 41:57). If private property rights were absolute, would Scripture view this redistribution so favorably?

Also, in the nation of Israel there seems to have been some public administration of poverty relief. As mentioned earlier, the third-year tithe was to be made available to "the Levite, the alien, the fatherless and the widow." The scriptural information concerning this tithe "appears to instruct the land-owners to deposit the third-year tithe in the town, which suggests central administration."[8]

The need for redistribution—Even if we can accept that public sector involvement in the poverty problem is not forbidden by Scripture, is such redistribution by the state necessary or wise? Would we not be better off relying on private charity alone to cope with the needs of the poor? There are good reasons for believing otherwise. Can one identify a nation at any time in history in which the needs of the poor have been adequately met without some involvement by the state? How, then, is this to be explained?

Here again, the Bible is most helpful to us in understanding the dilemmas of humankind. Because of the Fall, sin is in the world and so is injustice. The selfishness inherent in sinful human beings implies that God's ideal for justice would not be attained even if all were Christians, for the process of sanctification is incomplete. In a largely nonChristian society, the attainment of God's ideal for justice is even less likely. Therefore, the structures of society should be constructed to curb man's inherent selfishness and to work toward the ideal of justice set forth in Scripture.

Economic theory provides a rationale for poverty alleviation as a public good. A public good is characterized as lacking excludability and exhaustibility.[9] That is, if the good is provided, there is no way to exclude those who have not contributed to its cost from benefiting from the fact that it has been provided. Also, once it has been provided, it costs no more for millions of people to consume it than for one person to do so. National defense is one example of a public good. Poverty alleviation is another.[10]

Economists say that in the case of public goods the market fails, in the sense that such goods would not be provided in sufficient quantities by the free market. The reason for this is the "free rider" problem. Because of the nonexcludable character of public goods, those who do not contribute to the cost of them cannot be excluded from benefiting from their provision. So while everyone may agree that poverty relief is very desirable, many will not contribute voluntarily toward its provision since they believe that it will be provided anyway, whether or not they contribute. Or, conversely, they would be willing to contribute their fair share toward the alleviation of poverty, but are not willing to contribute more than their fair share to compensate for the free riders who are contributing nothing. Or, finally, some do contribute what they consider to be their fair share, so that some poverty relief is provided, but less than the optimal amount is provided because of the free riders who contribute nothing.

The power of the state is used to solve the free rider problem in regard to public goods. In a democratic society, the public decides through the political process the desired amount of the good. The state then ensures through its powers of taxation that everyone contributes a fair share toward the cost of providing it. Thus, some goods important to national and individual welfare are provided that would not be provided, or would be provided in less than desirable amounts, in the absence of state action.

In this connection, two other points should be mentioned. First, there will always be some losers from the operation of a market system. For this reason, some sort of poverty relief is probably required for such a system to have the widespread support that it needs to survive.[11] And in the long run, the wealth-generating capacity of the market system has the greatest potential for alleviating poverty. This is so not only for the United States, but particularly for the less-developed countries of the world. Second, there is a strong case for providing firm limits on the state's power to redistribute wealth. Otherwise, much of the wealth transfer will go not to the poor but to the more politically powerful elements of society. And through the resultant increases in both prices and taxes, the poor may be less well off than before.[12] The selfishness of sinful human beings makes this precaution necessary.

The effectiveness of redistribution—We have seen that there is a rationale for having the government involved in poverty alleviation and that this rationale is consistent with biblical statements about the nature of fallen human beings. What, then, are we to make of assertions that governmental efforts at poverty alleviation have been ineffective? Have the state's efforts to alleviate poverty been a total failure and actually made matters worse? According to the most respected economists working in the field of poverty research, the answer is no.

In a recent review article of the extensive economic literature on the poverty problem in the United States, Isabel Sawhill concludes that anti-poverty programs definitely have been effective in reducing the amount of poverty.[13] Because of the complexity and imprecision of economic analysis, one cannot say by exactly how much these programs have reduced the amount of poverty. But the overwhelming evidence from hundreds of studies by professional economists refutes the more casual empiricism of Charles Murray and other popular writers on the poverty problem.[14] Likewise, the success of Canada, Japan, and parts of Western Europe in combining a higher degree of income equality with economic progress refutes the notion that some state involvement in the economy leads necessarily to either economic impotence or totalitarianism.

In her assessment of the numerous studies to date, Sawhill estimates that all governmental *cash* transfers in the United States removed 27.3 percent of the pretransfer poor persons from poverty in 1967. This figure had risen to 34.5 percent by 1985. When *in-kind* transfers (such as food stamps and medical care) are included, around 28 percent were removed from poverty by all transfers in 1967 as compared to 41.6 percent in 1985.[15]

Much of this progress is attributable to the impact of cash social insurance programs (which include social security, workmen's compensation, unemployment insurance, etc.) on the economic status of the elderly.

For example, in 1967 an estimated 44.9 percent of the pretransfer elderly poor were removed from poverty by cash social insurance while another 6.3 percent were removed from poverty by other cash transfers (welfare payments, supplemental security income), for a total of 51.2 percent as a result of both. By 1985, 71.3 percent of the pretransfer elderly poor were removed from poverty by cash social insurance, and another 14.0 percent by other cash transfers. Thus, 85.3 percent of the pretransfer elderly poor were removed from poverty by the combined effects of the two.

By contrast, between 1967 and 1985 the percentage of nonelderly poor persons who were removed from poverty by cash social insurance increased from a mere 11.0 percent to only 15.4 percent. The percentage of nonelderly poor persons removed from poverty by other cash transfers actually declined, from 4.7 percent to 4.1 percent, in this same period. This decrease can be attributed to the reductions in such transfers during the 1980s.

Expressed in 1986 dollars, total social welfare expenditures of the United States in 1984 were $476 billion, of which 79 percent was from social insurance programs and 21 percent from means-tested public assistance programs. This total amounted to 13.4 percent of the gross national product and $2,007 per person in the United States.[16] The means-tested public assistance programs involved expenditures of $100 billion, which amounted to approximately $422 per person in the United States or about 2.8 percent of the gross national product.[17]

Only a very slight decline in the officially measured poverty rate occurred between 1967 and 1985, which has caused some to conclude that the tremendous expenditures on antipoverty programs during this period yielded no progress. However, the officially measured rate disregards significant in-kind transfers, and several other reasons account for the small official poverty rate decline during this period.

One factor is demographic changes that began in the 1950s before the War on Poverty but accelerated during the 1970s and continued into the 1980s. Changes in the age, race, and sex composition of household heads have put substantial upward pressure on the poverty rate. Murray and others have argued that the increase in female-headed households can be attributed directly to the antipoverty programs themselves. Yet Sawhill finds that

> (1) there is little or no evidence that welfare encourages out-of-wedlock children . . .; (2) there is some (although not entirely consistent) evidence that welfare increases divorce rates and that it discourages remarriage although both effects are modest . . . ;
> (3) there is evidence that welfare has large effects on the living

arrangements of young single mothers, encouraging or permitting them to establish independent households.[18]

As Sawhill further notes, while the benefits available to a family with no other income have, after adjustment for inflation, been declining since 1970, the trend toward female-headed households has continued to increase.[19] This is certainly true of the nonpoverty population as well. The erosion of moral standards and the breakdown of the traditional family have been caused by a variety of influences, not the least of which must have been declining influence of the Christian religion in U.S. society. They can hardly be blamed entirely on the antipoverty programs.

Another factor tending to inflate the poverty rate in 1980 as compared to 1967 is the rate of unemployment. Several studies have shown a very close relationship between the amount of poverty and the level of unemployment. The unemployment rate in 1967 was only 3.7 percent; in 1980 it was 7.1 percent.[20] Mainly because of a decline in unemployment, the official poverty rate fell from 15.2 percent of the population in the recession of 1984 to 13.6 percent by March 1987. It has no doubt declined further during the remainder of 1987 and during 1988 as the unemployment rate continued to fall.

So when they are analyzed carefully, the governmental poverty programs in the United States are seen to have significantly reduced poverty, particularly among the aged. That is not to say, however, that governmental programs for the prevention and alleviation of poverty have been nearly as effective as they might have been. In terms of the "leaky bucket" analogy of the late Arthur Okun, there have been many holes in the bucket used to transfer income from the more fortunate in society to those less fortunate.

Just how leaky is the transfer bucket? It cannot be determined exactly. Estimates in the range of 25 percent to 30 percent of income lost due to reduced work efforts of the poor and the disincentive effects of taxation necessary to fund the programs are not uncommon. In addition, the welfare bureaucracy creates huge costs.

Weaknesses in the system of redistribution—One reason for the disappointing effectiveness of poverty programs in the United States is their disregard of scriptural principles. Seldom has there been a work requirement, even for the able-bodied poor. The Bible repeatedly condemns laziness. The Apostle Paul established the rule that "if a man will not work, he shall not eat" (2 Thess. 3:10). There is a sense of fairness here in that each person who is not disabled should contribute to his or her own support.

But the importance of work goes beyond that. Udo Middelmann has stated, "Only in creative activity do we externalize the identity we have as men made in the image of God. This then is the true basis for work."[21] Because of this we can appreciate the significance of poverty prevention as opposed to poverty alleviation. The provisions in the Old Testament for dealing with poverty gave opportunities to the poor to glean for food, and the instructions regarding the Jubilee meant that families would not over time become deprived of the means with which to earn a living. The intention apparently was that all would be enable to live a life of dignity and productivity, exercising their inherent creativity and thereby more fully establishing their identity as unique creatures of God.

Several states have been experimenting with a work requirement for welfare recipients since about 1982. Preliminary results indicate that these experiments have been quite successful in reducing the welfare rolls. Such indications have not emerged because people have been deterred from applying for welfare benefits by the work requirement, either. Instead, the job experience, work habits, information, and contacts gained through the work programs have enabled the recipients to obtain gainful employment.[22] Fortunately, the recent federal poverty legislation includes a work requirement, albeit a modest one. Its effectiveness remains to be seen. Much will depend on how it is enforced.

Various other measures have been proposed for encouraging work effort by persons in poverty. One possibility is a wage rate subsidy program as an alternative to welfare payments. Recent research indicates that a wage rate subsidy is potentially much more efficient in alleviating poverty than are cash grants.[23] Other suggestions include offering tax incentives for corporations to operate in high unemployment areas, such as the inner city, and abolishing the minimum wage for teenagers so that the poor may have more opportunities to gain work experience and on-the-job training.

United States poverty programs have fallen short in failing to realize the fundamental importance of the family unit. The family was ordained by God as the basic unit of society, and poverty alleviation programs as well as other governmental programs should be designed to strengthen rather than weaken this institution. In many states two-parent families do not qualify for welfare assistance, even when both parents are unemployed. The increasing number of female-headed households among the poverty population has resulted largely because minors have not been required to live with their parents to qualify for assistance. This could be easily changed. Also, more vigorous enforcement of child support laws would discourage abandonment and thus tend to strengthen the position of the family.

Finally, the biblical principle of accountability can help to get at the roots of the poverty problem. Parents must be held accountable for supporting and taking care of their children. Schools must be held accountable for accomplishing their task of providing the basic educational skills necessary to function in modern society. The laws and institutions of society should reinforce the premise that the individual must bear responsibility for his or her own actions. These things, in one way or another, involve the state in preventive measures that are partial solutions to the poverty problem.

SUMMARY AND CONCLUSIONS

Nothing in Scripture expressly forbids the state's involvement in poverty prevention or alleviation. There is a rationale provided by economic theory for having poverty prevention and alleviation financed through the state as a public good. In most societies the Christian Church cannot realistically be expected to bear the entire burden of poverty alleviation. Even if this were feasible, it would not be wise. Through the state, all citizens can be required to pay their fair share in alleviating poverty so that the resources of the Christian Church can instead be focused on evangelization and other aspects of ministry.

That is not to say that the Christian Church does not have a critically important role in preventing and alleviating poverty. Many things can be done within the household of faith to prevent unemployment or other misfortune from causing fellow believers to have to rely on public assistance. (Many suggestions are made in the excellent chapter in this volume by T.M. Moore.) Also, there will always be gaps in any publicly administered assistance program that will have to be filled by concerned Christians. Finally, and perhaps most important, Christians can, through proclaiming the values taught in Scripture, provide a blueprint for preventing poverty throughout society.

Studies have shown that persons who attain a high-school education, remain consistently employed at any job, and stay married, very seldom end up persistently poor.[24] The Church can help to develop attitudes in society that will go a long way toward dealing with the poverty problem. These would include an understanding of the inherent value of work and our obligation to do it; an appreciation of the intended permanence of marriage and the fundamental importance of the family unit; and the accountability of individuals for their own actions and their responsibility to develop their God-given talents. Through communication of these biblical principles, the Church can help to ensure that the state's role in preventing or alleviating poverty will be minimized.

EDITOR'S PERSPECTIVE

It is clear that those of us who live under "special grace" are called on to care for the legitimate needs of the poor, especially the needs of our brothers and sisters in Christ. It is also abundantly clear that those who govern and operate under "common grace" are expending a lot of energy and money to address numerous perceived "needs" affecting the poor, without regard to their faith premises. These realities raise several questions that cry out for answers, but their answers are not always apparent. For example, should the government, operating under common grace, be a primary participant in society's efforts to redress the problems associated with poverty? Can people with an unbiblical world view have an accurate understanding of human nature that will enable them to establish policies, procedures, and institutions that will actually help the poor in the long run, or are their good intentions doomed to ultimate failure because they lack a true understanding of mankind's fallen nature? Is the Christian Church meeting the needs of the poor who profess the name of Christ and who are identifiable through their association with a local church?

The differences between the work of T. M. Moore and that of Joe McKinney are really matters revolving around the empirical answer to the second question just raised: Are the government's efforts to address the issues of poverty effective? T. M. Moore holds up the work of Charles Murray, *Losing Ground: American Social Policy 1950–1980,* and the article by Lawrence Mead entitled "Why Murray prevailed" as evidence that the government's efforts have not been very effective and, in fact, have created some counterproductive side effects. Joe McKinney, on the other hand, perceives that the work of Charles Murray was probably not as reliable as it could have been had he used more rigorous empirical tools of analysis; therefore, he calls on an article by Isabel Sawhill that appeared in the *Journal of Economic Literature* in which she extensively reviews the poverty literature and concludes that the government's efforts have produced some significant and measurable benefits for the poor.

T. M. Moore urges us to "labor to see that government does not exceed its bounds in attempting to care for the poor," and Joe McKinney tells us the Scripture's scanty statements about communities' responsibilities for the poor leave the Christian community free to decide how to balance the involvement of the Church and the state in attending to the needs of the poor. Others might argue that Scripture's clear call to the Christian community to care for the poor, and its relative silence regarding the role of the public sector, is prima facie evidence that the responsibility was given to the Church and that an appeal to Scripture's silence is not an appropriate basis for believing the state should be involved. But others contend that while Scripture was given to the Church for its instruction, it was not intended to be a manual for the operation of the state; therefore, the state is both obligated and free to seek its own means of doing good for its citizens (see Rom. 13:1-7). The debate goes on.

The editor believes the Christian community must start where it finds itself in contemporary society and do several things: (1) obey Christ's clear call to care for the poor in the "church family" and strive to develop diaconal ministries that will first identify and then assist the poor; (2) always be prepared to meet acute and immediate needs—cover the naked, warm the cold, and feed the hungry; (3) participate in the affairs of government and seek to influence public actions so that they reflect as much wisdom as possible in helping the poor to eventually help themselves; and (4) foster governmental efforts as long as they provide encouragement and incentives to every segment of the private sector to engage the issues of poverty.

But should we ever encourage those who govern to become directly involved in addressing the issues of poverty since all government funds must first be taken from its citizens by taxation and then redistributed? The editor answers with a qualified yes—provided the four steps outlined in the above paragraph are given a higher priority and are being diligently pursued. If the state still discerns biblically recognized needs among the citizens after these four steps have been taken, I would *not* try to shut off the wellspring of compassion flowing from common grace. I would be grateful for both the desire and the effort of those who govern to help the poor when I had exhausted my abilities and the Church and other segments of the private sector had exhausted theirs.

I now want to examine a foundational presupposition of our entire economic modus operandi and look at how the application of this assumption creates a genuine structural consequence seriously affecting the distribution of wealth. This issue needs to be discussed thoroughly by the Christian community. At this time I have no better alternatives or solutions to offer as responses to my observations and reservations because these particular concerns have been coming into focus in my mind only over the past several years. Their implications are so far-ranging that I have not yet decided if any "cure" is worse than the "illness" and, therefore, nothing should be done. To act or not to act, that is the question.

If we think back to chapters 4 and 5, which were written by Ron Nash and David Jones, we will recall that these two men discussed subjective and normative economic values as they relate to economic systems, and that they both defended a free market system resting on some form of *utility theory* that asserts we can place meaningful values (subjective or teleological) on all economic activity. Nash made his points empirically and philosophically, and Jones rested his case on the norms of Scripture. But behind their penetrating discussion of utility theory is still another assumption about whether mankind's state of "natural equality" or "natural inequality" should be the normative base for determining what is fair and just when distributing wealth.

Let me explain. If we believe that our natural equality—we are all equally human and, therefore, have equal inherent worth—should be the governing principle by which we distribute wealth, need or equal (proportional) shares should become the normative standard by which we would distribute wealth in an economic system. If, on the other hand, we believe that our natural human inequalities—our physical, mental, and experiential differences—and their application to a task should govern how we distribute wealth, we should build an economic system that distributes wealth according to people's efforts, contributions, and merit.

A free market system rests wholly on the belief that our natural differences (inequalities) should serve as the governing and normative grounds for determining the just distribution of wealth. This means that people with inherent physical and mental advantages come out of the starting blocks of life with a natural advantage over those who are less endowed. Furthermore, when we build an economic system based on the appropriateness of this reality, we soon discover that wealth is indeed distributed unequally and that those with the advantages, however they are measured, will obtain a larger share of the wealth.

This does not mean, for example, that a bright person will always get more wealth than a less intelligent individual, because the bright person may be lazy, or bright in an area with little economic value attached to it, while the less intelligent person may have other offsetting abilities—the will to persevere, wise use of the money available to him, a good sense of timing with regard to the market—that allowed him to excel. But the fact is, personal inequalities give rise to economic inequalities. Persons advocating a free market system implicitly accept natural inequality as the normative grounds on which to establish economic justice.

The editor accepts human inequality as the basis for economic justice in the *short run*, too, because it is the most consonant with the many biblical principles that address individual moral choice, personal responsibility and accountability, work, rewards, and other weighty biblical ideas. But I do not accept it for the perpetual or long-run, uninterrupted operation of an economic system for the reason that Scripture does not seem to, either.

The Jubilee, which is mentioned twenty-one times in Leviticus (chapters 25 and 27) and one time in Numbers 36:4, was obviously intended to accomplish several things for God's children. First, any purchaser of land in Israel was really understood to be leasing the land. The purchaser had obtained a time-defined and limited-life benefit, not a perpetual one. He was leasing the seller's family inheritance, which was to be perpetual and was a stewardship trust from God. Second, personal mistakes of judgment, natural calamities of life, and/or poor moral character that shaped the lives of one generation were not to be allowed to have a perpetual or multigenerational impact beyond a defined period of time. And finally, the Jubilee guaranteed that a family could not be cut off perpetually from the opportunity to own, work, and share in the generally available resources God had given everyone.

Having pointed to the problems associated with distributing wealth on the grounds of natural inequality, and the Scripture's presentation of the Jubilee as a remedy for perpetual inequality, I still have no suggestion for overcoming the economic injustices in a fallen world because (1) the Jubilee was never actually practiced in history; (2) the concept was given to a nation of God's people and not a heathen or pluralistic society; and (3) the plan was given to God's children when they were entering a land that needed to be subdivided, and it was not given to them for implementation after there was a long and established due process in place for determining legitimate property claims.

I am not at ease, however, with an economic system deeply rooted in the acceptance of human inequality as a grounds for determining economic justice when very sinful people are involved in the system's operation and people have such different power bases related to their inherent advantages and disadvantages. Such a system has no way of redressing perpetuated inequalities that can and do arise, in part, from sinful injustices. But all my thoughts and concepts to redeem the situation merely create another set of injustices and a new set of problems. Injustices seem to be inherent in a fallen world, and our task seems to call for identifying, reducing, or minimizing them, but not eliminating them.

CAN A "LOVE ETHIC" BE APPLIED IN THE MARKETPLACE?

What is love? Can it be manifested effectively in the marketplace without its being compromised, sentimental, or smothered by natural economic laws that govern the marketplace and seem so uncaring in their consequences for those with mental, physical, and experiential disadvantages? Or to ask it another way, are "love" and "business" complementary or antithetical? How Christlike can a businessperson be and still succeed in business?

Such questions arise more frequently than we might like to admit. We are not always sure that we can be completely committed to Christ and function successfully in business. Many Christians have lingering doubts about the appropriateness of trying to take an ethic of love into the rough-and-tumble arena of the marketplace.

When we are completely honest with ourselves, though, we must admit that it is very difficult for us to be absolutely committed to Christ in any area of life—social, political, family, or business—because we are so easily distracted, tempted, and led astray. The marketplace is filled with things that appeal to our old nature, and Christians know this all too well. Awareness of our moral frailties confronts us regarding our ability to truly love our neighbors in the marketplace. We have experienced our personal failures and observed the inappropriate conduct of so many others that we sometimes wonder if love and business are like oil and water and don't mix. We must dispel such self-doubts. For that reason, let us examine in considerable depth the question: Can biblical love function effectively in the marketplace?

Love is not an easy concept to define, and it can be just as hard to discern because it manifests itself in so many ways and is so easily counterfeited by people who believe that its feigned presence offers them the hope of a profit.

For example, what often seems at first to be a good opportunity really turns out to be someone else's opportunity to use us, not love us. Feigned appearances and deception occur frequently in the marketplace. We should not be surprised, though, for even Eve in her moral perfection (and innocence) was deceived by Satan, who disguises himself as an angel of light whenever he can (see 2 Cor. 11:14). We need a standard by which we can identify true love so we can keep from being manipulated or entangled and confused by our emotions, desires, and personal beliefs that may still be out of conformity with true godly love.

When the Apostle Paul wrote the Philippians about his intentions to send Timothy to them, he said, "I have no one else of kindred spirit who will genuinely be concerned for your welfare. For they all seek after their own interests, not those of Christ Jesus" (Phil. 2:20-21). *Agape*, the distinctive biblical concept of love, is an attitude of the heart that expresses itself through words and deeds reflecting a genuine godly concern for doing what is in the best interest of our neighbors. Furthermore, the concern expressed must be in keeping with the revealed interests of Christ and must be carried forward in a way that nourishes the recipient with the fruit of the Spirit and those attributes of love described in 1 Corinthians 13:4-7.

Is such an other-directed interest in people capable of surviving in the maketplace where people are generally oriented toward their own interests, even when such self-interest is generally prudent enough to foster service for others? Can love be sustained and business survive when others get tough, shave corners, and operate by low ethical standards? Or must love be put on the shelf when the economic going gets rough? Richard Longenecker and Richard Land explore these questions, for the answers to them are extremely important to any Christian's sense of well-being, contentment, and personal integrity in the marketplace as he or she works amidst the "hard sell," "quick buck," and "be successful" pressures.

Richard Longenecker sets the stage by discussing the nature and quality of Christian ethics embodied in the biblical principle that people, and our relationships with them, are more significant than the production and consumption of things. People should be given the higher priority in our thinking and conduct. Does exhibiting Christ's love mean putting the well-being of others ahead of our material interests? Dr. Longenecker does not believe that an *agape* ethic is mutually exclusive from the idea of running a successful business, but he does note marketplace behavior that is antithetical to godly love. In fact, some of his colleagues at the Colloquium believed the thrust of his paper was a bit harsh toward the business community, particularly in the section entitled "The Nature of Business." The editor, however, believes he delineates a fair picture of what is generally promulgated by the nonbusiness media and, therefore, what the general populace is led to believe regarding the ethics of business. Though it is true that the overwhelming majority of business transactions are carried out ethically, there are reasons to believe that the reported unethical behavior is only the tip of the unethical iceberg. In any case, our central question—Can Christians take the *agape* ethic into the marketplace and function successfully?—is still compelling.

Richard Land is not as pessimistic as Richard Longenecker. He maintains that *agape* love can function in business, and when understood from a balanced biblical perspective, it is the only sound and wise way for people to operate in the marketplace. From his perspective, *agape* love need not be out of step with "hard bargaining" that is fair to all parties, or constructive correction of people who have exhibited inadequate behavior.

Dr. Longenecker—while agreeing in principle with Dr. Land and believing that the marketplace is an appropriate place to be called into service as a Christian—is not very optimistic about the typical Christian's ability to be "tough with regard to the 'hard stuff' (production, efficiency, markets, etc.) and tender with regard to people." To use a military metaphor, he simply believes that the marketplace is the equivalent of a mined battlefield with many risks for the Christian to be wounded. He has the compassion of a military commander who loves his troops, but who acknowledges the just cause that motivates him to order them into battle with the full knowledge, and even expectation, that some will be killed or injured.

CHAPTER 12

O TEMPORA! O MORES! — ON BEING A CHRISTIAN IN BUSINESS TODAY

Richard N. Longenecker

Richard N. Longenecker is the Ramsay Armitage Professor of New Testament at Wycliffe College, and Graduate Professor at the Centre for Religious Studies, both at the University of Toronto in Canada. He received his B.A. from Wheaton College, his M.A. from Wheaton Graduate School, and his Ph.D. from the University of Edinburgh New College. He taught at Wheaton College, Wheaton Graduate School, and Trinity Evangelical Divinity School before moving to Toronto. His various responsibilities at the University of Toronto have included being the Director of Advanced Degree Studies (Wycliffe College) and Chairman of the Advanced Degree Council at the Toronto School of Theology. He is the author of six books and numerous articles.

One of the more memorable expressions of antiquity is that of Marcus Tullius Cicero (106–43 BC), the Roman statesman and orator, who in 63 BC lamented, "O tempora! O mores!" — "Oh, what times! Oh, what standards!" The expression appears at the beginning of Cicero's speech in the Roman senate against Lucius Sergius Catiline, who had earlier been on the wrong side in the Roman civil wars and was at the time planning another insurrection. Cicero's *Against Catiline* exposed his plans, resulting in Catiline's immediate departure from Rome and later defeat.

Cicero lived in times that were badly out of joint. He was not a great thinker. Often he bemoaned and eulogized more than analyzed or spoke constructively. He was, however, a great orator who knew how to capture the minds and hearts of his audiences. And "O tempora! O mores!" encapsulated for many the mood and temper of the day.

The expression, of course, has primary reference to the political turmoil that Cicero saw all around him, which none but the blind could deny. Yet "O tempora! O mores!" also seems a somewhat appropriate response to what is going on with regard to ethical standards, or the lack of them, in business and the marketplace today.

True, our day may not be unique in what appears to be its pervading— though, thankfully, not universal—disregard of ethics. Nonetheless, our day, with its underlying secularism and rampant materialism, has in its emphases on money over morals and power over people all too frequently rivaled the ethical callousness of previous times. In the name of profits, weakened by a disease termed *affluenza* and driven by what may be called *performance paranoia*, ethically insensitive managers have presented us with such disasters as thalidomide, Love Canal, the Dalkon Shield, and Bhopal, and we've added to the list of sharp, unscrupulous operators such names as Ivan Boesky and Dennis Levine. Likewise, impelled by a mania for power and personal aggrandizement, governmental leaders using their posts for their own advantage, politicians entrapped in duplicity while claiming to be above-board, and television preachers doing in private what they denounce in public, have become the objects of public scrutiny.

Even our families, churches, colleges, and universities are affected by the current ethical malaise, with reports surfacing of the breakdown of morals in these venerable institutions established for the well-being of society. So colleges and universities across the land, attempting to fill the ethical vacuum, have inaugurated various ethical components into their curricular structures, taking particular care to have such an ethical component in their schools of business. And so we as Christians are called on to think seriously about what it means to be a Christian in a secular, materialistic society—particularly what it means to live out our biblical ethic in the marketplace, the place of business and human affairs.

THE NATURE OF BIBLICAL ETHICS

Christians avow that God has revealed Himself and His purposes in the pages of Holy Scripture, both Old and New Testaments. So Christians insist that life must be viewed from the perspective of divine revelation, and they attempt to work out a biblical ethic in their daily lives (though, of course, with varying degrees of success). A major problem, however, arises right at the start, for Christians differ widely as to the nature of biblical ethics. Some stress laws and seek to regulate life in terms of prescriptions; others emphasize love alone, apart from any laws or prescriptive principles.

Between these two extremes are a myriad of views on the nature of biblical ethics.

It is necessary, therefore, to be clear about what we as Christians believe regarding the essence of our faith before asking how we should act in society, the world of business, and the marketplace. What do we mean, for example, when we speak of an "ethic of love"? How specifically Christian is it? How does it relate to other types of ethics? How is it to be worked out in our lives and in society?

It is impossible in this brief discussion to lay out in any adequate manner all the features of a fully orbed Christian ethic. Certain basic features, however, can and must be highlighted, particularly those having to do with a Christian in business today. And this we will attempt to do here.

The priority of people and relationships—God's plan for mankind involves the achievement of a truly personal relationship between Himself and His people, and so between people themselves. In working out their ethic, Christians must always give primary attention to people and to relationships between people: first, to God, the Supreme Person, and to the relationship He has established in Christ Jesus; also, and of corollary importance, to others and relationships with them. Christian ethics begins with God and being "in Christ," which is Paul's way of expressing that truly personal and inexpressibly intimate relationship established by God with His people. But Christian ethics also builds on the premise that Christians are to treat others as God has treated them—that is, with genuine concern for others' welfare and appropriate action in expressing that concern.

In the opening chapters of Genesis the focus is on people and relationships. The creation accounts of Genesis 1–2 portray the origins of everything that exists, but the climax of those accounts is on the creation of mankind, both male and female, to whom was given the distinct honor of bearing God's image. And Genesis 3 is the first of many recitals of relationships broken because of human sin, but restored through God's initiative and redemptive activity.

This focus on people and relationships continues throughout the Bible. God's words of instruction to His people in the Ten Commandments are, first of all, "I am the Lord your God, who brought you out of Egypt, out of the land of slavery," which are then followed by statements explaining how His people are to conduct their lives before Him (see Exod. 20:2-17; Deut. 5:6-21). The messages of the Old Testament prophets to God's wayward people were always predicated by some such consciousness as expressed in Isaiah 43:1:

This is what the LORD says—
  he who created you, O Jacob,
  he who formed you, O Israel:
"Fear not, for I have redeemed you;
  I have summoned you by name; you are mine."

Jesus' response in the gospels as to which is the most important commandment has two parts: "The most important one . . . is this: 'Hear, O Israel, the Lord our God, the Lord is one. Love the Lord your God with all you heart and with all your soul and with all your mind and with all your strength.' The second is this: 'Love your neighbor as yourself.' There is no commandment greater than these" (Mark 12:29-31). And Paul's final words in the body of what is probably his most bombastic letter, Galatians, are that Christians are to "do good to all people, especially to those who belong to the family of believers" (Gal. 6:10).

Biblical ethics, then, concentrates on people and relationships. Everything that has to do with plans, procedures, and the exercise of power, however proper each may be in context, is subjugated in the biblical scheme of things to people and truly personal relationships. Means to an end are inevitable and necessary, but people and truly personal relationships are the ends themselves, never means to an end for some other purpose. If we are to speak of a biblical ethic of business, we must start here by keeping people and relationships as the apex in the hierarchy of factors in all our theory and practice.

The significance of righteousness—Of great importance as well in a biblical ethic is the concept of righteousness. In the Bible the word *righteous* is used both as an attribute of God and as a status given by God to people in a right relation with Him. So Christians, being "in Christ," are justified by faith and accounted righteous before God. But being accounted righteous also means (1) that we are in the process of being made righteous in our everyday living, and (2) that we are to express righteousness in all that we do. Ethically, we are to view our lives and actions in terms of righteousness, not just in terms of propriety—that is, in terms of what God has done for us and how we are to treat others in response, not just in terms of the prevailing customs and usages of our culture.

The Deuteronomic legislation of the Pentateuch is a case in point where righteousness, and not mere propriety, is stressed for the life of God's people. Mosaic legislation, of course, was not the first set of laws promulgated to regulate societal living. The Code of Hammurabi (eighteenth century BC)

certainly antedates the laws of Moses, the Code of Bilalama of Eshnunna
precedes that of Hammurabi by about a century, and the fragmentary Code of
Lipit-Ishtar takes us back even further. Many of the particulars in these
collections of legal maxims are similar simply because the social conditions
of people are similar. The Mosaic law code can be paralleled at many places
with such codes as those of Hammurabi, Eshnunna, and Lipit-Ishtar, yet its
orientation and spirit differ significantly. Legislation in these earlier codes is
enforced by specific punishments, often of a rather severe nature, but in the
Mosaic code, reflecting as it does a theocratic community, legislation is
supported by the "absolute imperative" of the divine word. Likewise, these
other codes stress social propriety, but the Mosaic code emphasizes righteousness that works itself out in terms of justice in society. True, the upper
part of the stone tablets of Hammurabi depicts in bold relief Hammurabi
receiving a scepter and ring from Shamash, the Babylonian god of law and
justice—and so, by juxtaposition of relief and text, it is implied that the
nearly three hundred laws are divinely given. Beyond that, however, there is
very little suggestion in the Code of Hammurabi of any vertical orientation
for ethical living.

A theocentric orientation continues in the New Testament as well. The
Sermon on the Mount, for example, serves in Matthew's Gospel (see chapters
5–7) as the epitome of our Lord's ethical teaching. The caption to Jesus'
words on such diverse topics as anger, lust, divorce, oaths, retaliation, love
for enemies, giving to the needy, prayer, fasting, money, and judging others
is this: "Unless your righteousness surpasses that of the Pharisees and the
teachers of the law, you will certainly not enter the kingdom of heaven"
(Matt. 5:20). The factors of a Godward orientation and the stress on
righteousness in the biblical ethic call on us to think both vertically and
horizontally in living out our lives as Christians, not just horizontally or in
terms of accepted practice alone.

The "law of Christ" and the "mind of Christ"—In a biblical ethic, while
the basis is laid in the Old Testament, the focus resides in the New. Both
Testaments set before God's people an obligatory ethical task, which in the
Old Testament is Torah-centered and in the New is Christ-centered. For the
most part, this task is presented in the New Testament in terms of following
Jesus' example and teachings, which are given (1) to set a standard for
conduct pleasing to God, (2) to indicate the direction in which Christian
morality should be moving, and (3) to signal the quality of action to be
expressed.

As a standard, the example and teachings of Jesus "help towards an intelligent and realistic act of 'repentance', because they offer an objective standard of judgment upon our conduct, so that we know precisely where we stand in the sight of God, and are in a position to accept His judgment upon us and thereby partake of His forgiveness."[1] As indicating direction and quality, "they are intended to offer positive moral guidance for action, to those who have, in the words of the gospels, received the Kingdom of God."[2]

Thus, Paul speaks expressly of "the law of Christ" in Galatians 6:2, where he says that in bearing one another's burdens his converts are fulfilling "the law of Christ," and in 1 Corinthians 9:21, where he refers to himself as not lawless but "under Christ's law" (lit. in-lawed to Christ). The New Testament writers habitually reflect Jesus' teachings in their ethical exhortations (see Rom. 12–14; 1 Thess. 4:1-12; James) and appeal to Jesus' example as the pattern for Christian living (see Phil. 2:5-11; 1 Pet. 4:1).

But Christian ethics is not to be considered only a discipline of following Jesus' example and teachings. A vital factor is God's immediate and personal direction by His Spirit. Paul refers to this as having "the mind of Christ" (1 Cor. 2:10-16), by which he seems to mean that Jesus' example and teachings become operative in Christian lives through the activity of the Holy Spirit.

In the New Testament, the Christian life is shown to be dependent for both its inauguration and its continuance on God's Spirit, who in His ministry confronts men and women with the living Christ, brings them into personal fellowship with God through Christ, and sustains them in all aspects of their new lives in Christ. Thus, Christians are said to live "in the new way of the Spirit, and not in the old way of the written code" (Rom. 7:6), and Christian ministry is portrayed as being "not of the letter but of the Spirit" (2 Cor. 3:6). This realization caused Paul to speak of the Christian as a "spiritual" person (1 Cor. 2:15; 3:1) and of the Christian life as a "fellowship with the Spirit" (Phil. 2:1) as well as a "fellowship with [God's] Son Jesus Christ" (1 Cor. 1:9). Without the "mind of Christ," the "law of Christ" remains remote and unattainable. When the two are in harmony, however, direction is supplied for Christian living.

The "love of Christ" — To know, however, is not the same as to do. Biblical ethics calls for not only knowledge as to what is right, but also for a will to do what we know to be right. Most of our problems regarding ethics have to do more with the will than the intellect. So in a truly biblical ethic, love must be at the heart of matters—love that motivates our living and conditions our actions.

Many religions and systems of ethics emphasize love in human relations, and in this, by common grace, they are right. The Biblical ethics elevates the concept of love to the level of a response to God's love and actualizations of that divine love on the part of God's own to all people in their various needs. In the Old Testament, for example, the believing Israelite responded to God's great redemptive act of love in freeing His people from Egyptian slavery, and so felt compelled to express that love in righteous conduct before God and in justice toward others (see Exod. 20:2-17; Deut. 5:6-21). In the New Testament, God's love is depicted as preeminently expressed in Jesus Christ (see John 3:16). As Paul phrases it, "Christ's love compels us" (see 2 Cor. 3:14) now to act in ways that both respond to and reflect the magnanimity of God. Christ's love for us and our love for Christ are contained in the expression "the love of Christ," and on the basis of that love Christians find motivation and the proper conditioning for ethical living.

Some have supposed that "the love of Christ" in biblical parlance is just another way of saying "the law of Christ" (appealing to such verses as Rom. 13:10, which says that "love is the fulfillment of the law," and James 2:8, where "the royal law found in Scripture" is defined as, "Love your neighbor as yourself"), and so have denied any objective standards or propositional principles for living the Christian life. In Paul's letters, however, where these expressions come to the fore, "love of Christ" and "law of Christ" are not so much equated as they are balanced, the latter being one important factor in the direction of Christian living and the former spoken of as a motivating and conditioning activity, receiving guidance from Christ. God, who in great love acted redemptively on behalf of humanity, "has poured out his love into our hearts by the Holy Spirit, whom he has given us" (Rom. 5:5). Now love has come to characterize a truly Christian lifestyle (see Jesus' parting words to the twelve disciples in John 13:34-35: "A new command I give you: Love one another. As I have loved you, so you must love one another. By this all men will know that you are my disciples, if you love one another"). And as love provides the matrix and context for the ethical lives of Christians, so the Spirit of God provides the dynamic and strength. The same God who raised Jesus Christ from the dead also gives life to our "mortal bodies through his Spirit" (Rom. 8:11).

Much more should be said for any full treatment of the nature of biblical ethics. These points, however, are particularly pertinent in speaking of Christian ethics in the world of business. It remains, in what follows, to parallel what has been said about the nature of biblical ethics by a discussion of the nature of business and then, finally, to deal directly with the question of the Christian in the marketplace.

THE NATURE OF BUSINESS

Business, as the dictionaries tell us, "pertains broadly to all gainful activity, though it usually excludes the professions and farming."[3] Yet even the professions and farming have large business components so that the term *business* rightfully applies to all human activity involving financial gain.

Skeptics, with a more jaundiced eye, have suggested that a truer definition of *business* might be something like "the acquisition of another's wealth on the pretext of providing for another's welfare" or "the conduct of public economic affairs for one's own personal advantage"—perhaps also "the competition of offered services following a game-plan of the survival of the fittest, with the goal being the gaining of a monopoly." And sadly, skeptics all too often speak from experience, having encountered certain businesspeople whose only interests seem to be the financial bottom line and not leaving too much money on the table.

Business, like every facet of human activity, is assuredly rife with corruption, but enumerating such corruptions does not tell us what business is. The power of business to corrupt is simply a reflection of the tremendous power inherent in business, for, to paraphrase a cliché, "all power has within it the power to corrupt—tremendous power to corrupt tremendously; absolute power to corrupt absolutely." Such power to corrupt must cause us to be skeptical, in large measure, about every human activity. Yet no legitimate human activity should be defined simply by its corruptions. In defining business, we must focus on its purposes and goals. In particular, with biblical ethics being primarily interested in people and relationships, we need to consider if the marketplace is inherently impersonal and insensitive to people and their needs.

Business and society—The basic function of business is to be an enabler of society. By attending to society's needs for goods and services, business sets people free for other pursuits. By generating wealth for workers, owners, and governments, it liberates people from the enslavement of poverty and allows them to take advantage of opportunities. Indeed, the degree to which such disciplines as philosophy, the arts, medicine, and education flourish or falter depends largely on the commercial vitality of a nation.

Ancient civilizations viewed business enterprises as service industries whose whole purpose was to support whatever facet of society they were connected to—whether government, religion, the arts, or one of the professions. In the cultures of Mesopotamia, Egypt, Asia Minor, Greece, and Rome, the "businessman" of the day was often a slave or freedman whose activities in generating wealth benefited primarily those for whom he worked. For example, when Jerusalem fell to the Babylonians in the sixth century BC, Jewish young men of royal and noble stock were taken as slaves to Babylon to be trained for civil and commercial service on behalf of the king—among them were Daniel and his three companions (see Dan. 1:3-7). So it was in Jerusalem's fall to the Romans in AD 70 and 135; a great number of people were deported as slaves, and many became agents of commerce.

Business has long since, of course, shed its lowly origins. The rise of business and businesspeople to the highest levels of society—and of schools of business to the largest and most prestigious departments in our colleges and universities—deserves extensive chronicling. Nevertheless, business in its proper form is still a service industry.

Business and people—What, then, can be said regarding business and people? Is the marketplace, like nature, "red in tooth and claw," where only the fittest survive and people are expendable? Is the marketplace inherently impersonal and insensitive to people and their needs?

The robber barons of the late nineteenth century thought so. Fueled by the social Darwinism of British philosopher Herbert Spencer (1820–1903) and others, they exploited people and systems for their own advantage, blatantly arguing that only a favored few are worthy enough to receive the benefits of the earth's resources. These sentiments have reappeared, seemingly in cycles, in the Roaring Twenties, the Fulsome Fifties, and the Awesome Eighties of the twentieth century. When there is a booming economy, there seems to be an increase in the claims that business is somehow separate and apart from society, that business cannot be held to the standards applicable to the way ordinary people treat one another, and that the introduction of noneconomic factors into business would upset the workings of a free market. Attitudes like these are particularly rampant today.

Yet business in its proper role is an enabler of society, and society has to do with people and relationships. Business cannot trample or ignore the rightful concerns of people and avoid ultimately being called to task. In the short term, ruthlessly disregarding people can accumulate money. Sadly, the list is long of sharp, unscrupulous operators who have taken the money and run. Over the long haul, however, history has shown that business is only truly successful as it takes seriously the legitimate concerns of people—both those of its employees and those of its customers. Every business must ask: How does our production affect our workers? How do our policies and practices affect our staff? How does our product affect our customers?

Examples of business's disregard for people over profits are abundant.

They include sweatshop conditions, dangerous machinery, unsafe exposure to contaminants, chemical dumping, the foisting on the public of products lacking intrinsic value, and the continued production and sale of products known to be hazardous—for example, thalidomide, the Dalkon shield, or Ford Pintos.

On the other hand, in many businesses, both large and small, people are important and profits seem not to override their concerns. All of us can cite certain local merchants whose concern for their staff and customers is legendary in the community and who take pride in keeping it that way. In the early sixties, when the J. C. Penney Co. was alerted that a radio sold in their stores caught fire at times in customers' homes, it stopped selling the line, alerted the manufacturer, placed national ads informing the public of the potential danger, and offered immediate refunds. In 1982, when Johnson & Johnson learned that some Tylenol capsules had been contaminated with cyanide, it stopped sales and recalled $100 million worth of the product from supermarket and drugstore shelves, even though Tylenol accounted for the largest share of the company's profits. The motto of the Canadian steelmaker Dofasco is: "Our product is steel; our strength is people." Whether or not such a claim always rings true, that is the stance necessary for good business. Business is more than business; it concerns primarily people and society.

Business and profits—If business concerns primarily people and society, what part do profits play? Is not the balance sheet with its bottom line important? Can business exist without regard for profits?

For many businesspersons, their great commandment says to "maximize profits." Making as much money as possible for their companies—and, in the process, as much as they can for themselves—is for many people the primary moral obligation of life. Hard, measurable performance criteria such as costs, sales volume, and profits tend to drive out softer, less measurable criteria such as quality of production, ethical practices, and social responsiveness. Companies become profit driven more than principle driven; employees cease to view their employment with loyalty, creativity, and pride, coming to consider it mainly in terms of income and consumption. Fixation on profits results in the love of money for itself, with business losing its real purpose for existence and workers losing the real value of work.

Yet business cannot exist without reasonable profits. Profits are like fuel to the fire of business—with business, in turn, geared for the benefit of people and society. Only governments, churches, and charities can exist on a not-for-profit basis, but even their budgets must be balanced in the long run or they, too, will go bankrupt. Profits, like money, are not evil of themselves;

the love of money and the fixation on profits are evil. If profits are the end in themselves, people, morality, society, and all else become simply means to an end, and business is seriously skewed. If, however, reasonable profits are seen as an auxiliary goal, with the ultimate goals being the good of people and the welfare of society, business has a proper perspective and is in a position to flourish.

Business and ethics—Nothing inherent in business makes it either ethically good or morally bad. Business, while an enabler of society, is also a creation of society. And its ethics reflect those of the society that has created it and that it serves.

There are not, however, just a few business leaders who hold to the deep-rooted belief that business is accountable to a lower standard of ethical conduct than society at large. This belief is held by many managers of business, whose slogan seems to be, "If you want to get along, go along." It is also the belief of the great proportion of people today, who have both a history of business and their encounters with certain business types to inform them.

Business has the potential for either great good or great evil simply because it controls the purse strings of every institution it serves, and "he who pays the piper calls the tune." It is vulnerable to the lack of wisdom and the lack of morality of its managers. A single decision, undergirded by both economic and ethical considerations, can have repercussions for good in the lives of large numbers of people, while a similar decision, made without concern for ethics or people, has the potential for great destruction. The ethics of those who manage business are reflected in the business ethics of the day, which is a fact often obscured when corporations are large and the chain of command in them seems impersonal.

People tend to think of the ethics of society too highly and the ethics of business too lowly. The problem is that society itself is diseased, and business, with its economic power and high profile, only brings that disease out into the open. The disease of society is its rampant materialism, which has roots in secularism. The expression of that disease is greed, which, because of public exposure, is most clearly seen in the world of business.

There is no sinister design behind those evils that do appear occasionally in business—no conspiracy of planners to make workshops injurious, machinery unsafe, factories explode, products dangerous, rivers and lakes polluted, medicines to have disastrous side effects, or workers summarily dismissed. At times, of course, such evils are the result of a lack of thought, bad planning, or poor foresight by owners, directors, and managers. More often, simple greed has led many companies and individuals astray—wanting to get to the market in a hurry, and make more money, setting aside moral constraints to "get ahead" and being oblivious to consequences. There is, therefore, a desperate need for ethical considerations to be brought back into society in general, and into business in particular, for only as life and work are principle oriented rather than simply profit oriented will society and business be healthy.

CHRISTIANS IN THE MARKETPLACE

By all appearances, business today is booming. Wealth is being generated at an unprecedented rate, stock markets are flooded with new companies and new issues, business activity is at new highs, the lifestyle of the rich is trumpeted in the media, young urban professionals are taking over and setting new styles of management, and schools of business have become growth industries, often the largest and most dominant departments of the colleges and universities of North America. Yet business in the 1980s is also suffering moral decay, with dry rot evident in the underpinnings and portions of the facade falling off. And this despite the round of antitrust legislation and pure food and drug laws enacted in the early part of this century to protect people from the likes of the robber barons; and the legislative reforms of the 1930s designed to protect society from shoddy goods, stock market manipulations, and bank failures; and the additional reforms inaugurated during the 1960s and early 1970s to provide further legal safeguards for the public.

Legislation, of course, is necessary. But a secular, materialistic society seems able to find new ways to circumvent laws to its own advantage, and greed rules the day too often when power and money converge. So, despite legislation, banks continue to collapse because of mismanagement and criminal activity by managers; organized crime continues to get its money laundered through respectable fronts; rivers and lakes continue to be polluted by the dumping of toxic wastes; products known to be dangerous continue to be sold to an unsuspecting public; defense contractors steal governments blind; bribes, kickbacks, and expense-account padding continue to be prevalent; corporate raiders continue to extort gigantic sums from publicly traded companies; inside information continues to be a curse in the stock markets; and unscrupulous real estate deals continue to be made. Business today is in a moral crisis of epidemic proportions. And it seems that this crisis will be sustained for some time, for reports from various schools of business indicate that the present generation of students likes it that way, much preferring money over morals.

What, then, about Christians in the marketplace? How can biblical ethics be worked out in the world of business today? Where are the conflicts? What perspectives should we take, and what strategies should we carry out? There are, of course, no specific rules to be given. Christians are not robots, and situations differ considerably. Five general observations, however, need to be stated here.

In the first place, the Christian needs to recognize that he or she, by God's grace, is different from others and called upon to express that difference in ways meaningful to the situation at hand. As a new creation through Christ's redeeming work, the Christian has a different set of ethical values from that of the marketplace. So the Christian is urged, "Do not conform any longer to the pattern of this world, but be transformed by the renewing of your mind" (Rom. 12:2), and challenged to be salt and light in the world, letting "your light shine before men, that they may see your good deeds and praise your Father in heaven" (Matt. 5:13-16). The Christian must determine to be different from others in the conduct of business, preferring always to be in accord with biblical principles rather than secular, materialistic practices at points of conflict. The Christian needs to see business as a calling of God and a means of witness for God.

Second, the Christian in business needs to maintain a sharp focus on people and their needs. Amidst the many pressing issues involved in planning, production, programs, selling, and the like, the Christian needs constantly to keep in mind the people who produce the product or service and the people who consume it, for every business is a service industry meant to enable society and meet the needs of people. Some object that to concentrate on the "soft stuff" of people values is to lose the tough-mindedness necessary to deal with the "hard stuff" basic to success in business. Yet the paradox is that many truly successful businesses have owners and managers who are both tough with regard to the "hard stuff" and tender with regard to people. Because of the combination of factors, such businesses have succeeded over the long haul.

Third, the moral tone of companies is set by those respective companies' highest ranking executive officers, who consciously and consistently commit themselves and their companies to doing well by doing good. Many corporate employees have behaved improperly simply because they felt themselves without guidance from the front office or because they mistakenly believed that management would approve their activity if it produced profits. So the Christian in an executive role needs to take seriously the formal directives regarding morality given within his or her company and the ethical tone set by his or her example.

A fourth matter concerns formal ways of instructing in ethics within a company, whether they be codes of conduct, training programs in ethics, ethics committees, ombudsmen, special hot lines to handle ethical concerns, or some combination of these. Admittedly, some endeavors to insert an ethical component into business are more face-saving or promotional exercises than real endeavors to alter the tone of business. Nevertheless, when drawn up by top-level executives and supported enthusiastically by them, codes of conduct and the like are meaningful. And Christians need to be at the forefront of such endeavors.

Fifth, and finally, the injection of ethical components into the curricula of our schools of business is laudable. Courses on ethics in business are threatening to become a growth industry, though all too often they are seen more as supplements to the curriculum than as integral parts of every course. Nevertheless, the pendulum is beginning to swing in our schools of business from simply imparting management skills, a facility with numbers, and a craving for wealth to attempting to inculcate a sense of honor and what is ethical. And this endeavor, too, though only in its infancy, needs to be applauded and encouraged.

The Christian always lives within the tension of a dual citizenship and dual responsibilities. He or she is a citizen of this world and of a particular society and must generally obey those laws; but he or she is also a citizen of the Kingdom of God and must always live out Kingdom ethics. Where there is conflict between the two, the Christian's loyalty must be to God. That is what Jesus meant when He said, "Give to Caesar what is Caesar's, and to God what is God's" (Luke 20:25). That is what all Christians have found to be true as they attempt to live out their faith in a secular, materialistic society.

It may seem somewhat unrealistic to expect individual Christians to do much to change a society that is rampantly materialistic and the world of business that thrives on greed. Nevertheless, as those who are God's own, Christians are called to struggle with the ethical issues of business and to be involved in taking risks. Indeed, if God makes His appeal through us (see 2 Cor. 5:20), society generally and the world of business in particular will hear that appeal only as it is lived out in action. The verbal word is important, but it must be matched by the lived-out word. And the businessperson, probably above all others, has not only the greatest challenge but also the greatest opportunity to live out God's Word in our world and society today.

EDITOR'S REFLECTIONS

While Dr. Richard Longenecker does not deny that the love ethic modeled and called for by Christ and developed in us by the Holy Spirit can be carried into the marketplace and practiced without compromise, he clearly views business in a somewhat somber and distrustful manner. But Scripture does the same thing when it draws attention to the motives and behavior of those who do not follow Christ but instead pursue their own desires.

For example, Christ said, "The sons of this age are more shrewd in relationship to their own generation than the sons of light" (Luke 16:8). The context of this statement shows that Christ is not commending the shrewdness being described, but is simply pointing out that people who reject God's standards operate by worldly criteria as they look out for their own interests rather than Christ's. People who have their identity attached to the rewards of the marketplace create their own standards and do such perverse things as remain silent when silence is equivalent to a lie, tell half-truths, act deceptively, make promises they do not intend to keep, and perform other acts of ethical corner-cutting.

This reality, plus the apparent prospering of the wicked, really bothered many people in the Bible. For example, Asaph envied the prosperity of the wicked (see Ps. 73:3, 12); Job complained that the "blameless man is a joke" while "the tents of the destroyers prosper" (Job 12:4, 6); Jeremiah asked God, "Why has the way of the wicked prospered?" (Jer. 12:1); and others like Amos, Habakkuk, and Micah noted the ease and prosperity of the wicked.

It is perfectly fair for Dr. Longenecker to point out some of these same realities in our day. The wicked often materially prosper, and they frequently get by with their unethical behavior. But God has revealed their end to us; they stand in slippery places; and they will give their final accounting to Christ (see Ps. 73:15-20; Rom. 14:12). The ungodly are exchanging a priceless and eternal inheritance for more material wealth in this life (see Ps. 17:14; Luke 16:25). Christians should not be naive, though. The ungodly, who are as technically capable and proficient as God's children and who are often willing to use an unethical tactic to gain unfair advantages for themselves, play on a field that is tilted in their favor and where the rules of play are not the same.

Christians must do a superior job in the marketplace if they are to be godly and compete successfully. However, the notion that godliness is good *because* it helps us obtain material wealth is a heresy of major proportions (see 1 Tim. 6:6). The acid test comes when we perceive that godliness and success are mutually exclusive. Will we then choose godliness over worldly success, or will we rationalize compromise (see Prov. 25:26)?

The specific question we still want to pursue in this section is this: Can the biblical concept of *agape* love (a volitional commitment to seek the best for our neighbor) be brought to the marketplace without ruinous economic consequences for the person practicing it? Richard Land believes very strongly that the answer is YES! And he also believes that today's declining level of ethics in the marketplace actually offers Christians a special opportunity to be salt and light in the business community. To be recognized as people of superior integrity can be used by God to open doors for us "to give an account for the hope that is in [us]" (1 Pet. 3:15). Dr. Land is right!

CHAPTER 13

THE ETHICS OF LOVE CAN SUCCEED IN THE MARKETPLACE

Richard D. Land

Richard D. Land is the Executive Director of the Christian Life Commission of the Southern Baptist Convention in Nashville, Tennessee. He received the A.B. degree, magna cum laude, from Princeton University and holds the Ph.D. degree from Oxford University. Dr. Land also received a M.Th. degree from New Orleans Baptist Theological Seminary where he served as student body president and received the Broadman Seminarian Award as the outstanding graduating student. Dr. Land, a sixth-generation Texan, served from February 1987 to May 1988 as Administrative Assistant to the Governor of Texas while on leave of absence from Criswell College where he was Vice President for Academic Affairs and Professor of Theology and Church History.

What is a Christian love ethic? Is such an ethic compatible with business, and can one employ it in the marketplace successfully?

The question of ethics in business is a very timely topic. The decline of American values into a morass of relativism and hedonism, coupled with a dizzying acceleration of technological innovation, has spawned a business scene increasingly populated with commercial buccaneers as rapacious as any nineteenth-century robber baron. Such people, embracing greed as a virtue, are as distressingly shallow, and as abjectly philistine, as any George Babbitt of Sinclair Lewis's imagination.

The havoc wrought by such people's behavior has merited notice in numerous and varied forums. A recent *Time* magazine cover story asked questions that served as its commentary on the current American scene: "What's wrong? Hypocrisy, betrayal and greed unsettle the nation's soul. . . . At a time of moral disarray America seeks to rebuild a structure of values."[1] A definition of the problem, however, does not automatically suggest definitive answers. *Time* was much more certain of the problem than of the solution's source, much less the solution itself.[2]

An article by Daniel E. Maltby asserts that "corporate America, reflecting the larger society, is confused and searching for its ethical identity." By significant margins, business majors perceive American business to be unethical. The ethical dilemmas facing the modern executive have led to a mushrooming presence of ethics courses in the curricula of business schools. Business ethics books, virtually nonexistent ten years ago, have skyrocketed to over five thousand published titles today.[3]

The central thrust, however, appears to be "the study of values, not the teaching of values."[4] America's current relativistic presuppositions apparently preclude anything other than a subjective, individual, or sociological basis for "dealing with what is good and bad and with moral duty and obligation," which is *Webster's* definition of *ethics*.[5]

Some seem to have reduced the argument for business ethics to a neo-utilitarian or "success" approach, asserting *The Power of Ethical Management* with a dust jacket that proclaims "INTEGRITY PAYS! YOU DON'T HAVE TO CHEAT TO WIN."[6] Even *Reader's Digest* recently printed an article condensed from *Nation's Business* lauding "that ethical edge."[7] One does not have to disagree with the argument that high ethical standards are a good long-term business practice to be disturbed that an appeal for such standards would be based on mere profitability.

Even if high ethical standards contribute to long-term profitability through such results as product excellence, customer satisfaction, and employee loyalty, the question of the Christian ethic of love and its compatibility with the opportunity to function successfully in the marketplace would remain unanswered. The radical standard of Christian love, as illustrated and explained in the New Testament, subsumes and goes far beyond any ethic founded merely on a principle of prudentiality or mutual beneficiality.

Many have discussed the New Testament concept of *agape* love as embodied in the Person of Jesus Christ and as explained by Him and by His apostles.[8] Jesus Christ came to fulfill the law, not to abolish it (see Matt. 5:17-19). Numerous commentators have noted that the essence of God's law is summarized in the Decalogue. The first table's four commandments relate man's obligation to love God, and the second table's six commandments summarize man's responsibility to his fellowman.

When Jesus was asked, "Which is the great commandment in the law?" He further summarized God's requirements when He responded,

You shall love the Lord your God with all your heart, and with all your soul, and with all your mind. This is the great and first commandment. And a second is like it, You shall love your neighbor as yourself. On these two commandments depend all the law and the prophets. (Matt. 22:36-40)

God's love encompasses God's law. Paul reiterates this when he declares love as the fulfillment of the law's second table of commandments:

For he who loves his neighbor has fulfilled the law. The commandments, "You shall not commit adultery, You shall not kill, You shall not steal, You shall not covet," and any other commandment, are summed up in this sentence, "You shall love your neighbor as yourself." Love does no wrong to a neighbor; therefore love is the fulfilling of the law. (Rom. 13:8-10)

If the New Testament's revelation of *agape* love in and through Jesus Christ did not negate the Old Testament's revelation of the law, it certainly radically clarified it. This clarity emphasized the supernatural nature of its origin and the comprehensiveness of its demands. The New Testament's writers were searching for a somewhat amorphous word that they could infuse with all the incredibly new and enlarged understanding of the nature and requirements of God's love they had acquired through their experience of the Christ. In *agape* they found their answer.

Agape and its derivatives had little substantive pre-New Testament history. It did not have "the power or magic" of *eros*, it had "little of the warmth" of *phileo*, and its meanings were "still imprecise."[9] Within three decades the Church had developed its own dictionary of words and meanings in an attempt to convey and describe the magical life in and by the Holy Spirit made possible by the Christ event. Concerning this phenomenon, *agape*, which "had acquired so specialized and rich a meaning that it seemed almost a neologism," furnished the premier example.[10]

Anders Nygren has declared that *agape* is "a quite new creation of Christianity" without which "nothing that is Christian would be Christian."[11] *Agape* is

essentially a Christian word standing for something that is essentially Christian. It was this love, none other and nothing less, that brought the Lord Jesus into the world to die upon the Cross. It is a love that does not depend upon any worth at all in the object of it; it is God's love showered freely upon all men, and to be realized by every man who turns to God in repentance and faith.[12]

Agape, transformed, "demands the exercise of the whole man" to the whole world. The Christian is to love the unlovely, the wicked, and the enemy (see Matt. 5:43-48).[13] The Christian is to love God more than man and people more than things, and in loving people, the Christian is to "love the whole man, not just his soul."[14]

Agape also involves renunciation. Two forces of particular interest that Christ calls upon His followers to repudiate in their love for God are "mammon and vainglory."[15] The "love of money is the root of all evils" (1 Tim. 6:10) and the "pride of life . . . is not of the Father but is of the world" (1 John 2:16), and both are antithetical to *agape.*

Both antonyms of *agape* bear upon the question of the Christian ethic of love and the marketplace. In American culture, it is virtually impossible to separate money and prestige, mammon and vainglory. To seek these idols of the world's worship is to deny *agape.*

Agape is "unnatural in the sense that it is not possible for the natural man."[16] A Christian can experience this divinely initiated *agape* love only through conversion, and then he or she is enabled to exercise this love, which is a "fruit of the Spirit" in the yielded, obedient believer's life (see 1 John 4:8-10, 19; Gal. 5:22).[17]

The all-consuming nature of *agape* and its ethic is illustrated by the Apostle Paul's statement to the Galatians: "It is no longer I who live, but Christ who lives in me" (2:20). Paul describes *agape* at some length in the thirteenth chapter of 1 Corinthians. R. C. H. Lenski has movingly explained the deep and comprehensive meanings of that sublime passage; he states that *agape* always seeks sacrificially the highest good of the other.[18]

Is such a Christian love ethic compatible with the marketplace? Yes, if both love and the marketplace are understood properly. *Agape* love is self-sacrificial and service oriented, and as noted earlier, it encompasses the whole being, material as well as immaterial.

However, *agape* love is not indulgent or sentimental. If it were, it could not be consistently compatible with the marketplace. First, it would often actually do what is harmful to its recipient. Second, it would set up conflicting priorities among differing groups and individuals. To indulge one person or group would often lead directly to injustice for another person or group, which would be inconsistent with *agape. Agape,* properly understood, will express "concerns for the ultimate welfare of all mankind, a passion to do what is right, and enforcement of appropriate consequences for wrong action."[19]

The marketplace must also be understood properly. It may be defined under "business" as

> the array of socially-accepted customs and usages which allocate scarce resources and determine levels of output, income, and human welfare. Ostensibly, business activity—producing, exchanging, distributing and consuming—is undertaken to achieve the greatest good for the "greatest number of people."[20]

Such a definition is unrealistic in the present business milieu, but illustrates what a marketplace could and should be. Does this indicate that capitalism is in any meaningful sense peculiarly Christian? The answer is both simple and complex. The simple answer is no, capitalism is not intertwined with a definitive biblical mandate. The complex answer is that while capitalism—as it has developed in America into a more or less mixed economy with economic checks and balances—is not synonymous with the biblical mandate, it is more compatible than many economic systems.

Alternatively, capitalism has developed in the West with several presuppositions that are nonbiblical. Adam Smith (deism), Herbert Spencer (social Darwinism), and Milton Friedman (libertarianism), the intellectual defenders of free market capitalism, all share certain common views antagonistic to Christianity.[21] Brian Griffiths remarks,

> *They are all an attempt to present economic life as something which is impersonal, amoral, which can be expressed as a "system" and which, as a system, has a natural tendency to equilibrium.* In short, they are all derivative of a Renaissance and Englightenment worldview in which God is pushed into the background and economic life made autonomous of anything Divine or indeed, ultimately, of human as well.[22]

These autonomous ideologies and the philosophy of possessive individualism, which penetrates so much of the modern market economy, must be identified by Christians and rejected. If the Christian ethic of love is to be compatible with the marketplace, and if the market economy is going to be reclaimed from its worst excesses, Christians must identify, expose, and separate from such philosophies and the practices they spawn.[23]

This does not mean that the capitalist system should be completely overturned. First, capitalism, especially industrial capitalism, has proven capable of producing tremendous wealth that has drastically raised the living standards and met the material needs of large numbers of people:

> In Britain alone in the nineteenth century there was a 1600 percent rise in goods and wages. It was as if the human race had at last hit upon an effective formula for raising whole populations from poverty to unheard of standards of wealth. The capacity of capitalism to generate wealth is unparalleled in history, and quite possibly one of the greatest single blessings bestowed on humanity. No system has been so helpful to the poor and provided such opportunity to rise out of suffering. It has done so chiefly by reason of the fact it allows wealth to be diversely controlled and be freely invested in new causes. Real wealth is not the possession of natural resources. It is human creativity and ingenuity and that is what democratic capitalism releases in good measure.[24]

Second, capitalism is compatible with Christ's statements in which He did not condemn wealth or praise poverty; He only warned about the "spiritual hazards" accompanying wealth.[25]

Third, capitalism is consistent with the biblical concept that we are to be responsible stewards of those resources God has entrusted to our use, and that includes the world in which God has placed us.[26]

To balance capitalism with a Christian perspective, a proper recovery of the Reformation concept of work as a vocation is essential.[27] The Reformers reacted against the ascetic ideal and emphasized that all creation was "God's good gift to men to be used responsibly. . . . This was a mandate not to exploit the earth, but to develop its resources." The recovery of a Christian concept of work means that "the priority is changed from an emphasis on rewards to the ideal of service."[28] Oliver Barclay makes the point that "service, not profit, is the Christian's first motive. To reverse that order is paganism."[29] Christianity needs to recover the biblical perspective whereby, as Carl Henry put it in a remarkably prescient essay over twenty years ago,

> work becomes a way-station of spiritual witness and service, a daily-traveled bridge between theology and social ethics. In other words, work for the believer is a sacred stewardship, and in fulfilling his job he will either accredit or violate the Christian witness.[30]

A truly biblical perspective on work must include an understanding that Adam worked *before* the Fall, making work "a creation ordinance" that was "spoiled only to some extent by sin."[31] The Christian objective should be not to see the abolition of work, but to make work "serve its true purposes."[32] The New Testament conceives the believer as doing "all work as a spiritual service," reclaiming the workshop and the marketplace as legitimate arenas of spiritual endeavor.[33] Carl Henry comments,

> The Reformation did not eliminate the priesthood but rather did away with a non-priestly laity; every follower of Jesus Christ was reminded anew of his calling to full-time priestly service. This emphasis did not so much secularize the ministry as it sanctified the laity. The Christian workman becomes a priest among his fellow-workers; he serves both God and neighbor as a daily sacrifice.[34]

Reclaiming the Reformation heritage in the work arena would enable the Christian believer to exercise the *agape* love ethic as an employer or as an employee. Whatever the work, as long as it did not dishonor God through immorality, would be rendered "with a good will as to the Lord and not to men" (Eph. 6:7).

Paul's explanation in the Ephesian letter revealed the revolutionary impact of the Christian faith on every human relationship and sphere of activity, including the economic:

> Slaves, obey your human masters loyally with a proper sense of respect and responsibility, as service rendered to Christ; not only working when you are being watched, as if looking for human approval, but as servants of Christ conscientiously doing what you believe to be the will of God. Work cheerfully as if it were for the Lord and not for a man. You may be sure that the Lord will reward each man for good work irrespectively of whether he be slave or free. And as for you employers, act toward those who serve you in the same way. Do not threaten them, but remember that both you and they have the same Lord in Heaven, who makes no distinction between master and man.[35]

When one remembers that the primary subject addressed in this passage is the master-slave relationship, one perceives the way in which even the most outrageously exploitive worldly relationships will soon be redeemed beyond recognition by a consistent application of New Testament principles grounded in Christian love by all participants in the relationship.

What is often not so readily understood is the extent to which transformation takes place when only one participant in the relationship, acknowledging the lordship of Christ, obeys the biblical mandate. The most menial task, the least skilled labor, is elevated to the realm of service, a service done for the Lord, and in such a manner that the worker can gladly "offer it to him as a piece of service."[36]

Such elevation of even the most menial labor to the spiritual level does not entail acquiescence to slavery, discrimination, or any other injustice by the Christian. One may engage actively in attempting to change a relationship, a situation, or an institution while still acknowledging and affirming the worth and dignity of all work (not immoral or illegal) done "as to the Lord."

The early Church has often been charged with acquiescence to the Greco-Roman world's slavery. It should be clear that the apostles and the early Church assaulted slavery at its foundation, and ultimately slavery, its foundation undermined, crumbled under the onslaught.

In the modern era Christians face a prospect different from the ascetic and monastic denial of the world opposed by their Reformation forebears. Today the Christian is called to bear witness against the false philosophies that idolize "profit" and "career" and those who perceive the "idle rich" as worthy of emulation.[37] Oliver Barclay elaborates on this idea:

> The Christian believes . . . that a workload of reasonable proportions is in fact God's intention and something that serves man's health and well-being. At the same time, Christians have often been foremost in attacking the excessive workload that has been placed on employees. . . . It was necessary to create labor unions and to bring in legislation to limit working hours. . . . The Christian ideal is neither the workaholic who lives for his work nor the person who has very little work to do.[38]

With this proper balance, Christians may enter a marketplace transformed first and foremost in their own minds, ready to live an *agape* ethic. Whatever they are called upon to do, they do it as an act of service to God. When they perceive a relationship, situation, or institution out of kilter with the biblical perspective, they must labor to change it by peaceful and persuasive means. Christians must repent of their lack of understanding of the "disparity between a Christian man in business and a Christian businessman." The Christian community must resolve to eliminate thinking that perceives of no "Christian way of doing business."[39]

Christians must also understand that, as Lord Acton so sagely observed, "power tends to corrupt and absolute power corrupts absolutely."[40] Capitalist managers, labor union leaders, government bureaucrats, and elected political leaders are all susceptible to the corrosive acid of power. Consequently, in America an economic system has evolved that is roughly analogous to the political system's checks and balances, with executive (management), legislative (unions), and judicial (government) branches each checking the power and prerogatives of the other two.

In such a system a Christian should preach and practice a Christian love ethic in every situation, and he must work to alter those situations that fall short of a Christian definition of what they should be. He should not be reticent about doing this, either because of a faulty understanding of Church-state separation or because he has been infected with the relativistic ethos of the modern era.

The Southern Baptist Convention's confessional statement, while championing Church-state separation in the best Baptist tradition,[41] also says that

> every Christian is under obligation to seek to make the will of Christ supreme in his own life and in human society. . . . The Christian should oppose in the spirit of Christ, every form of greed, selfishness, and vice. He should work to provide for the orphaned, the needy, the aged, the helpless, and the sick. Every Christian should seek to bring industry, government, and society as a whole under the sway of the principles of righteousness, truth, and brotherly love.[42]

Relativism has infected modern Christians, even those who still retain strong personal convictions. Many such Christians are reluctant to express their convictions in a business milieu, and when they do so, they "apologetically explain that their ideas of morality are . . . just preferences . . . and that they certainly would not want to impose them on anyone else."[43]

This kind of thinking must be changed. Morals and values are *not* just matters of personal opinion. It should profoundly concern evangelicals that a recent study of the next generation of likely evangelical leaders indicates that they have been significantly swayed by relativistic ideas. The study concludes with these sobering words:

> The story of conservative Protestantism in America is in some ways the story of the pilgrim in John Bunyan's epic allegory. In his journey from the City of Destruction to the Celestial City, Bunyan's pilgrim stumbles . . . from the Slough of Despond to Doubting Castle; from the Town of Vanity to the Valley of Humiliation; from Hill Difficulty

to the Valley of the Shadow of Death . . . not to mention his encounters with such unsavory figures as Mr. Worldly Wiseman, Mistrust, Timorous, Pliable, and the like. Yet what our pilgrim (Evangelicalism) endures and Bunyan's does not is a long and sustained season in the Labyrinths of Modernity. Not only does he emerge a little dizzy and confused, but out of the experience our traveler is transformed. The pilgrim becomes a tourist. Though still headed toward the Celestial Country, he is now traveling with less conviction, less confidence about his path, and is perhaps more vulnerable to the worldly distractions encountered by Bunyan's pilgrim.[44]

Modern America needs Christian pilgrims, not Christian tourists. Christians must recognize "the Labyrinths of Modernity" for the temptation they present and resist and thwart their influence in the lives of believers.

As the Christian pilgrim journeys through the labyrinths of modernity, he is called to apply the Christian ethic of love to all areas of his life, including the marketplace. The question often arises as to whether the Christian love ethic is a general welfare principle of an impersonal nature or is instead focused on personally directed motives and actions. The answer is not either/or, but both/and. The Christian love ethic is radically inclusive in that it embraces the whole world, both corporately and individually. Christian love is to be applied to a business, a school, a city, a country, *and* to every individual working, learning, or residing therein. Christian love cannot be confined either to the corporate group or to the individual person. It must minister to and seek the highest good for all, but never to the injustice of the one.

As noted earlier, the Christian must exercise *agape* love to the whole man, spiritual and physical. Consequently, one cannot express *agape* to others and ignore economic benefits in that expression. True *agape* will follow the example of God who, Jesus explained in the course of commanding His disciples to love even their enemies, "makes his sun rise on the evil and on the good, and sends rain on the just and on the unjust" (Matt. 5:45). The significance of this illustration is often missed in a nonagricultural society. Without sun and rain, crops would not grow, and people would be reduced to starvation. It does not get any more basic or physical than food and survival.

The Christian pilgrim may very well be called to serve God in corporate management. If so, his or her opportunity and responsibility increase in relation to bringing the Christian love ethic to bear on the marketplace. Recent studies have revealed the enormous impact of leadership on a corporation or an organization.[45]

People who have studied large numbers of firms have concluded that individual leaders must set the example of high ethical standards. One author stated, "If he is beyond reproach, if he rewards right behavior in others, and if he is totally intolerant of wrongdoing, the chances are that nearly everyone in an organization will also behave ethically."[46] It has been noted that "in high ethics firms, responsibility is individual rather than collective, with individuals assuming personal responsibility for actions of the firm."[47]

Christian businesspersons today are operating at a propitious moment in history because people are seeking ethical models. If Christians will muster the courage to live out their convictions daily in the workplace, many will follow their lead.

How tragic it would be if, at precisely the moment in the twentieth century when the inadequacy and sterility of the modern pantheon of false gods became apparent, when their followers paused to listen, they heard only an uncertain, hesitant trumpet instead of the rich orchestral symphony of the good news. They need to hear that Jesus has a whole message for the whole man of love and justice for the whole world, which will generate and sustain life that nourishes the soul, feeds the hungry, treats the sick, instructs the ignorant, and liberates the mind.

May God give all Christians the grace to take their places in His orchestra and help make the music of the gospel as they apply the Christian love ethic to ever-increasing areas of their daily lives. May He give them vision so that they can victoriously traverse the labyrinths of modernity and lead the way so others can do the same.

EDITOR'S PERSPECTIVE

Richard Land's strong contention that the biblical concept of love (*agape*) can be carried successfully into the marketplace is, in the editor's opinion, a correct understanding of God's intentions, but it does require, as Land pointed out, a great deal of wisdom to do it.

Perhaps one other caveat is also in order. If we truly accept the full implications of *agape*, we must include the fact that *agape* can call on us to voluntarily sacrifice a portion of our personal wealth, as well as our time and energy, as we relate to others (see Deut. 15:7-8, 10; Prov. 21:26; Matt. 5:42; Luke 6:30, 35; 10:25-37).

Entrepreneurs and people who run their own businesses have the right to use their business resources as they would their personal savings, but a professional manager who is acting as an agent in a corporate environment has no such freedom or right because the agent manager is overseeing the personal assets of other people.

If we allow for this one qualification, Richard Land is right on target in his belief that those of us who are called to work in the marketplace are to love our peers, superiors, employees, customers, suppliers, and competitors.

Christian managers operating in the marketplace with an *agape* ethic must go one step further and ask an additional question: What ethical *standards* can we expect our employees to follow? The editor has concluded that there are three tiers of ethical standards, and two of these can be required of employees. One tier is beyond the volitional reach of the unregenerate. The three levels are outlined on the following page and will be discussed individually.

277

TIERS OF ETHICAL STANDARDS

Top Tier

Make a volitional commitment to enhance the well-being of my neighbors, even if it calls for some form of self-sacrifice.

Middle Tier

Subject all decisions and actions to the "sunlight" test and ask, Would both interested and impartial observers of my decisions and actions find them to be (1) mutually beneficial to all affected parties, and (2) prudent (practical, sound, discreet, circumspect, wise, informed, etc.)?

Lower Tier

Does my action obey the law and respect the cultural mores that bear on this decision and action?

Some Christians erroneously believe that nonChristians can never function on the top ethical tier, but occasionally people who do not love Christ are observed behaving in a manner consistent with that tier. This is possible because God's common grace can bring about a commitment to doing right that is strong enough to produce self-sacrificing behavior even in the lives of nonbelievers (see Rom. 5:7). Common grace will not, however, create in such a person's heart a *motivational base* that is the same as if the person had an intimate, personal knowledge of Christ's love. The true knowledge of Christ's love, when embraced in the innermost recesses of a Christian's heart, sets the expression of *agape* love apart from all other motivated responses in the human experience (see 1 John 4:16-19).

Philosophical altruism—an unselfish concern for others—can and does exist in specific cases in the lives of unbelievers, but this is not sufficient grounds for equating a particular altruistic act with the *agape* love of Scripture because a love for Christ is absent in humanitarian altruism. Such selfless acts illustrate the potential in God's image bearers for true love, but altruism without Christ still misses the biblical mark because the motive is unsustainable and doomed to revert to some form of self-righteousness. Because of this, Christians should not appeal to their fellow workers to act in a self-sacrificing, altruistic manner. They cannot will altruism into existence.

The middle tier of ethical standards can be more easily fostered and taught in the business environment because self-sacrifice isn't required in either prudentiality or mutual beneficiality. If persons in positions of leadership will practice mutual beneficiality and prudentiality with regard to others, and reward others for doing the same, those under them in the hierarchy will generally reflect their superiors' operating standards because it is prudent and in their best interest to do so. Workers know that their pay raises and promotions are attached, in part, to their compliance with their superiors' values.

The lower tier of standards—civil law and cultural mores—comprehends the minimal standards that a civilization can survive with. If these are ignored, the society will become anarchical. In fact, there seems to be an inverse relationship between the level of morality in a society and the number of laws necessary to govern it.

Christians can experience distress and anxiety when they suddenly find themselves in a society whose mores, practices, customs, and habits were not shaped by values compatible with the Judeo-Christian standards. Those of us who have lived in the United States all our lives are spoiled because our customs and mores were deeply influenced by the Judeo-Christian precepts. We are generally ill-equipped to handle mores shaped under different ethical persuasions.

To illustrate, the custom in Italy of reporting and paying a much lower income tax than the one actually owed, for the purpose of establishing a starting place for haggling with the tax authorities, is foreign to our very sense of honesty. The Italian business community, however, finds this practice acceptable and normal. To further illustrate the point, we are also offended—and rightly so from a biblical perspective—when bribes become a necessary and routine part of the business and political fabric of a society. But much of the world "greases" its operations through monetary payments. In many parts of the world, goods languish on the loading docks, or transportation papers are not forthcoming, when there is no "grease." Such methods often make it very difficult for Christians to live and function effectively in areas of the world where these practices prevail.

Therefore, we can conclude three things: (1) the *agape* ethic can function and does belong in the marketplace; (2) Christian leaders cannot expect nonChristians to practice *agape* love or altruism as a matter of everyday practice, but they can call for behavior that mirrors the attributes of mutual beneficiality and prudentiality; and (3) we must become like Christ in our very nature and character if *agape* love is to truly exist and be a force in the world. Our nature and character must be transformed by the Holy Spirit before this can happen, for we are totally dependent on the enabling work of Christ's Spirit to be able to love in a godly way. Yes, we are called to take the love of Christ to the marketplace, but the real love of Christ that counts others better than ourselves must be created in us by God. It is tough to work in the world and maintain a Christlike attitude, but God is capable of keeping our spiritual knees from bowing to the gods of mammon. The Holy Spirit must *dwell in us* so that Christ can be *formed* in us and we can have His *mind* and thereby be empowered to do *His will* (see 1 Cor. 2:16; Gal. 2:19–3:5; 4:19).

CHAPTER 14

THE FOUNDATION PRINCIPLES
IN REVIEW
Richard C. Chewning

G od has provided numerous biblical principles for our guidance that are operationally discernible in the natural order. Although these principles can be either overlooked or embraced, the natural consequences of either rejecting or following them cannot be avoided. And so it is with God's principles that have a bearing on business and economics. We cannot ignore God's revealed will without hurting ourselves or others. Conversely, if we diligently seek and follow God's directives, positive rewards will result. There are physical laws and there are spiritual laws, and they may not be ignored with impunity. Christ expressed this thought when He said,

> "Everyone who hears these words of Mine, and acts upon them, may be compared to a wise man, who built his house upon the rock. And the rain descended, and the floods came, and the winds blew, and burst against that house; and yet it did not fall, for it had been founded upon the rock. And everyone who hears these words of Mine, and does not act upon them, will be like a foolish man, who built his house upon the sand. And the rain descended, and the floods came, and the winds blew, and burst against that house; and it fell, and great was its fall." (Matt. 7:24-27)

Because few businesspeople are theologians and few theologians have been businesspeople, we have failed in the past to identify and disseminate those biblical principles that should direct our thinking regarding the biblical infrastructure for business and public policy. Neither have we looked for the biblical principles that should guide us as we perform our particular functions in the economic arena. This deficiency led to the CHRISTIANS IN THE MARKETPLACE series. The first two books have been specifically designed to ferret out precisely what the Bible has to say about the infrastructures God wants us to use as bases for our economic activities.

When buying a house, few people inspect its foundation. People are more likely to buy because of the aesthetics and the price of the house than the quality of its construction. But wise people also check to see if the home is structurally sound. The first two books of this series have done just that as they have examined the theological foundations of business and economics. Twenty-four of the world's finest scholars have expounded on the biblical principles that should undergird any system of economics. The third and fourth books rest on these foundations and are devoted to discovering and setting forth the specific biblical principles that apply to the functional areas of business (accounting, management, informations systems, marketing, etc.) and the application areas of public policy (national unemployment policy, health care policy, education policy, and so forth).

Two things are now in order as we conclude. First, a summary will be given of the foundational biblical principles that have been presented by the scholars in *Biblical Principles and Business: The Foundations* and in this book. The principles will be reviewed, and the location in the text of the two books where they were discussed will be noted by using a system of abbreviations. For example, if a principle was covered in book 1, chapters 3 and 7, and also in book 2, chapter 12, it would be designated: (bk. 1, chaps. 3, 7; bk. 2, chap. 12). And finally, a sample of the work done in developing the biblical principles that specifically apply to the functional areas of business and public policy will be provided so the reader will have an idea of the exciting intellectual journey that lies ahead.

Before we summarize the foundational principles, though, a comment is necessary. All the work in the CHRISTIANS IN THE MARKETPLACE series rests on the substantive belief that Scripture is God's absolutely accurate communication conveyed to His children for their care and instruction; and the writing of Scripture has been perfectly overseen by the Holy Spirit so that it comes to us with God's full authority and is, in the hands of the Spirit of God, a pure, healing light to be shined on every area of life—temporal *and* spiritual.

Furthermore, it is accepted that Scripture is (1) internally consistent, (2) expanding but not altering its revelation as it moves from Genesis to Revelation, and (3) self-interpreting. This last point means that Scripture, by providing multiple propositions or examples on the same subject, elucidates itself, albeit from various angles and in different contexts. Biblical principles are derived from the aggregation of these revelations on the same topic.

The books in our series, however, do not attempt to elaborate on or to defend these assumptions. They are simply accepted as "givens" throughout the work; their defense transcends the scope of the current project.

FOUNDATION PRINCIPLE 1

God created us to work and have dominion over the created order. This truth, though not the exclusive reason for our existence, was set forth before the Fall and was restated after the Fall. When we couple this fact with our innate capacity and desire to be creative and relate it to our inherent social characteristics, we soon realize that God created us to both engage in and enjoy the functions and rewards of exchange—economic, social, and intellectual. Economic activity is thus ordained by God and is a part of His intended will for us. God has declared all of this to be "very good," and He has imparted instructions to help us carry it forward. (See bk. 1, chaps. 2, 10; bk. 2, chaps. 1, 5, 6, 8, 9.)

FOUNDATION PRINCIPLE 2

God has given us clear directives on establishing and maintaining families, undertaking work, and fulfilling our needs for rest and worship, all of which are referred to theologically as the "creation mandates." God has also commanded us to evangelize the world and make disciples of persons who give their allegiance to Christ. We have been redeemed and set apart as a special people who are to know God and thereby become holy in character and righteous in behavior, even as He is.

These three dimensions of God's intentions for us are harmonized in that God specifically calls some people to focus on evangelism, while others are called on to engage in the making of disciples, thus incorporating all the creation mandates. This is concretely seen in the reality that *God calls many Christians to work in the economic arenas of life and be His agents there.*

Those called to labor for God's glory in the marketplace, however, need His special help as they (1) have the mind of Christ formed in them so they are enabled to think and behave as Christ would in the marketplace; (2) strive to constructively influence those with whom they work so that the group's behavior will be more righteous; and (3) pray and work for the synergistic transformation of society so that the creation mandates have a greater overall impact on culture. (See bk. 1, chaps. 2, 3; bk. 2, chaps. 12, 13.)

FOUNDATION PRINCIPLE 3

There is parity between and within the teachings of the Old and New Testaments. Because so much of the Old Testament was delivered in the context of an established theocratic state, more of it than the New Testament is devoted to civil and community matters. The Old Testament precepts are neither superior nor inferior to the civil and community matters discussed in the New Testament. In the same way, it can be fairly stated that Christ's teachings were predominantly focused on the attitudes, needs, and behavior of individuals and less focused on civil and public matters, but His life and teachings neither negated nor overshadowed the Old Testament revelations pertaining to personal ethics. Christ calls us to a higher level of personal sacrifice when He calls us to follow His personal example in fulfilling the intent of God's expressed will, but the ethic He taught is the same one found in the Old Testament. From this, we conclude that the Old and New Testaments together comprise the whole counsel of God and shape our understanding of God's intentions for us in the marketplace. (See bk. 1, chaps. 4, 5; bk. 2, chaps. 8, 13.)

FOUNDATION PRINCIPLE 4

The perfect and absolute will of God is revealed in its static form in the Law of God and disclosed in its dynamic and living form in Christ. Christians frequently experience real tensions, though, when they try to be obedient to the absolute will of God. They know that their fallen nature precludes them from being perfectly obedient, and they are completely dependent on the inner work of the Holy Spirit to enable them to manifest the will of God in their character and behavior. They are also aware that the absolutes of God are to be applied in situations requiring subjective moral judgments because (1) contemporary situations are often not perfectly analogous to biblical ones; (2) the absolute under consideration frequently applies to an abstract aspect of godly character (God is holy; therefore, we are to be holy), which makes it difficult to concretize the absolute in a dynamic situation; or (3) human finitude and imperfections render individuals relatively inept.

Christians must realize that *while God's Word is absolute in character and truth, we are nevertheless responsible in our finitude and imperfections to assess situations and make responsible judgments for which we are accountable.* This reality should not undermine our belief in absolutes or diminish our resolve to seek God's help in becoming holy and righteous so that our business practices can more perfectly reflect His will. Instead, this reality should stimulate us to seek a closer personal relationship with Christ in which we acknowledge our complete dependence on His grace and mercy. (See bk. 1, chaps. 6, 7; bk. 2, chaps. 12, 13.)

FOUNDATION PRINCIPLE 5

We are moral creatures, making moral choices with moral repercussions, who are morally responsible for our decisions and actions. Persons who reject Christ are as responsible before God for their moral choices as persons who love and obey Christ. But they are not motivated by His loving character and behavior, and they do not seek to glorify Him in what they do. Scripture clearly reveals that the evidence of God's existence, His attributes, and His nature and power are truly understood by them but they mentally suppress these realities. This truth leads us to a threefold conclusion. First, all people, apart from the regenerative work of the Holy Spirit, are truly dead in their sins, which renders them mentally, volitionally, and emotionally incapable of having the godly motive so essential for any act to be truly righteous. The unregenerate reside in a state of utter depravity.

Second, all people innately possess a sense of right and wrong. They may be approached forthrightly in the marketplace and called on to do what is universally understood to be right on the grounds of *natural law.* In fact, they can be approached on any one of three ethical levels: (*a*) it is our obligation to try to enhance the well-being of our neighbors, even when doing so may require self-sacrifice on our part; (*b*) it is good to be *prudent* (sound, discreet, circumspect, wise, informed, practical) and to seek those actions that produce *mutually beneficial* results; or (*c*) it is our minimal obligation to respect and obey the laws and cultural mores of society when they are not in conflict with God's standards.

Third, the prevention of civil anarchy that flows from the full-blown consequences associated with the first point above and the realization of any effective benefits from appealing to the natural law (the second point above) require God to create, by common grace, a moral climate that is able to incorporate godly principles into the woof and warp of the society. (See bk. 1, chaps. 8, 9; bk. 2, chaps. 1, 12, 13.)

Being endowed with a moral capacity also means we have the power of discretion. Our ability and concurrent obligation to choose is an essential aspect of our nature. Our capacity to make real moral choices cost Christ His life on the cross. Adam's choice to follow Eve's lead in eating the forbidden fruit caused Adam and all his heirs to fall, necessitating Christ's death to redeem mankind. The presence of this discretionary capacity in our nature points to an element at the heart of the truth that we are personally and morally responsible for our actions.

We are responsible for every choice we make, and we make moral choices or have moral opinions about every person and event we encounter. This concept, coupled with the biblical concept of our having been created to work (Foundation Principle 1), leads us to the necessary conclusion that our inherent capacity to choose is central to our personal responsibility to make choices resulting in meaningful contributions to society's welfare. This precept ought to become a building block on which to construct a society's economic system.

When God cursed the ground (because of Adam's sin) and removed Adam from the garden, and required him to toil and expend his energy to overcome the ground's resistance to his rule, God did not exempt Adam, or any of his descendants, from the harsh consequences of the Fall. Nor has God ever revealed that indolence—making poor moral choices that inhibit or preclude persons from being effective workers—should be materially rewarded. He is clear in establishing evidence to the contrary! (See bk. 1, chaps. 10, 11; bk. 2, chaps. 4, 5, 6, 7, 8, 9, 10, 11.)

FOUNDATION PRINCIPLE 6

God did not bestow a label such as capitalism or socialism on an economic system to reflect His preferences, but He has revealed many things about attitudes, capacities and characteristics, interpersonal relationships, the need to work, and other insights that help us know what a godly steward ought to be and do. *We can know those things that make an economic system compatible with His revealed will and with the created order.* We must acknowledge, though, that over the centuries God has sovereignly ruled the universe in a way indicating His willingness to allow His image bearers to accept or reject His discernible will regarding the type of economic arrangement that will serve mankind's needs more effectively, and His kindness and patience in giving people ample opportunities to walk in His ways or to go their own way until natural temporal judgments fall on them.

We must first discern and then speak out for the type of economic processes that ought to be in place if a business system is to reflect God's normative will. We should work hard to bring about understanding and behavior that foster the advancement of economic arrangements embodying God's normative standards—personal freedom to exercise responsible moral choice; opportunities to be productive, creative, and responsible; the right to own private property; and other personally enhancing and socially enhancing characteristics mentioned in chapters 2, 4, 5, 6, and 9 of this book. (See bk. 1, chaps. 2, 6, 7, 10; bk. 2, chaps. 2, 4, 5, 6, 7, 8, 9, 13.)

FOUNDATION PRINCIPLE 7

The fall of mankind gave rise to human misperceptions and perversions and, most of all, for the creation of attitudes that are self-serving (not God honoring) and inappropriately attached to the things of this world. For this reason, Christian ethics is concerned with the thoughts, attitudes, intentions, and motives of people. God looks on the heart as well as outward appearances. *Inner states and outward actions are equally important to God.* This is why Scripture says that the rich should not be arrogant or put their hope in riches, for these reflect attitudes of the heart.

When we understand the significance of our attitudes to God, we can recognize why God would want us to be free of the temptation to establish our righteousness through self-made religion that takes delight in self-abasement, personal accomplishments, self-righteous acts, status, and wealth (see Col. 2:18-23). Instead, we are to delight in Christ's righteousness and its imputation to us. We are to see everything in the light of God and praise Him who has given us everything for our enjoyment. We ought to appreciate and thank God for the value of gainful employment, the beauty of the operation of a successful business, the benefits of material wealth, and the place of an appropriate temporal self-interest, for they are compatible with His intentions for us and are His gifts to us. Scripture does not reveal a dichotomy between the sacred and the secular. God made everything and declared it to be very good. (See bk. 1, chaps. 2, 3, 8, 10; bk. 2, chaps. 2, 4, 5, 6, 8, 9, 13.)

FOUNDATION PRINCIPLE 8

A major biblical principle associated with stewardship is the necessity for the existence of personal property and the concomitant opportunity for stewards to exercise their free moral choice with regard to the administration of their personal property as they care for their families, churches, and others. This is another reason why the biblical principles are so important to the development of a healthy economic system. When people are denied opportunities to legitimately acquire and administer personal property, they are going to be retarded in their personal development. This observation should not surprise anyone, though, for the majority of adults spend the greatest portion of their waking hours engaged in some form of exchange—

producing, selling, buying, consuming—and these practices allow us to make a strong moral declaration about what we value and cherish the most, God or mammon. *Private property is central to the ideas of stewardship and personal moral choice, and it is an integral part of God's intended will for us to fulfill the creation mandates and carry out the Great Commission.* For this reason, we should want everyone to have the best opportunities possible to gain in a responsible way a reasonable amount of personal wealth. (See bk. 2, chaps. 5, 6, 7, 9.)

FOUNDATION PRINCIPLE 9

Some biblical truths seem to compete with one another, but they are really intended to be kept in balance in the purposeful tension God designed for them so that heresies (partial or imbalanced truths) can be avoided. A number of these tensions are either explicitly or implicitly involved with the foundation principles we are reviewing. For example, tensions can exist between the creation mandates and the Great Commission; the emphases of the Old and New Testaments; the adherence to absolute truths and the necessity for subjective judgments; the sovereignty of God and the responsibility of man; the spiritual and the temporal; and human equality and inequality. Christians have a difficult time dealing with the tension of being morally responsible individuals (see Foundation Principles 5, 6, and 8) who are simultaneously members of a community with responsibilities toward family, church, business, city, or nation. This is a vital foundation principle—*we are individuals with responsibilities toward our neighbors.*

Christians have responsibilities toward family, other Christians, and people in the wider community—in that order. Many of our scholars have noted that Scripture speaks of persons in positions of ruling authority (and individuals like Job) coming to the aid of the afflicted, needy, oppressed, orphans, poor, and widows. Besides, those who govern have the God-ordained authority to tax and use the revenues for the good of the governed.

Many American Christians feel uncomfortable when "government assistance" becomes the focus of conversation because for generations we have elevated "individualism" to great heights in our culture. The Bible, on the other hand, has a balanced perspective on this subject, and we in the Christian community desperately need to comprehend it. Only the Spirit, however, is capable of creating a proper world view in us that will allow us to seriously consider our relationship with and responsibilities toward the wider community. God pours out His temporal blessings on the righteous and the unrighteous alike. What are we to do? A biblical study of God's righteousness readily discloses that His compassion embodies an active concern for the downtrodden, hurt, needy, and oppressed. Are we not to be like God in this respect? (See bk. 1, chaps. 1, 2, 3, 11; bk. 2, chaps. 3, 7, 10, 11, 12, 13.)

FOUNDATION PRINCIPLE 10

God created us with motivational characteristics. Much of our creative energy is either released or shut down by the level of our motivation. We are also constituted so that we are capable of being influenced by both external and internal motivators—external rewards and punishments; internal desires, drives, and felt needs that activate or constrain the will. We are repeatedly confronted with temptations and opportunities to either try to manipulate others for our own self-serving ends or identify godly motivators and set them before people in an open and fair manner. To ignore or misunderstand our motivational nature is to risk creating an environment that fosters apathy and lethargy or that stimulates ungodly desires promoting self-centeredness.

When we combine this biblical principle with the previously discussed principles of work, moral choice, private property, and personal responsibility, we quickly realize just how integral this dimension of our humanity is to God's intentions regarding the creation of an economic system. An economic system must motivate those in it, or it will eventually fail. (See bk. 1, chaps. 12, 13; bk. 2, chaps. 8, 9.)

FOUNDATION PRINCIPLE 11

A fundamental biblical statement is this: "We have come to know and have believed the love which God has for us. God is love, and the one who abides in love abides in God, and God abides in him" (1 John 4:16). Love, the commitment to seek the good of another person or group even at the cost of self-sacrifice, is the highest expression of godliness. Christ has placed this calling before us all. In issuing the call to love, Christ shifted the standard from "love your neighbor as yourself" to "love one another, even as I have loved you" (John 13:34). He identified this as a *new* commandment because the standard was shifted from self to Christ.

Christians are to manifest Christ's love in all aspects of life: being with our families, serving and relating to other Christians, pursuing leisure activities, and working in the marketplace. There is no more evident principle in all Scripture. We are called to love our neighbor even as Christ has loved us. This absolute call applies seven days a week and in everything we do. We are not to conceive of the commandment to love others in some restrictive way, for Christ loved us when we were still His enemies. (See bk. 2, chaps. 12,13.)

FOUNDATION PRINCIPLE 12

God intends for us to have the "mind of Christ" and thereby acquire a true Christian view of life and the world (see 1 Cor. 2:16). The opening chapter of *Biblical Principles and Business: The Foundations* pointed out that being Christian does not automatically or necessarily give us an accurate or godly view of life. Chapters 12 and 13 of that book showed how a Christian's interpretation of Scripture could influence his or her world view and that an individual's world view is crucial. A mature Christian world view is developed incrementally by the Holy Spirit through the use of biblical precepts impressed on the heart. These precepts are in turn integrated with one another and our observations of the world until a larger and more complete understanding of reality is generated, enabling us to act according to God's expressed will. Those who have matured to this point are people of wisdom, and we know that wisdom comes from truly knowing and relating to God. Such a relationship results in our being like Him in character and conduct. This being true, we ought to seek God as the true "End" of all life. (See bk. 1, chaps. 1, 12, 13; bk. 2, chaps. 1, 8, 13.)

THE FOUNDATIONS ARE LAID

The twelve foundational principles named here are not an exhaustive list of biblical principles that could have been identified. Furthermore, much more could be said about our creation in the image of God or our fallen nature; these realities also yield significant foundational principles (see bk. 2, chap. 1). But these twelve principles are sufficient to establish that God wants His children to have the opportunity to exercise responsible moral choices in every area of life, including the economic realm. Our need to be free to exercise responsible moral choices points to a central aspect of our nature. This human quality should deeply influence our thinking about business and the economic arrangements nurturing it.

People need the freedom to be able to serve others, create, and produce without being artificially or unjustly cut off from those aspects of life that would help them to mature so they can participate in the fulfillment of the creation mandate. Unemployment, for example, for those who are willing to work and capable of working, regardless of their relationship with Christ, is probably one of the most dehumanizing economic conditions persons can encounter on earth. We were created to work, and to be kept from it, for whatever reason, is to attack our very identity and thwart part of the reason for our existing. People need to be able to work, sell, acquire, trade, succeed, fail, change jobs, and do a host of other things related to choice making. In addition, those who work in the public sector have an obligation to foster the things mentioned above and to act to eliminate every manmade obstruction hindering genuine, responsible freedom in the marketplace.

A SAMPLE OF THE FUTURE

At this point, it will be helpful to get a glimpse of what lies ahead. The third book in this series rests squarely on the foundations laid in these first two volumes and builds on them by identifying specific biblical principles applicable to twelve functional areas of business: strategic management, management, marketing, accounting, personal investments, advertising, informations systems and operations research, banking, organizational behavior, insurance, law, and human resources.

For example, Dr. Tom Harrison, the author of the chapter on accounting, focuses on six specific biblical principles that should guide Christians in that field. These include such things as God's concern for accountability, disclosure, and deceit. When we ask ourselves why each functional field of business exists, we quickly realize that it represents special tasks that are relational in character. That is why something as mechanical as accounting is completely undergirded by moral judgments and actions that affect those who have an interest in the records of business.

The scholars have not yet begun duplicating the principles that are being identified with the individual functional areas. (If you'll remember, one of the objectives of this series is to discover if there are many or only a few biblical principles.) It is too early to authoritatively make a final ruling on this point, but it would appear that there are many principles.

It is the editor's great hope that readers of the next two volumes in the series—about applying biblical principles to business and to public policy—will become excited about the material, whether or not it relates to their areas of professional expertise. It is hoped that a growing awareness of the richness and true applicability of biblical truths to the areas of business and public policy will stimulate a hunger to learn even more about God's great love for us as we work in the marketplace. For example, it was a thrill to see the scholars give Dr. Rae Mellichamp an enthusiastic ovation when he completed his presentation "Applying Biblical Principles in Information Systems and

Operations Research." They found his comments incredibly insightful, even though most of the scholars do not consider themselves professionals in the field of computer technology. But they became enthused when they learned how God had addressed, centuries ago, the ethical and moral considerations intricately and contemporarily involved in the management and use of this technology. Those of us who are responsible for the development of this series believe the readers will share their enthusiasm.

NOTES

CHAPTER 2

1. Taken from Paul Samuelson, *Economics: An Introductory Analysis* (New York: McGraw-Hill, 1967), pages 15-16.
2. Warren T. Brookes, "Goodness and the GNP," in *Is Capitalism Christian?*, ed. Franky Schaeffer (Westchester, Ill.: Crossway, 1985), page 24.
3. *The Limits to Growth: A Report for the Club of Rome's Project on the Predicament of Mankind,* ed. Donella H. Meadows et al. (New York: Universe Books, 1972).
4. *The Resourceful Earth: A Response to Global 2000,* ed. Julian L. Simon and Herman Kalin (Oxford: Blackwell, 1984), page 3.
5. Of course, there are other reasons why Christians have chosen to adopt a "simple" (or "simpler") lifestyle, such as (1) to be able to give more to others; (2) to develop Christian character and live more closely in imitation of Christ; (3) to forgo present reward and increase future heavenly reward; and (4) to live within the constraints of a low level of personal income.
6. Brookes, "Goodness and the GNP," page 45.
7. Michael Novak, "The Ideal of Democratic Capitalism," in *Is Capitalism Christian?*, page 52. On pages 61-64 Novak notes that truly enlightened self-interest includes not only the desire for profit but also an interest in preserving familial and community values and fulfilling religious, moral, artistic, and scientific interests, as well as interests in justice and peace. Thus, he can speak of "virtuous self-interest" (page 61), a large measure of which is necessary for democratic capitalism to function

effectively. Similar arguments are made by Warren Brookes, "Goodness and the GNP," see esp. pages 19-25, 40-45.

8. "The theory of the Communists may be summed up in the single sentence: Abolition of private property" (Karl Marx, *Communist Manifesto* [New York: International Publishers, 1948], page 23).

9. This is the argument of Ronald J. Sider, *Rich Christians in an Age of Hunger* (Downers Grove, Ill.: InterVarsity Press, 1984), page 96.

10. *The Constitution of the People's Republic of China* (Beijing: Foreign Languages Press, 1983), page 14.

CHAPTER 3

1. Jerry Falwell, *Listen, America* (Garden City, N.Y.: Doubleday, 1980), page 13.

2. Falwell, *Listen, America,* page 71.

3. George Gilder, "Where Capitalism and Christianity Meet," *Christianity Today,* February 3, 1983, page 27.

4. John C. Cort, *Christian Socialism* (Maryknoll, N.Y.: Orbis, 1988).

5. Stephen C. Mott, "How Should Christian Economists Use the Bible?" (Paper delivered at Biblical Perspectives on a Mixed Market Economy Consultation, Wheaton, Illinois, September 18-20, 1987), pages 36-37.

6. Nicholas Wolterstorff, "The Bible and Economics: The Hermeneutical Issues," *Transformation,* vol. 4 (June-December 1987), pages 17-18.

7. Stephen C. Mott, "The Contribution of the Bible to Economic Thought," *Transformation,* vol. 4 (June-December 1987), page 27.

8. Walter L. Owensby, *Economics for Prophets* (Grand Rapids, Mich.: Eerdmans, 1988), page xvii. This book is a thoughtful introduction to contemporary economic problems from a Christian perspective, and it is written in laymen's terms.

9. James W. Skillen, "The Economic Theory of Stewardship," *Eternity,* January 1988, page 12.

10. John White, "The Golden Cow: Materialism in the Twentieth-Century Church" (Downers Grove, Ill.: InterVarsity Press, 1979), page 38.

11. Stephen C. Mott, *Biblical Ethics and Social Change* (New York: Oxford University Press, 1982).

12. Mott, *Biblical Ethics,* pages 59-60, translates the Greek word *dikaiosyne* in this passage as "justice." The RSV, NIV, and other versions translate it as "righteousness," but Mott argues that when the word is used in the context of social responsibility or oppression, "justice" would be a better rendition.

13. Mott, *Biblical Ethics,* page 62.
14. Ronald J. Sider, *Rich Christians in an Age of Hunger* (Downers Grove, Ill.: InterVarsity Press, 1977), pages 59-85. See also Sider, *Cry Justice: The Bible Speaks on Hunger and Poverty* (Downers Grove, Ill.: InterVarsity Press, 1980), a Bible study book based on all the Scripture texts that pertain to questions of hunger, justice, and the poor. It is hardly necessary to point out that a vast body of literature has grown up around the theme of God's concern for the poor. Sider's work, however, has had the greatest impact on evangelical thinking because he is an evangelical, and unlike most writers on liberation, he holds to a high view of Scripture.
15. Owensby, *Economics for Prophets,* page xviii.
16. An especially egregious example of this is the parody on Sider's work by David Chilton, *Productive Christians in an Age of Guilt Manipulators* (Tyler, Tex.: Institute for Christian Economics, 1982).
17. William Graham Sumner, *The Challenge of Facts and Other Essays* (New Haven: Yale University Press, 1914), page 90.
18. Herbert Spencer, *Social Statics* (New York: Appleton, 1872), page 415.
19. A. G. Keller and M.R. Davie, eds., *Essays of William Graham Sumner* (New Haven: Yale University Press, 1934), vol. 2, page 56.
20. J. Philip Wogaman, *Economics and Ethics* (Philadelphia: Fortress, 1986), page 21.
21. Dietrich Bonhoeffer, *Letters and Papers from Prison* (New York: Macmillan, 1967), page 210.
22. Owensby makes the point forcefully. *Economics for Prophets,* pages xix-xx.

CHAPTER 4

1. One of the more notorious examples of such an error is Karl Marx's theory of surplus value. See my discussions in Ronald Nash, *Poverty and Wealth: The Christian Debate Over Capitalism* (Westchester, Ill.: Crossway, 1986), page 34, and in Ronald Nash, *Freedom, Justice and the State* (Lanham, Md.: University Press of America, 1980), pages 162-164.
2. Bettina Bien Greaves, *Free Market Economics* (Irvington-on-Hudson, N.Y.: Foundation for Economic Freedom, 1975), page 175.
3. The word *marginal* is used with respect to an addition or subtraction that changes the status quo. The marginal utility (value) of some commodity is what some person is willing to sacrifice to obtain one more unit or what he insists on receiving as his price for having one less unit. Economic value should be measured not in terms of the total value (whatever this

might mean) but in terms of one more or one less unit of the good or service. Humans weigh their choices regarding the acquisition (or loss) of some economic good in terms of what they take to be the benefits (or costs) of one additional unit. This judgment is always made in terms of the situation at that particular time. To secure one additional unit of some good at one time, I may be willing to incur a particular cost. At some later time that follows my acquisition of one unit of the good, I contemplate the new cost I am willing to incur to obtain one more unit of the good. The second situation is different from the first; I have just satisfied a want by acquiring one unit of the good. For this reason, the marginal utility of an additional unit of the good may be different in the second case.

4. Greaves, *Free Market Economics*, page 175.

5. There are nonmoral uses of the word *good*. We say that so-and-so is a good baseball player, that a certain restaurant serves good food, and that Lassie is a good dog. The economic use of *good* described above is equally nonmoral.

6. Obviously, the price of an economic good will reflect other things as well, such as a person's ability to bear the cost to acquire it.

7. Careful attention should be paid to the way I word this point. It would be wrong, of course, to think that all Christians would agree about the contents of any list of economic choices that ought to be criticized. All I am claiming is that an acceptance of the subjective theory of economic value is consistent with *any* person's criticizing particular economic choices on *moral* grounds. But having the right to make such objections is distinct from being right in those judgments. Anyone who presumes to make such judgments should be prepared to defend his claims. Naturally, any debate that might ensue would not be a debate about economics.

8. Positive or scientific economics is descriptive in the sense that it seeks to determine and report *what is the case*. Normative economics builds on the information supplied by positive economics and makes value judgments about the alternative policies that can be pursued. Normative economics makes judgments about *what ought to be the case*. For more on this distinction, see Nash, *Poverty and Wealth*, pages 14-18.

9. Charles W. Baird, review of *The Economics of Time and Ignorance*, in *The Review of Austrian Economics*, vol. 1 (1986), page 190.

10. Karen Vaughn, "Does It Matter That Costs Are Subjective?" *Southern Economic Journal*, vol. 46 (1980), pages 708-709. For more on the role of markets in all this, see Nash, *Poverty and Wealth*, chapter 5.

11. Israel Kirzner, "The Open-Endedness of Knowledge," *The Freeman*, vol. 36 (1986), page 87.

12. See Nash, *Poverty and Wealth,* chapters 12 and 13.
13. See Nash, *Poverty and Wealth,* chapters 8 and 11.
14. James M. Buchanan, "Introduction: L.S.E. Cost Theory in Retrospect," in *L.S.E. Essays on Cost,* ed. J. M. Buchanan and G. F. Thirlby (New York: New York University Press, 1981), page 14. The letters *L, S,* and *E* in the title refer to the London School of Economics.
15. Buchanan, "L.S.E. Cost Theory," pages 14-15.
16. Greaves, *Free Market Economics,* page 218.
17. Arman A. Alchian and William R. Allen, *University Economics,* 2nd ed. (Balmont, Calif.: Wadsworth, 1967), pages 15-16.
18. Alchian and Allen, page 20.
19. Kirzner, "Open-Endedness of Knowledge," page 87.
20. Kirzner, "Open-Endedness of Knowledge," page 88.
21. A *successful* entrepreneur is one whose beliefs about an opportunity prove to be correct. Every entrepreneur takes risks based on his beliefs. Since there is no certainty in economic behavior, entrepreneurs sometimes win and sometimes lose.
22. Stephen C. Littlechild, *The Fallacy of the Mixed Economy* (San Francisco: The Cato Institute, 1979), page 74.
23. By "capitalism," I do not mean the interventionist or mixed economy that often passes for capitalism in the United States. See Nash, *Poverty and Wealth,* chapters 6–11.
24. For one statement of von Mises's argument, see Ludwig von Mises, *Socialism* (New Haven: Yale University Press, 1951).
25. Giovanni Sartori, "The Market, Planning, Capitalism and Democracy," *This World* (Spring-Summer 1983), page 59.
26. Tom Bethell, "Why Socialism Still Doesn't Work," *The Free Market,* November 1985, pages 6-7.
27. Thomas Sowell, *Economics: Analysis and Issues* (Glenview, Ill.: Scott, Foresman, 1971), page 83.
28. Some socialists sought to counter von Mises's argument. For a discussion of how that counterattack fails, see Nash, *Poverty and Wealth,* pages 84ff.

CHAPTER 5

1. George J. Stigler, *The Economist as Preacher and Other Essays* (Chicago: University of Chicago Press, 1982), page 3. Stigler's observation is confirmed by Amartya Sen: "If one examines the balance of emphasis in the publications in modern economics, it is hard not to notice the eschewal of deep normative analysis, and the neglect of the influence of

ethical considerations in the characterization of actual human behavior"
(*On Ethics and Economics* [Oxford: Blackwell, 1987], page 7).

2. Stigler, *Economist as Preacher,* page 3.

3. Deontological: from the Greek *deon,* meaning "duty" or "obligation";
teleological: from the Greek *telos,* meaning "end" or "goal."

4. Cf. Lisa Sowle Cahill, "Teleology, Utilitarianism, and Christian
Ethics," *Theological Studies,* vol. 42 (1982), pages 601-629.

5. *Nicomachean Ethics,* 1. 7. 10.

6. Augustine, *City of God,* 22. 30. Cf. Calvin, *Institutes,* 3. 25. 2. For an
elaboration of the biblical basis of the Augustinian teleology, see the
author's article "The Supreme Good," *Presbyterion: Covenant Seminary
Review 11* (1985), pages 124-141.

7. Stigler, *Economist as Preacher,* page 26.

8. Christini Ammer and Dean S. Ammer, "Utility," in *Dictionary of
Business and Economics,* rev. ed. (New York: Free, 1984). Cf. Ricardo:
"If a commodity were in no way useful — in other words, if it could in no
way contribute to our gratification — it would be destitute of exchange-
able value" (cited by John Kenneth Galbraith, *Economics in Perspective:
A Critical History* [Boston: Houghton, 1987], page 82).

9. Nicholas Georgescu-Roegen, *Encyclopedia of Economics,* ed. Douglas
Greenwald (New York: McGraw–Hill, 1982), page 934.

10. *An Introduction to the Principles of Morals and Legislation* (1789), cited
by Galbraith, *Economics in Perspective,* page 118.

11. Georgescu-Roegen, *Encyclopedia of Economics,* page 934.

12. Cf. Ludwig von Mises, *Epistemological Problems of Economics,* trans.
George Reisman (Princeton: D. Van Nostrand, 1960), pages 151-152.

13. Milton and Rose Friedman, *Free to Choose: A Personal Statement* (New
York: Avon, 1981), page 135.

14. Friedman, *Free to Choose,* pages 18-19.

15. Von Mises, *Epistemological Problems of Economics,* page 150.

16. Alfred Marshal, cited by Galbraith, *Economics in Perspective,* page 5.

17. *Webster's New World Dictionary of the American Language, College
Edition* (New York: Simon and Schuster, 1980).

18. Thomas Chalmers, *On Political Economy, in Connexion with the Moral
State and Moral Prospects of Society* (Glasgow, 1832), page iii.
Chalmers was concerned with finding a remedy for "pauperism" or, as
we would say, "chronic poverty."

19. Chalmers, *On Political Economy,* page iv.

20. *Westminster Shorter Catechism,* questions 74-75. The *Larger Catechism*
is remarkably comprehensive:

The duties required in the eighth commandment are, truth, faithfulness, and justice in contracts and commerce between man and man; rendering to everyone his due; restitution of goods unlawfully detained from the right owners thereof; giving and lending freely, according to our abilities, and the necessities of others; moderation of our judgments, wills, and affections concerning worldly goods; a provident care and study to get, keep, use, and dispose these things which are necessary and convenient for the sustentation of our nature, and suitable to our condition; a lawful calling, and diligence in it; frugality; avoiding unnecessary lawsuits, and suretyship, or other like engagements; and an endeavour, by all just and lawful means, to procure, preserve and further the wealth and outward estate of others, as well as our own. (question 141)

The sins forbidden in the eighth commandment, besides the neglect of the duties required, are, theft, robbery, man-stealing, and receiving anything that is stolen; fraudulent dealing, false weights and measures, removing landmarks, injustice and unfaithfulness in contracts between man and man, or in matters of trust; oppression, extortion, usury, bribery, vexatious lawsuits, unjust inclosures and depopulations; ingrossing commodities to enhance the price; unlawful callings, and all other unjust or sinful ways of taking or withholding from our neighbor what belongs to him, or of enriching ourselves; covetousness; inordinate prizing and affecting worldly goods; distrustful and distracting cares and studies in getting, keeping, and using them; envying the prosperity of others; as likewise idleness, prodigality, wasteful gaming; and all other ways whereby we do unduly prejudice our own outward estate, and defrauding ourselves of the due use and comfort of that estate which God hath given us. (question 142)

21. *Larger Catechism*, question 8.141. Cf. Leviticus 25:35; Philippians 2:4.
22. Cf. Calvin: "Not only are those thieves who secretly steal the property of others, but those also who seek for gain from the loss of others, accumulate wealth by unlawful practices, and are more devoted to their private advantage than to equity" (*Commentaries on the Four Last Books of Moses Arranged in the Form of a Harmony*, trans. Charles William Bingham [Grand Rapids, Mich.: Eerdmans, 1950], vol. 3, page 111).
23. The repetition of the verb is generally assumed to be necessary, but there are other grammatical possibilities, e.g., "Love your neighbor as [one like] yourself," i.e., as a person with rights and responsibilities before God the same as you. For a fuller presentation, see the author's "Love: The Impelling Motive of the Christian Life," *Presbyterion: Covenant*

Seminary Review, vol. 12 (1986), pages 65-92.

24. Galbraith, *Economics in Perspective,* page 64.

25. *Westminster Shorter Catechism,* 8.104.

26. Sen, *On Ethics and Economics,* pages 22-28.

27. *The Theory of Moral Sentiments* (1790), cited by Sen, *On Ethics and Economics,* page 23.

28. Galbraith, *Economics in Perspective,* page 233.

29. Galbraith, *Economics in Perspective,* page 291.

30. For a Christian approach to the problems of unemployment in Great Britain, see Alan Storkey, *Transforming Economics: A Christian Way to Employment* (London: SPCK, 1986).

31. *Sine qua non:* an essential condition; indispensable; an absolute prerequisite. *Raison d'etre:* reason for being; justification for existence.

32. Chalmers, *On Political Economy,* p. iii.

33. Henry Hazlitt, *Economics in One Lesson* (New York: Harper, 1946), page 211.

34. Peter L. Berger, *The Capitalist Revolution: Fifty Propositions About Prosperity, Equality, and Liberty* (New York: Basic, 1986).

CHAPTER 6

1. Hans van der Geest, "AIDS und die TREUE," in *Reformiertes Forum* (Basel, Switzerland), February 11, 1988, pages 8-9.

2. Karl Barth, *Protestant Theology in the Nineteenth Century* (Valley Forge, Pa.: Judson, 1972), esp. chapter 1.

3. This thesis of the liberation theologians is echoed by Ronald J. Sider in his influential work *Rich Christians in an Age of Hunger* (Downers Grove, Ill.: InterVarsity Press, 1984).

4. Harvey A. Cox, *The Secular City* (London: SCM Press, 1965).

5. Roland Huntford, *The New Totalitarians* (New York: Stein & Day, 1972).

6. Hannah Arendt, *The Origins of Totalitarianism* (New York: Harcourt Brace Jovanovich, 1973 [1951]), pages 305ff., 318. This theme is also developed by Friedrich Georg Junger in *Maschine und Eigentum* (1950).

7. Thomas Molnar, *Utopia: The Perennial Heresy* (New York: Sheed & Ward, 1967).

CHAPTER 7

1. U.S. Roman Catholic Bishops, "Economic Justice For All: Catholic Social Teaching and the U.S. Economy," *Origins: NC Documentary*

Service, vol. 16 (November 27, 1986), pages 409-456.

2. Abraham Kuyper, *Christianity and the Class Struggle*, trans. D. Jellema (Grand Rapids, Mich.: Piet Hein Publishers, 1950), pages 17-20.

3. Kuyper, *Christianity and the Class Struggle*, pages 19, 51-52.

4. Jean-Jacques Rousseau, *The Social Contract*, trans. W. Kendall (Chicago: Gateway, 1954), page 41.

5. Rousseau, *The Social Contract*, page 41.

6. Daniel Bell, *The Cultural Contradictions of Capitalism* (New York: Basic, 1976), pages 10-12.

7. Bell, *Cultural Contradictions*, pages 14-15.

8. Bell, *Cultural Contradictions*, pages 15-30.

9. See Bernard Zylstra, "A Neoconservative Critique of Modernity: Daniel Bell's Appraisal," *Christian Scholar's Review*, vol. 7, no. 4 (1978), pages 337-355.

10. Irving Kristol, *Two Cheers for Capitalism* (New York: Basic, 1978), pages 66-68.

11. Harry M. Kuitert, *Signals from the Bible*, trans. Lewis B. Smedes (Grand Rapids, Mich.: Eerdmans, 1972), pages 30-33.

12. Kristol, *Two Cheers*, pages 66-68.

13. John Locke, *Two Treatises of Government* (New York: Hafner Publishing, 1947), pages 51, 65-66, 136.

14. Gerald Vandezande, *Christians in the Crisis: Toward Responsible Citizenship* (Toronto: Anglican Book Center, 1983), pages 63-64.

15. Max L. Stackhouse, *Public Theology and Political Economy: Christian Stewardship in Modern Society* (Grand Rapids, Mich.: Eerdmans for Commission on Stewardship National Council of Churches, 1987), page 120.

16. Stackhouse, *Public Theology and Political Economy*, page 120.

17. Stackhouse, *Public Theology and Political Economy*, pages 132-135.

18. See Robert Bellah et al., *Habits of the Heart: Individualism and Commitment in American Life* (Berkeley, Calif.: University of California Press, 1985), pages 152-154, 281-283, 286.

CHAPTER 8

1. Jean L. McKechnie et al., eds., *Webster's New Twentieth Century Dictionary of the English Language*, unabridged 2d ed. (New York: Collins & World, 1977), page 921.

2. *Webster's Dictionary*, page 1853.

3. See *Webster's Dictionary*, page 574. But see especially the standard

economists' definition of economics in Thomas Sowell, *Economics: Analysis and Issues* (Glenview, Ill.: Scott, Foresman, 1971), page 2.

4. This does not presuppose that shipping corn to Ethiopia is, *ipso facto,* either good or bad. The Ethiopian government intercepts many food shipments and resells them on the world market in exchange for arms, which it uses to kill its people.

5. Modern economists speak of "cost" more specifically as "opportunity cost"—i.e., all the opportunities lost by our choosing to use resources one way instead of another. Cost is measured, then, not in dollars or other monetary units but in opportunites—things far less susceptible of precise measurement and hence less easily dealt with by materialistic, "econometric" economics.

6. Forty-six incentives that I found revealed in Genesis 1–21 are biological reproduction and rule over the earth (1:28; cf. 8:17; 9:1, 7; 16:2; 19:32); preservation of life (2:17; cf. 3:3; 6:13-14; 19:15, 17; 20:3, 7); marital union (2:24); knowledge and self-determination (3:5); food (3:6); Zaesthetics/beauty (3:6); wisdom (3:6); embarrassment (3:8); fear (3:10; cf. 3:24; 4:15; 9:5-6; 12:12-13, 18-20; 16:6; 18:15); peer pressure (3:12-13; cf. 3:17); malevolence, or simple evil (3:14; cf. 6:5; 8:21; 13:13); hatred of evil, love of righteousness (3:15); will to power (3:16); desire for eternal life (3:22); desire to gain God's approval (4:3-4, 7); anger (4:5); desire to master or defeat sin (4:7); jealousy (4:8; cf. 13:7; 16:5; 20:10); self-centeredness, neglect of others (4:9); discontent (4:12); resentment and vengeance (4:23; cf. 9:25); sexual lust (6:2; cf. 19:5); benevolence, or simple righteousness (6:9); disrespect for parents (9:22); respect for parents (9:23); gratitude (9:26-27); fame (11:4; cf. 12:2); ethnic/cultural preservation, unity, and pride (11:4); desire to gain God's blessing (12:3); desire to avoid God's curse (12:3); obedience to God's command (12:4; 17:23); physical necessity (13:6); peacemaking (13:8; 21:22-24); greed (13:10; cf. 14:11-12); family loyalty (14:14ff.— or is this justice? or both?—cf. 20:11); honor to God's spokesman (14:20); integrity (14:22-24); faith (15:6); unbelief (16:1-6; cf. 18:12); pride or contempt (16:5); cowardice (16:6; cf. 20:2); reverence or fear of God (9:6; cf. 17:3); doubt (17:17); hospitality or generosity (18:3-8; cf. 19:2); laziness (19:19); security (21:22-24).

7. For discussion, see the chapter by Ronald Nash in this collection. See also E. Calvin Beisner, *Prosperity and Poverty: The Compassionate Use of Resources in a World of Scarcity* (Westchester, Ill.: Crossway, 1988), chapter 8, "Value and Price," and references cited there. The most extensive analysis of economic value is Eugen von Böhm-Bawerk's

Capital and Interest, trans. George D. Huncke and Hans F. Sennholz, 3 vols. (South Holland, Ill.: Libertarian Press, 1959), vol. 2, *Positive Theory of Capital,* Book 3, *Value and Price,* pages 121-256.

8. This understanding lies at the root of many economists' objections to wage and price controls as countereffective and inconsistent with the subjective theory of economic value. See Beisner, *Prosperity and Poverty,* chapter 12, "Stewardship and Economic Regulation: Price Controls."

9. See Ronald H. Nash, *Poverty and Wealth: The Christian Debate Over Capitalism* (Westchester, Ill.: Crossway, 1986), page 72.

10. This leads to the principle of *marginal utility.* See Beisner, *Prosperity and Poverty,* chapter 8, and Böhm-Bawerk, *Capital and Interest,* vol. 2, Part A, esp. chapter 3.

11. This is true of *altruistic* people. But people may also give charity where it isn't appreciated or beneficial.

12. Two other kinds of incentive are rarely—if ever—much involved in *economic* choices. They are genuine (unmixed) benevolence and genuine (unmixed) malevolence. Genuinely benevolent acts are done for the sole purpose of complying with God's revealed moral will and so doing good to others, without regard to personal costs (see Rom. 13:8-10). Genuinely malevolent acts are done for the sole purpose of violating God's revealed moral will and so harming others, without regard to personal benefits.

13. James M. Buchanan, "Methods and Morals in Economics," in *Science and Ceremony,* ed. William Breit and W. P. Culbertson (Austin: University of Texas Press, 1976), pages 163-174, reprinted in Buchanan, *What Should Economists Do?* (Indianapolis: LibertyPress, 1979), pages 201-217. The citation is from the latter, page 207.

14. There are exceptions, such as when one says to himself, "If I stick to it and finish this homework assignment tonight, I'll treat myself to an ice-cream sundae when I'm done." One can offer himself a reward, but generally rewards and punishments come from others.

15. St. Augustine, *Expositions on the Book of Psalms,* on Psalm 73:25; paraphrased from A. Cleveland Coxe's translation in *A Select Library of the Nicene and Post-Nicene Fathers of the Christian Church,* ed. Philip Schaff, series 2, Part 1 (Grand Rapids, Mich.: Eerdmans, 1979), vol. 8, page 341.

16. Whether regenerate or not, Adam Smith was certainly more than a deist. His theological presuppositions were closer to those of orthodox Christianity. In his *Theory of Moral Sentiments* (Indianapolis: LibertyPress/Liberty-

Classics, 1976) he clearly affirmed the existence of Heaven and hell and of the Final Judgment, and referred distinctly to Christ as our Savior.

17. In Smith's moral philosophy, the "impartial spectator" was more than a rhetorical device (though it was that). It represented the well-formed conscience that judged impartially the prudence, justice, and beneficence of every person's acts.

18. Smith, *Theory of Moral Sentiments,* page 156.

19. See the discussion of Romans 13:1-10 in Beisner, *Prosperity and Poverty,* chapter 11, "Stewardship and Limited Government."

20. Smith, *Theory of Moral Sentiments,* pages 166ff., emphasis added.

21. Russell Kirk, *The American Cause* (Chicago: Regnery, 1957, 1965), pages 103ff.

22. This argument echoes a point made by Russell Kirk more than thirty years ago: "We may call this system of free enterprise 'capitalism,' if we like, though that Marxist word does not really mean very much. 'Capital' is simply those goods—tools, machines, buildings, ships, trains, and the like—which are used to produce other goods. Any civilized society, therefore, is 'capitalistic,' since capital goods always are required to produce consumer goods. A communistic society requires capital quite as much as a 'capitalistic' society does. But what Marx meant by 'capitalism' is the ownership of capital by private persons" (*American Cause,* page 100).

23. Cited in William D. Whitney et al., eds., *The Century Dictionary: An Encyclopedic Lexicon of the English Language,* 6 vols. (New York: Century, 1889), vol. 1, page 805.

24. A good historical survey of the social and economic changes that accompanied the transition from feudalism to "capitalism" is Nathan Rosenberg's and L.E. Birdzell's *How the West Grew Rich* (New York: Basic Books, 1986), chapter 4, "The Evolution of Institutions Favorable to Commerce," and chapter 5, "The Development of Industry: 1750-1880."

25. Kirk, *American Cause,* pages 154-156.

26. On the proper role of civil government in the economy, see Beisner, *Prosperity and Poverty,* chapter 11, "Stewardship and Limited Government."

27. See Friedrich A. Hayek, *The Constitution of Liberty* (South Bend, Ind.: Gateway, 1960, 1972), page 422, notes 5, 6.

28. Ludwig von Mises, *Socialism: An Economic and Sociological Analysis,* trans. J. Kahane, 2d ed. (London: Jonathan Cape, 1951, 1969), page 194.

29. This transition from feudalism to the free market economy and its ties to

the growth of towns and trading, along with the growing recognition of the connection between private property ownership and freedom, is chronicled in Rosenberg and Birdzell's *How the West Grew Rich,* esp. chapter 2, "The Starting Point: The Middle Ages," and chapter 3, "The Growth of Trade to 1750."

30. Friedrich A. Hayek's seminal warning against the destruction of Western liberties through socialism, *The Road to Serfdom* (Chicago: University of Chicago Press, 1944), hinges on this very understanding of the relationships between property and liberty, on the one hand, and between lack of property and serfdom (servility, slavery), on the other.

31. Similar mistaken notions of freedom plague some contemporary writings on economics by representatives of the evangelical left. See, for example, Ronald J. Sider, *Rich Christians in an Age of Hunger,* 2d rev. ed. (Downers Grove, Ill.: InterVarsity Press, 1984).

32. Kirk, *American Cause,* pages 107ff.

33. See Beisner, *Prosperity and Poverty,* chapter 12, "Stewardship and Economic Regulation: Price Controls."

34. See Beisner, *Prosperity and Poverty,* chapter 8, "Value and Price," and chapter 12, "Stewardship and Economic Regulation: Price Controls." See also von Mises, *Socialism: An Economic and Sociological Analysis,* Part 2, Section 1, chapter 2, "The Organization of Production Under Socialism," esp. section 2, "Economic calculation in the socialist community."

35. For a discussion on what is just, see Beisner, *Prosperity and Poverty,* chapter 4, "A Christian View of Economic Justice," and chapter 5, "Does Justice Demand Equality?"

36. Cited in Ludwig von Mises, *Planned Chaos* (Irvington-on-Hudson, N.Y.: Foundation for Economic Education, 1947, 1965), page 87. Reprinted from von Mises, *Socialism: An Economic and Sociological Analysis,* Epilogue, page 589; von Mises found the quotation in Friedrich Hayek, *The Road to Serfdom,* chapter 9.

37. See Beisner, *Prosperity and Poverty,* chapter 11, "Stewardship and Limited Government."

38. It may be argued that a truly free market is impossible given man's fallen nature. This may mean either that (1) that because man is sinful, he cannot be trusted to act righteously in a truly free market, and therefore, a truly free market is undesirable, or (2) that because man is sinful, he will never grant his fellows the full freedom God intends for them. The former meaning is equally valid as an objection to a controlled market. Sinful man cannot be trusted to act righteously when in control of others;

therefore, a truly controlled economy is undesirable. The second idea, that because man is sinful he will never grant true and complete freedom to his fellows, seems a much more likely explanation for the failure of mankind yet to achieve a truly and completely free market (in the proper sense of freedom). Since a free market permits greatly differing rewards for greatly differing behavior, and since fallen man is inherently envious and covetous, it seems unlikely that any society will overcome envy and coveting sufficiently to permit the full range of economic freedom God intends for man.

39. William E. Diehl defends such a system in his essay "The Guided-Market System," in *Wealth and Poverty: Four Christian Views,* ed. Robert G. Clouse (Downers Grove, Ill.: InterVarsity Press, 1984). Gary North's response to Diehl in the same volume indicates the theoretical and practical weaknesses of Diehl's program.

40. See Beisner, *Prosperity and Poverty,* chapter 8, "Value and Price," chapter 12, "Stewardship and Economic Regulation: Price Controls," and chapter 13, "Stewardship and Economic Regulation: Access Controls and Subsidies."

41. Any discussion of the state's role in the economy must recognize that the distinguishing feature of the state, in contrast to any other institution, is its possession of the monopoly of force. Aside from limited punishment of children by parents and limited use of force in self-defense, only the state is ordained by God to use force to gain people's compliance with its mandates.

42. Von Mises, *Planned Chaos,* page 29. This work is included as an epilogue to von Mises's *Socialism: An Economic and Sociological Analysis,* where this paragraph appears on page 538.

CHAPTER 9

1. For a definition of *incentive,* see pages 169-171.

2. A valuable insight of the public choice school of economics is that, because civil employees are morally no different from private persons, they are as likely to formulate public policy with their self-interest in mind as private persons are to make private decisions with their self-interest in mind. (Self-interest must not be equated with selfishness. See the chapter in this book by Ronald Nash.) This insight is consistent with the biblical doctrine of the sinfulness of man and undercuts the common assumption that civil employees are necessarily more altruistic than private persons.

3. One of the most extensive and valuable studies of motives is Adam Smith's *Theory of Moral Sentiments* (Indianapolis: Liberty*Press*/Liberty*Classics*, 1976), first published in 1759 and still rewarding to careful readers. References to it in this chapter are to this Liberty*Classics* edition.

4. Carl F. H. Henry, *Christian Personal Ethics* (Grand Rapids, Mich.: Baker, 1977 [1957]), page 528.

5. Henry, *Christian Personal Ethics*, page 532.

6. An implication of the argument of the previous chapter is that the free market economic system performs better in this respect than the controlled economy.

7. Henry, *Christian Personal Ethics*, page 184.

8. Adam Smith, *An Inquiry into the Nature and Causes of the Wealth of Nations*, ed. Edwin Cannan (Chicago, Ill.: University of Chicago Press, 1976 [1776]), vol. 1, page 476 [Bk. 4, ch. 2, sec. (2)].

9. Smith, *Theory of Moral Sentiments*, page 90.

10. Smith, *Theory of Moral Sentiments*, pages 71-72.

11. These are summarized in E. G. West's introduction to *Theory of Moral Sentiments*, pages 27-29.

12. Jim Halteman, *Market Capitalism and Christianity* (Grand Rapids, Mich.: Baker, 1988), pages 24-27.

13. In agreement, see Ronald C. Doll, "Motives and Motivation," in *Baker's Dictionary of Christian Ethics*, ed. Carl F. H. Henry (Grand Rapids, Mich.: Baker, 1973), pages 437ff.

14. Henry, *Christian Personal Ethics*, pages 531, 533.

15. Henry, *Christian Personal Ethics*, pages 529-548.

16. Henry, *Christian Personal Ethics*, page 530. See the *Heidelberg Catechism*, Third Part, in *Creeds of Christendom*, ed. Philip Schaff, 3 vols. (Grand Rapids, Mich.: Baker, 1977 [1877]), vol. 3, pages 338ff.

17. Walter Bauer, *A Greek-English Lexicon of the New Testament and Other Early Christian Literature*, trans. William F. Arndt and F. Wilbur Gingrich, rev. F. Wilbur Gingrich and Frederick W. Danker, 2d ed. (Chicago: University of Chicago Press, 1979), page 467.

18. This idea forms a central theme in my *Psalms of Promise: Exploring the Majesty and Mystery of God* (Colorado Springs: NavPress, 1988), a study of man's covenantal relationship with God as revealed in eighteen selected psalms.

19. The verse brings to a climax a discussion of the proper recipients of systematic financial support from the Church, a context starting at 5:3. I have discussed this at length in *Prosperity and Poverty: The Compassion-*

ate Use of Resources in a World of Scarcity (Westchester, Ill.: Crossway, 1988), pages 203-205. See also E. Calvin Beisner, "The Poor Among Us: How Should Your Church Help?" and "How Much for How Many?" *Discipleship Journal*, vol. 9, no. 1 (1989), pages 17-20.

20. The ell was a measurement of length based on the distance from elbow to base of hand.

21. The Bible does not prescribe maximum interest rates on loans. Neither does it prohibit all interest. Rather, it prohibits interest on loans to the poor but leaves rates of interest on other loans open to mutual agreement. See Beisner, *Prosperity and Poverty*, pages 215, 276-277 (notes 21, 24), 258 (note 19).

22. *Heidelberg Catechism*, question 110.

23. St. Francis de Sales, *Introduction to the Devout Life*, trans. John K. Ryan (Garden City, N.Y.: Doubleday Image Books, 1972 [1608]), pages 162ff.

24. The tithe—10 percent of net income—is required in Scripture as a tribute payment in the believer's covenantal relationship with God. It is a minimum, not a standard, level for Christian giving. It is upheld, not abolished, in the New Testament. See Beisner, *Prosperity and Poverty*, pages 202, 270 (notes 18, 20). On overcoming the worship of wealth, see chapter 1 of the same work.

CHAPTER 10

1. Ronald H. Nash, *Social Justice and the Christian Church* (Milford, Mich.: Mott Media, 1984), page 1.

2. Charles Murray, *Losing Ground* (New York: Basic, 1984).

3. Cf. Daniel Patrick Moynihan, *Family and Nation* (New York: Harcourt Brace Jovanovich, 1987), pages 216-217. There are good reasons why Murray's analysis has stood up and has begun to convince even the skeptics. For a summary of those reasons, see Lawrence M. Mead, "Why Murray Prevailed," *Academic Questions,* vol. 1, no. 2 (Spring 1988), pages 23ff.

4. Myron Magnet, "The Homeless," *Fortune,* November 23, 1987, page 183.

5. American Enterprise Institute, *The New Consensus on Family and Welfare* (Milwaukee: Marquette University Press, 1987), page 101.

6. Cf. Moynihan, *Family and Nation,* pages 46-47; American Enterprise Institute, *Consensus on Family and Welfare,* pages 47-48.

7. Cf. Sean Wilentz, "God and Man at Lynchburg," *The New Republic,* April 25, 1988, pages 30ff.

8. Michael Harrington, *The New American Poverty* (New York: Penguin, 1987), page 61; American Enterprise Institute, *Consensus on Family and Welfare*, page 8; George Grant, *The Dispossessed* (Ft. Worth: Dominion Press, 1986), page 31.

9. Harrington, *New American Poverty*, page 9.

10. Harrington, *New American Poverty*, page 67.

11. Ronald H. Nash, *Poverty and Wealth* (Westchester, Ill.: Crossway, 1986), pages 172-173.

12. Nash, *Poverty and Wealth*, pages 172-174.

13. Nash, *Poverty and Wealth*, page 71.

14. American Enterprise Institute, *Consensus on Family and Welfare*, page 51.

15. Magnet, "The Homeless," page 180; American Enterprise Institute, *Consensus on Family and Welfare*, page 14; Moynihan, *Family and Nation*, pages 45-48, 95, 111.

16. Grant, *Dispossessed*, page 16; Harrington, *New American Poverty*, pages 8, 11, 58, 60.

17. Grant, *Dispossessed*, pages 33ff.

18. Grant, *Dispossessed*, pages 33ff.

19. David Chilton, *Productive Christians in an Age of Guilt Manipulators* (Tyler, Tex.: Institute for Christian Economics, 1985), pages 46, 49.

20. Chilton, *Productive Christians*, page 50.

21. George Grant, *Bringing in the Sheaves* (Atlanta: American Vision Press, 1985), pages 74ff.; Chilton, *Productive Christians*, pages 56-57.

22. Grant, *Bringing*, pages 80-82.

23. Grant, *Bringing*, page 82.

24. Grant, *Bringing*, pages 58-60.

25. Grant, *Dispossessed*, pages 34-35.

26. Chilton, *Productive Christians*, pages 52ff.

27. Moynihan, *Family and Nation*, page 173.

28. Grant, *Bringing*, pages 60-61.

29. Grant, *Bringing*, pages 111ff.

30. Cf. John Grossman, "OIC: A Hand Up, Not a Handout," *American Way*, February 1982, pages 38ff.; Mark A. Thennes, *Creating Neighborhood Enterprise: A Primer for Nonprofits* (Washington, D.C.: National Center for Neighborhood Enterprise, 1984); Robert L. Woodson, "Helping the Poor Help Themselves," *Policy Review* (Summer 1982), pages 73ff. Most of the "secular" programs that work for helping the poor use principles deriving from a biblical approach to the problem. This is not to say that these principles are self-consciously adapted; rather, it is merely to

observe that what the Bible has to say about such things as encouraging responsibility, teaching skills, and providing ongoing support while the poor are getting back on their feet is coming to be acknowledged by directors of secular programs for poor relief as eminently reliable and valid. See, for example, the symposium, "Don't Give Up: Poverty Programs That Work," *Washington Monthly*, June 1988, pages 28ff.

31. Peter Goldberg, "Corporate America Should Speak Out on Social Issues," *Nonprofit Times*, vol. 1, no. 3 (June 1987), page 23.

32. Nash, *Poverty and Wealth*, pages 114ff.

33. Grant, *Dispossessed*, page 35.

34. American Enterprise Institute, *Consensus on Family and Welfare*, page 9.

35. Grant, *Bringing*, page 98.

36. Magnet, "The Homeless," page 190.

37. Chilton, *Productive Christians*, pages 45, 229ff.

38. American Enterprise Institute, *Consensus on Family and Welfare*, page 14.

39. American Enterprise Institute, *Consensus on Family and Welfare*, page 87.

40. Grant, *Bringing*, page 70.

41. American Enterprise Institute, *Consensus on Family and Welfare*, pages 99ff.

42. Ken Auletta, *The Underclass* (New York: Vintage, 1983).

43. C. John Miller, *Outgrowing the Ingrown Church* (Grand Rapids, Mich.: Zondervan, 1986), pages 81ff., 151ff.

44. Moynihan, *Family and Nation*, pages 116-117.

45. Moynihan, *Family and Nation*, page 168.

46. Moynihan, *Family and Nation*, pages 180-181; American Enterprise Institute, *Consensus on Family and Welfare*, page 15.

CHAPTER 11

1. This summary of the Mosaic law provisions relating to poverty draws heavily on John D. Mason, "Biblical Teaching and Assisting the Poor," *Transformation*, vol. 4, no. 2 (April-June 1987), pages 1-14.

2. Mason, "Biblical Teaching and Assisting the Poor," page 9.

3. For a forceful statement of this view, see E. Calvin Beisner, *Prosperity and Poverty: The Compassionate Use of Resources in a World of Scarcity* (Westchester, Ill.: Crossway, 1988). Others writers in this tradition include Gary North, *An Introduction to Christian Economics* (Nutley, N.J.: Craig Press, 1973), and David Chilton, *Productive Christians in an*

Age of Guilt Manipulators (Tyler, Tex.: Institute for Christian Economics, 1981). Related works would include Ronald H. Nash, *Social Justice and the Christian Church* (Milford, Mich.: Mott Media, 1983), and Ronald H. Nash, *Poverty and Wealth* (Westchester, Ill.: Crossway, 1986).

4. Important statements of Austrian school positions include Ludwig von Mises, *Human Action*, 3d rev. ed. (Chicago: Regnery, 1966), Friedrich von Hayek, *The Road to Serfdom* (Chicago: University of Chicago Press, 1944), and Murray Rothbard, *For a New Liberty*, rev. ed. (New York: Macmillan, 1978).

5. For a critique of the Austrian school's view of the state, and that of the Christian writers influenced by it, see Thomas E. Van Dahm, "The Christian Far Right and the Economic Role of the State," *Christian Scholar's Review*, vol. 12, no. 1 (1983), pages 17-37.

6. Charles Murray, *Losing Ground: American Social Policy 1950-1980* (New York: Basic, 1984). Also, see Nash, *Poverty and Wealth,* chapter 16.

7. Douglass C. North, *Structure and Change in Economic History* (New York: Norton, 1981), chapter 3.

8. Mason, "Biblical Teaching and the Poor." page 6.

9. William Baumol and Alan Blinder, *Economics* 4th ed. (New York: Harcourt Brace Jovanovich, 1988), chapter 29

10. See Richard B. McKenzie, *The Fairness of Markets: A Search for Justice in a Free Society* (Lexington, Mass.: Lexington Books, 1987), chapter 9. Also, see Milton Friedman, *Capitalism and Freedom* (Chicago: University of Chicago Press, 1962), chapter 10.

11. McKenzie, *Fairness of Markets,* page 166.

12. McKenzie, *Fairness of Markets,* pages 179-180.

13. Isabel V. Sawhill, "Poverty in the U.S.: Why Is It So Persistent?" *Journal of Economic Literature,* vol. 26 (September 1988), pages 1073-1119. Another important review article on the poverty problem is Sheldon Danziger, Robert Haveman, and Robert Plotnick, "How Income Transfer Programs Affect Work, Savings, and the Income Distribution: A Critical Review," *Journal of Economic Literature,* vol. 19 (September 1981), pages 975-1028.

14. For a specific critique of Murray's work, see Sheldon Danziger and Peter Gottschalk, "The Poverty of *Losing Ground,"* *Challenge,* May-June 1985, pages 32-38. For Murray's defense of his work, see Charles Murray, "Have the Poor Been 'Losing Ground'?" *Political Science Quarterly,* vol. 100 (1985), pages 427-485, and Charles Murray, "How to

Lie with Statistics," *National Review,* February 28, 1986, pages 39-41.

15. Sawhill, "Poverty in the U.S.," page 1100.
16. Sawhill, "Poverty in the U.S.," page 1098.
17. Calculated from data in Sawhill, "Poverty in the U.S.," page 1098.
18. Sawhill, "Poverty in the U.S.," page 1104.
19. Sawhill, "Poverty in the U.S.," page 1105.
20. Danziger and Gottschalk, "Poverty of *Losing Ground,*" page 34.
21. Udo Middelmann, *Proexistence* (Downers Grove, Ill.: InterVarsity Press, 1974), page 12.
22. Bradley R. Schiller, "As States Show, Workfare Gets the Job Done Fast," *Wall Street Journal,* June 28, 1988, page 26.
23. Charles L. Ballard, "The Marginal Efficiency Cost of Redistribution," *American Economic Review,* vol. 78, no. 5 (December 1988), pages 1019-1033. A comprehensive proposed alternative to the present welfare system is presented in Robert I. Lerman, "Nonwelfare Approaches to Helping the Poor," *Focus* (publication of the University of Wisconsin-Madison Institute for Research on Poverty), vol. 11, no. 1 (Spring 1988), pages 24-28.
24. Michael Novak, "The New War on Poverty," *Focus,* vol. 11, no. 1 (Spring 1988), pages 6-10.

CHAPTER 12

1. Quoting C. H. Dodd, *Gospel and Law* (Cambridge: Cambridge University Press, 1951), page 64.
2. Dodd, *Gospel and Law,* page 64.
3. William Morris, ed., *American Heritage Dictionary* (Boston: American Heritage and Houghton Mifflin, 1975).

CHAPTER 13

1. Walter Shapiro, "Ethics: What's Wrong?" *Time,* May 25, 1987, page 14.
2. Ezra Bowen, "Ethics: Looking to Its Roots," *Time,* May 25, 1987, page 26.
3. Daniel E. Maltby, "The One-Minute Ethicist," *Christianity Today,* February 19, 1988, page 26.
4. Maltby, "One-Minute Ethicist," page 26.
5. *Webster's New Collegiate Dictionary* (Springfield, Mass.: G. & C. Merriam, 1977).
6. Kenneth Blanchard and Norman Vincent Peale, *The Power of Ethical*

Management (New York: William Morrow, 1988). The virtual ubiquity of the question of ethics' place in present-day business and the appeal to its profitability is illustrated by the center page of a Southwest Airlines flight schedule that contains an advertisement exhorting businesspeople to "Be there," arguing that personal presence greatly aided business success. The tableau illustrating the advertisement is an open book with a stack of additional volumes, all on business subjects, and prominent among the books is *The Power of Ethical Management.* Blanchard and Peale's book actually says and argues for more than ethics for profitability, but that is the way it has been advertised.

7. Karen Berney, "That Ethical Edge," *Reader's Digest,* April 1988, pages 177-180, condensed from *Nation's Business,* August 1987.

8. Gerhard Kittel, ed., *Theological Dictionary of the New Testament,* trans. and ed. Geoffrey W. Bromiley (Grand Rapids, Mich.: Eerdmans, 1964), vol. 1, pages 21-55 (hereafter *TDNT*). Colin Brown, gen. ed., *The New International Dictionary of New Testament Theology,* translated, with additions and revisions, from the German *Theologisches Begriffslexikon zum Neuen Testament* (Grand Rapids, Mich.: Zondervan, 1975-78), vol. 2, pages 538-551. William Barclay, *New Testament Words* (Philadelphia: Westminster Press, 1964), pages 17-30. Norman L. Geisler, *The Christian Ethic of Love* (Grand Rapids, Mich.: Zondervan, 1973), passim, and Nigel Turner, *Christian Words* (Nashville: Thomas Nelson, 1981), pages 261-271.

9. Kittel, *TDNT,* vol. 1, pages 36-37.

10. Turner, *Christian Words,* page 262, quoting C. Spicq, *Agape in the New Testament,* 1963, St. Louis and London, ii., page v.

11. Anders Nygren, *Agape and Eros* (London: SPCK, 1953), page 48, quoted in Turner, *Christian Words,* page 262.

12. Norman Snaith, *Expository Times,* vol. 70 (1958), page 20 in Turner, *Christian Words.*

13. W. Barclay, *Words,* pages 20-21.

14. Geisler, *Love,* pages 39, 76-77, 80.

15. Kittel, *TDNT,* vol. 1, page 45, citing Matthew 6:24b and Luke 11:43.

16. W. Barclay, *Words,* page 22.

17. Cf. Brown, *Dictionary,* vol. 2, page 545.

18. R. C. H. Lenski, *The Interpretation of St. Paul's First and Second Epistles to the Corinthians* (Minneapolis: Augsburg, 1939, 1963), pages 544-574.

19. Millard J. Erickson, *Christian Theology* (Grand Rapids, Mich.: Baker, 1983-85), pages 297-298.

20. Sidney A. Williams, "Business Ethics," in *Baker's Dictionary of Christian Ethics*, ed. Carl F. H. Henry (Grand Rapids, Mich.: Baker, 1973) page 78.
21. Brian Griffiths, *The Creation of Wealth: A Christian's Case for Capitalism* (Downers Grove, Ill.: InterVarsity Press, 1984), page 106. Cf. also David L. McKenna, "Capitalism," in *Baker's Dictionary of Christian Ethics*, pages 82-84.
22. Griffiths, *Creation of Wealth*, page 107.
23. Griffiths, *Creation of Wealth*, pages 80-84.
24. Clark Pinnock, "A Pilgrimage in Political Theology: A Personal Witness," in *Is Capitalism Christian?* ed. Franky Schaeffer (Westchester, Ill.: Crossway, 1985), page 320, citing Paul Johnson in *Will Capitalism Survive?*, ed. Ernest W. Lofever (Washington: Ethics and Public Policy Center, 1979), page 4. This testimonial is all the more striking for having come from one who previously had been a scathing critic of capitalism.
25. Griffiths, *Creation of Wealth*, pages 46-47.
26. Griffiths, *Creation of Wealth*, pages 49-53.
27. Oliver R. Barclay, *The Intellect and Beyond* (Grand Rapids, Mich.: Zondervan, 1985), pages 110ff.
28. O. Barclay, *Intellect*, pages 111-112.
29. O. Barclay, *Intellect*, page 117.
30. Carl F. H. Henry, *Aspects of Christian Social Ethics* (Grand Rapids, Mich.: Eerdmans, 1964), page 31.
31. O. Barclay, *Intellect*, pages 42-43.
32. O. Barclay, *Intellect*, page 43.
33. Henry, *Aspects*, page 42.
34. Henry, *Aspects*, page 43.
35. Ephesians 6:5-9, *The New Testament in Modern English*, trans. J. B. Phillips, rev. ed. (New York: Macmillan, 1972).
36. O. Barclay, *Intellect*, page 113. Cf. also Henry, *Aspects*, pages 50ff.
37. O. Barclay, *Intellect*, pages 102ff.
38. O. Barclay, *Intellect*, page 103.
39. William J. Krutza, "The Nearsighted Ethics of Christian Businessmen," *Eternity*, September 1976, page 15.
40. Lord Acton, letter to Bishop Mandell Creighton, April 3, 1887, in *The Oxford Dictionary of Quotations*, 3d ed. (Oxford: Oxford University Press, 1980), page 1.
41. Herschel H. Hobbs, *The Baptist Faith and Message* (Nashville: Convention Press, 1971), page 139.
42. Hobbs, *Message*, page 128.

43. David Neff, "Integrity You Can Afford," *Christianity Today,* January 15, 1988, page 17.
44. James Davison Hunter, *Evangelicalism: The Coming Generation* (Chicago: University of Chicago Press, 1987), page 213.
45. Maltby, "One-Minute Ethicist," page 27; Griffiths, *Creation of Wealth,* pages 117-122.
46. Maltby, "One-Minute Ethicist," page 28, quoting James O'Toole, *Vanguard Management.*
47. Mark Pastin, *The Hard Problems of Management: Gaining the Ethics Edge,* quoted in Maltby, "One-Minute Ethicist," page 28.